Publishing
in the
Information Age

PUBLISHING
IN THE
INFORMATION
AGE

A New Management Framework for the Digital Era

Updated with a new Afterword

DOUGLAS M. EISENHART

 PRAEGER

Westport, Connecticut
London

The Library of Congress has cataloged the hardcover edition as follows:

Eisenhart, Douglas M.
  Publishing in the information age : a new management framework for
the digital era / Douglas M. Eisenhart.
      p.   cm.
  Includes bibliographical references (p.   ) and index.
  ISBN 0–89930–847–3 (alk. paper)
  1. Publishers and publishing—United States.   2. Communication and
traffic—United States.   3. Mass media—United States.   I. Title.
Z471.E55   1994
070.5'0973—dc20   93—5581

British Library Cataloguing in Publication Data is available.

A hardcover edition of *Publishing in the Information Age: A New Management Framework for
the Digital Era* is available from Quorum Books, an imprint of Greenwood Publishing Group,
Inc. (ISBN: 0–89930–847–3).

Library of Congress Catalog Card Number: 93–5581
ISBN: 0–275–95696–2

First published in 1994
First paperback edition 1996

Praeger Publishers, 88 Post Road West, Westport, CT 06881
An imprint of Greenwood Publishing Group, Inc.

Printed in the United States of America

The paper used in this book complies with the
Permanent Paper Standard issued by the National
Information Standards Organization (Z39.48–1984).

10 9 8 7 6 5 4 3 2 1

Copyright Acknowledgments

The author gratefully acknowledges the permission granted by the following organizations and
individuals for use of their material in this work: Christopher Burns, Christopher Burns, Inc.;
Harvard University Program on Information Resources Policy; NeXT Computer, Inc.; J. Kendrick Noble, Jr., Noble Consultants, Inc.; Professor Ronald Rice, Department of Communication, Rutgers University.

To My Steadfast Companion and Wife,
Gilly

Contents

Illustrations

FIGURES

TABLES

Preface

Every book has a story, and this one is no exception. I relate it here not only because it reveals the genesis of the study and my route to the subject, but also because my audience is (presumably) composed largely of publishers, a group that will have a special appreciation of the evolution of an idea from conception to embodiment.

The book got its start in the classroom twenty years ago when, as a teacher, I thought about creating materials that would do a better job of presenting concepts and inspiring my students than the poor texts I was expected to use. At that time I also became enamored with the television broadcast of several exceptional educational programming series intended for viewing by the general public, particularly Kenneth Clark's *Civilization* and later Jacob Bronowski's *Ascent of Man,* both of which had beautifully produced and successful book tie-ins.

I pursued this interest in communications through education school and into the publishing and television industries. In the late 1970s, when my job in book publishing was to manage the development of intellectual properties in other forms and markets, I became increasingly interested in questions concerning new media and information technologies and their potential role in the development and exploitation of a publisher's information assets. When I considered these questions they often seemed to raise even more fundamental questions about growth, direction, strategy, and basic definitions of the publishing business, but a precise vision of that changing business seemed difficult to grasp.

At the same time I also began to hear and see a great deal about the

"Information Age" and the "information industry"—the Information Industry Association was formed in 1969—but these designations were unclear. What exactly was meant by information industry? Were publishers included? These were new terms that tended more to obfuscate than clarify, yet they were and are now widely accepted and broadly applied. Trade book publishers might rankle at their inclusion in the information industry and see the term as too reductive when considering the richness of a Thomas Hardy novel or the delicate beauties of a folio of fine art prints. The term would seem equally inappropriate when applied to a Fellini film sold by a video publisher on videocassette or disc. Surely these aren't merely "information."

Confusion over terminology is only one of the symptoms of change. Other major concerns about publishing and its future continued to appear, including the effects of the proliferation and mass usage of the new technologies, the changing user habits these new communication forms engender, new and unknown industry competitors, and intensified merger and acquisition activity. These and other powerful effects spell great change, and although no one has a crystal ball (at least one that works) I wanted to know as best as I could what publishing would look like as we enter the next millennium, now less than a decade away.

Subsequent positions in programming and marketing in the cable television industry, and time spent consulting in video and software publishing, only served to heighten my interest in issues surrounding the new media. I began to focus on these issues in a more analytical, versus experiential, fashion while a student in business school. It was at that time, in 1983, that I had the excitement of discovering the Information Business Map created by the group at Harvard's Program in Information Resources Policy (*see* Chapter 1). The map was simultaneously a revelation and a confirmation. By putting the various components of the media—books, broadcast television, cable television, software, audio cassettes, and other print and electronic forms—into a single framework, the map made explicit my intuition that these components were related. This was a critical moment for me, for by validating my instinct on the subject it provided me with the necessary theoretical foundation, and confidence, to pursue my own ideas further.

Shortly thereafter, in early 1985, I moved to Boston and approached Benjamin Compaine, then Executive Director of the Harvard Program, with a proposal for a study of new publishing media. Feeling it was more appropriate as a book, Ben referred me to his successor in the editorial department at Knowledge Industry Publications, Ellen Lazer. Ellen liked the idea, and she suggested and subsequently accepted a revised outline for the project. After only a few months under contract with Knowledge Industry, however, the Communications Library series, in which the book was to appear, was sold to G.K. Hall, a Boston-based subsidiary of Macmillan, where I was initially taken in by Donna Sanzone and later adopted by the newly appointed Communications Library editor, Carol Chin. However, by the time I had submitted my final manuscript, G.K. Hall was in turn reorganized and my project was absorbed, along with part of the G.K. Hall imprint, into Macmillan Reference, whose line had no place for a study of this nature or for this intended market.

I then set about locating another publisher for the book—now peddling not a proposal but a completed manuscript—and was fortunate enough to connect with Eric Valentine, publisher of Quorum Books at Greenwood Publishing Group. Eric took the project under his wing, the saga came to an end, and the book came to life. Each of these persons has played a pivotal role along the way, and all deserve acknowledgment here.

There are several ideological and conceptual forefathers of this book, each of whom, through their own written work, informed my thinking in critical ways on different topics addressed in this study. This group includes Christopher Burns, Benjamin Compaine, Peter Drucker, Howard Gardner, Irving Louis Horowitz, Koji Kobayashi, Thomas Kuhn, John McLaughlin, Harvey Poppel, Michael Porter, Neil Postman, John Sculley, and Oldrich Standera. Their words, thoughts, and influence can be found throughout this book.

I am also indebted to all those I interviewed in the early phase of the book's research from 1986–1988. The theoretical and strategic aspects of this book were reinforced by the insights drawn from the broad-ranging experience, perspectives, and expertise of these individuals, most of whom continue to play active roles in shaping the industry's future (title and organizational affiliation are at the time of interview): David Altschul, Vice President, Legal Affairs, Warner Brothers Records; Gary Arlen, Publisher, Interactivity Report; Raymond C. Ashton, Vice President, Program Development, American Interactive Media; Walter S. Baer, Director of Advanced Publishing Technology, Times Mirror Company; Jennifer Bater, Media Specialist, Booz Allen Hamilton; William Bowman, Chairman, Spinnaker Software; Debbie Brienne, Senior Research Associate, Center for Children and Technology, Bank Street College of Education; Christopher Burns, President, Christopher Burns, Inc.; John Y. Cole, Director, Center for the Book, Library of Congress; Frank Collins, Acting Director, Radcliffe Publishing Course, Harvard University; Stan Cornyn, President, The Record Group; Richard Cross, Partner, The Berwick Group; Marshall Cutchin, Director of Operations, Veterinary Learning Systems; Don Edwards, Director of Video, WaldenBooks; Beth Fader, Director, Information Access Services, GTE of California; Stuart Karl, Chairman, Karl-Lorimar Video; Wes Kussmail, President, Delphi Videotex; Dan Lacy, Senior Executive Vice President, McGraw-Hill, Inc.; Mike Levinger, Marketing Manager, McCormack & Dodge; Rob Lippincott, Director, Interactive Technologies, WGBH, and Director of Market Development, Information Services Group, Lotus Development; Andrew Lippman, Director, Electronic Publishing Group, MIT Media Lab; James J. Lyle, President, Video Publishing Resources; Donald McLagan, Vice President, Information Services Group, Lotus Development; Kenneth Miller, Co-founder and President, Miller Associates; J. Kendrick Noble, Jr., analyst, Paine Webber; Lee Papayanopoulos, Director, Information Technology Project, Columbia Business School; William Phillips, Senior Editor, Little, Brown; Harvey L. Poppel, Partner, Broadview Associates; Ronald E. Rice, Professor, Annenberg School of Communications, University of Southern California; David Roux, Co-founder and President, Datext; Larry Sackett, Vice President, Telecommunications, Gannett; Tom Snyder, Founder and President, Tom Snyder Productions; Sol Stein, Founder and President, Stein & Day; Sam Tyler, Co-founder and President, Nathan/Tyler Productions; Christine Urban, Founder and President, Urban & Associates; and Kathy Wilson, Research Associate, Center for Children and Technology, Bank Street College.

In addition to those directly involved in the project, those who have read part or all of the manuscript at various stages and made comments include Benjamin Compaine, Harry Foster, Christopher Burns, Elizabeth Kubik, Jonathan Latimer, and Steve Vana-Paxhia. I thank them all for their helpful criticism and insights.

My thanks to Darci Mehall for her quick and expert rendering of all the figures and tables in the book. I have always felt that the visual encapsulations of my argument would be a critical part of the book's success, and she has brought these figures to life. My thanks also to Chris Coffin for her continuing interest and timely assistance at several points along the way.

I am also indebted to my friend Bart English for extending his help to a friend in need, making it possible for me to continue and complete this study.

I must mention the inspirational role played by the late Helen Doyle Venn, long-time director of the Radcliffe Publishing Course. In a sense, this book is a tribute to her belief in the power of communication. Finally, I must pay an enormous debt of gratitude to my loyal wife, who endured my absence, preoccupation, and countless other unmentionable irritations and idiosyncrasies of the author at his work throughout the entire early years of our married life, which also included having two children, changing jobs, and buying a house. It is no understatement to say that her belief in the ultimate worth of my labors and her support and understanding throughout this long process enabled me to fulfill my vision and complete this task.

Although many have contributed in ways great or small to the making of this book—and I apologize to those whom I have neglected to name here—it is, in the end, my own creation, my own synthesis, my own interpretation. Any inconsistencies, inaccuracies, irrelevancies, vaguenesses, or other shortcomings in the book are mine alone. Despite my efforts to bring these thoughts to light, I view this book as an initial statement that will need refinements, amendments, and up-dates over time. But however flawed it may be, it is my humble hope that it will prove of use to those involved in the changing world of publishing. If it provides some understanding, some useful vision of this evolving world, then I will have achieved my goal of making it possible for publishers to proceed with a greater degree of confidence in the brave new world of publishing in the Information Age.

Introduction

At our present juncture something indeed appears to be happening on the grander scale . . . a general reconstitution of the information procedures of the world.

—Erik Barnouw

Over the past several years it has become increasingly clear that powerful forces of change are at work which are challenging publishers' accepted view of their world, causing them to take note, to rethink the premises of their business, and to speculate on its direction for the future. As we head into the next millennium, publishers continue to ask, but now with greater urgency, a familiar litany of questions:

- How will people be informed and entertained in the future, and who will supply this information and entertainment?
- What forms will information products and services take, and how will they be used?
- Will books survive, or will computers and other undreamt of technologies, electronic or otherwise, supplant them?
- Will newspapers survive, or will they also be supplanted by screen-delivered news and entertainment?
- What will it take for firms to survive in the information business of the future? How will they plot strategy and sustain profitable growth?
- Will the big publishing and media companies that dominate the busi-

ness today be the power players of tomorrow, or will they be supplanted by technology, based on other firms? Will there be any room
for smaller firms?

- If we even bother to ask these questions, can there be any point in
studying the past if it is so quickly made obsolete by unprecedentedly
swift changes in technology and markets?

SYMPTOMS OF CHANGE

The forces of change are manifested in several symptoms in the publishing
industry environment, symptoms that suggest to publishers that it is no longer
business as usual.

Changing Definitions

The central metaphors in the world of mass communications continue to
be the book, the magazine, and the newspaper, but they are stretched to
include new media forms. Television shows such as "Masterpiece Theater"
gain their credibility (and their material) from the book world, displaying
sumptuous piles of leather-bound volumes in a gentleman's library. With the
advent of spoken word audio cassettes, we see "Books on Tape" and "Talking
Books." Sony's Data Discman plays optical discs known as "Electronic Books,"
and a new media publisher, Voyager, produces and publishes magnetic disk
"Expanded Books." The early videotex and teletext trials saw themselves as
"electronic newspapers," and it is no coincidence that many of the pioneers
in those trials were the newspaper companies themselves.

The definition of publishing itself is broadening, prompted by the range of
new media formats. If publishing means the packaging and sale of discrete
physical products—newspapers, books, magazines, and now videotapes, audio
cassettes, software disks and CD-ROM's—then what of electronic databases
delivered over phone lines or via satellite transmission? If publishing is increasingly involved in the packaging and delivery of electronic products, including databases and video and audio programs, then how is it to be
differentiated from broadcasting? Is pay-per-view cable television a form of
publishing? Do these distinctions even matter?

Stretched terminologies bespeak new players with different perspectives
and experiences. A shared understanding is prerequisite for industry progress,
and common language is an essential step in creating that understanding. But
with a lack of standard terminology in a broadening community with new types
of practitioners, this shared understanding becomes more difficult to achieve.
Due to industry conventions which have grown up and taken root over time,
practitioners from the various core industry segments—recording, broadcasting, cable, film, publishing, telecommunications, computers, and consumer

electronics—are talking to each other with different vocabularies. We need a common language to accommodate these colliding galaxies in one comprehensible universe.

Blurring Industry Boundaries

But industry definitions are also changing. Heretofore seen as separate core industries with their own sets of products, distribution networks, and industry conventions—we speak of the "book industry" or the "software industry" or the "film industry"—publishers of books, magazines and newspapers, radio and television broadcasters, computer hardware and software firms, and film companies are increasingly being viewed as component pieces of a new meta-industry—the information industry.

One striking example of such blurred boundaries is the convergence between interpersonal communications systems and mass communications media, until quite recently two distinct systems.[1] Long distance interpersonal communications, for point-to-point two-way exchanges of messages, have previously been accomplished only through the telecommunication networks, such as the telephones and telegraph. But these systems are now converging with mass communications systems, the one-to-many, one-way media designed for broad audiences, such as the broadcast media of radio and television and the print media of books, magazines, and newspapers. Text, for example, is available two-way over phone lines. Television has become a personalized item, via camcorders, as well as an interactive, point-to-point medium via video teleconferencing. Multimodal computer networks for desktop interactive voice, video, and data communications are around the corner.

Industry definitions and boundaries are important, for a firm's vision of the world points the direction in which it will head and the actions it will take. Thus as definitions and boundaries change businesses redefine themselves, a dangerous balancing act. If a business defines itself too narrowly, it will be blind to opportunities and lose out or possibly perish. But if it defines itself too broadly, it risks dissipating the strength of a central motivating vision, shared culture, and specialized skill base in order to become an organization that attempts to be all things to all people, a recipe for disaster. As Harvard Business School's Kenneth Andrews has stated, "All organizations must be focused in purpose in order to avoid outstripping their resources or squandering their distinctive advantage."[2]

New and Unknown Competitors

Blurring industry boundaries also mean that businesses will come up against new and different players, with differing goals and motivations, differing skills and experiences, differing resources, and differing worldviews. A book publisher moving into software publishing will be competing against firms from the computer industry whose skills, outlooks, and industry background are quite different from its own. What resources might they bring to the table that a book publisher cannot? Conversely, what advantages can a book publisher draw upon that they cannot? An educational book publisher venturing into software will be competing against a number of companies whose resources are wholly devoted to computer software, indeed whose founders often eat and breathe bits and bytes. Can it compete? Can a newspaper launching a videotex venture compete with the allied strengths of computer and retailing giants such as IBM and Sears in Prodigy? What information and resources do they have access to that the newspaper publisher does not?

New Processes and Products

The first step into electronic publishing for many newspaper and magazine publishers was in electronic process technologies, pre-press applications for the preparation of printed materials. Book publishers have been slower to move into this area as their production operations, unlike those of newspapers, are typically decoupled from the editorial operations, and their editorial and design process, compared to the deadlines of a daily metropolitan newspaper or a weekly or even monthly magazine, is protracted. But a mid-1980s study conducted by the Association of American Publishers reported that 80% of authors prepare their manuscripts electronically, providing a strong incentive for publishers to automate. Now most book publishers are implementing electronic processing in pre-press operations, and the typical book publisher of tomorrow, just like his colleagues in the newspaper and magazine industries today, will operate in an almost totally digital environment.

In addition to the advent of electronics throughout the pre-press end of print publishing, changes in media technologies have brought a proliferation of new electronic playback devices such as audio cassette players, compact audio disc (CD) players, videocassette recorders (VCR's), laserdisc players, microcomputers, and most recently a proliferation of various optical disc players, such as CD-ROM, CD-I, VIS, 3DO, and others. The widescale adoption and use of these devices has, in turn, created publishing opportunities for the program packages that go with them, such as audio cassettes, videocassettes, videodiscs, and floppy disk software and optical discs. This second type of electronic publishing—the delivery of material in electronic form versus electronic pre-press for delivery of material in print form—represents a new wave of electronic media—*publishing* media—after the first wave of electronic *broadcast* media in the first half of the century.

Does this new wave of electronic publishing media threaten the use of traditional print products as radio and television were thought to? The electronic products are sometimes more convenient to obtain or to use, sometimes cheaper for the consumer and more efficient for the producer, and if they are any or all of these things they can be viewed as competing directly with traditional print products for the user's time, attention, and money. Carried to its extreme, the traditional print publisher's nightmare portrays a totally electronic world, one in which users' habits, as we progress further and further into the Information Age, will change so drastically that the dependency on electronic information sources will completely displace the need for and use of books, magazines, newspapers, or any kind of printed material.

Changing User Habits

In 1964, some twenty years before "VCR" was widely known, iconoclast and media prophet Marshall McLuhan foresaw the coming of the personal moving image library: "Audio tape and video tape were to excel film eventually as information storehouses. . . . At the present time, film is still in its manuscript phase, as it were; shortly it will, under TV pressure, go into its portable, accessible, printed book phase. Soon everyone will be able to have a small inexpensive film projector that plays an 8-mm sound cartridge as if on a TV screen."[3] Two points are noteworthy in this 1964 image of the future: first, the metaphor and model McLuhan uses for the film industry's development is the publishing industry—referring to its "manuscript phase" and "portable, accessible printed book phase." Secondly the medium, McLuhan points out, would be driven toward this phase, whereby the consumer controls the time and place of film viewing just as he does with book reading.

Individual selection and control over film and video-viewed material marks a significant change in media consumption habits. Although McLuhan wrongly foresaw the use of individual 8-mm film projectors as the playback medium, he rightly foresaw the demand for individual consumer use of filmed or taped (and not just video but audio-taped) products, and correctly placed the film and television industries in their evolutionary phases. We are now at the point McLuhan foresaw where the means of playing back film and tape at the individual's discretion are widely available. As of this writing, nearly three-quarters of U.S. households have a VCR, and the widespread penetration of the devices has created a new industry, the video publishing industry. Thus the definitions of "publishing" and "library" must evolve as the storage media for mass-produced moving images are placed into the hands of the many. Information has become available for reproduction and repeated use not just in print form but in moving visual form, with sound. Nearly a hundred years of film production and fifty years of television production, heretofore locked in the vaults of distributors and broadcasters, are thus liberated and can be published for individual use. This enormous "backlist" is just the beginning, for new productions will continue to fill the pipeline to meet new demands and selected interests and needs, following the precedent of book publishing.

This is just one case of how a new media technology can create new user habits, new marketplace demands, and thus new publishing opportunities. The same analysis could be applied to computer software or online services. Information industry analyst Benjamin Compaine has suggested that all the changes in communications technologies may well force us to redefine our society's notion of literacy—for literacy, as Compaine says, is not static but "dynamic, a bundle of culturally relevant skills."[4] With millions of office workers spending their days in front of computer screens, with electronic calculators more the exception than the rule in our schools' mathematics classrooms, with video and audio formats increasingly in use as means of information transmission, this vision of literacy may well be true.

Strategic Alliances, Mergers, and Acquisitions

The 1980s saw many large publishing and media firms seeking to own, develop, and distribute content in all forms, print and electronic, throughout the world. Acquisitions, especially with international players, dominated the publishing news through the latter half of the 1980s. After this largely debt-driven feeding frenzy, we witnessed sell-offs and realignment of a number of the same purchased assets. As of this writing we are in a strategic alliance phase, where corporations are matching resources with each other to take advantage of the plethora of opportunities emerging in the digital era.

This type of activity, although historically characteristic of each segment of the industry, is now spreading across the media—witness microcomputer software firm Microsoft's purchase of a stake of British book publisher Dorling Kindersley in early 1991. While international combines will continue to realign their assets, new avenues for growth will also be sought via the younger, emerging media technologies as they continue to develop and achieve broad user acceptance and profitable levels of penetration.

Beyond the media mergers are the hardware-software mergers, the purchase by consumer electronics firms of content firms, most notably Sony's purchase of CBS Records and Columbia Pictures and rival Matsushita's purchase of MCA. In addition to consumer electronics firms, computer and telecommunications firms may also seek increasing control of content as hardware systems become less proprietary, more open, and more commodity-like. The 1991 ruling allowing the local telephone operating companies' ownership of information services provides one avenue for such activity.

New Research, Conferences, and Publications

Perhaps as clear an indication as any that there are fundamental changes occurring in publishing is the extent of the new research in the field, as well as the recent growth in the number of trade shows, conferences, and publications in the area. Several groups in university-based programs and in private sector consulting and research organizations have been at the forefront of the new research. The Harvard Program in Information Resources Policy, established in 1972, has developed several important new theories, including the Information Business Map (*see* Chapter 1) and other seminal concepts. Under the direction of Harvey Poppel (now a partner in Broadview Associates), the information technology group at Booz Allen Hamilton, management and technology consultants, developed a range of important concepts based on their work with Fortune 500 and other clients in the industry. The group headed by Nicholas Negroponte at the MIT Media Laboratory, as well as research being conducted at the Bank Street College of Education, the Xerox Palo Alto Research Center, and other sites, are both basic and applied research efforts on the new media technologies and their uses. At these and other private and public institutions, and throughout the affected industries, fundamental questions of publishing, communications, and information are being raised.[5]

If the research activity indicates possible change, the proliferation of conferences and publications in the new media arena are sure signs not only of change but of economic activity. New media conference producers and newsletter, journal, and magazine publishers are converging from all points, including print publishing, the computer industry, and entrepreneurial ventures straddling two or more of the converging industries.

FUD: Fear, Uncertainty, and Doubt

A few years ago a *Harper's* magazine cover article asked "Will Books Survive?" In the article a group of senior book publishing executives at an American Booksellers Association roundtable discussion traded views on the fate of their industry and offered their prognostications. Most of the talk, as the article's title suggests, was pessimistic, and it was not a manufacturers' fear of foreign competition or declining productivity, but a fear that the primary demand for their product—books—might simply disappear in an increasingly crowded, commercialized, and electronic media marketplace.

Why should there be such dire speculation? Do we see the leaders of other industries banding together to consider their collective doom? Do we see roundtable discussions of auto executives asking whether cars will survive? Usually not. Yet many print-based publishers seem to be particularly fearful that there are uncontrollable forces at work that will somehow have a hand in determining their fate. Hence, FUD—fear, uncertainty, and doubt.

While we cannot completely divine the fates of the individual media formats, we can take some comfort in communications analyst Efrem Sigel's conclusion that "For many years, books themselves will continue to be published by the tens of thousands, bought by the hundreds of millions, or billions. They will remain highly familiar objects, not relics of the past. But," adds Sigel, "as the landscape of communications changes, so will their role, and our perception of it. The evolution of that landscape will be very gradual but persistent, and one of its distinguishing features in the 21st century will be that those involved in communications will no longer consider it a question of the moment to ask, 'Does the book have a future?' "[6]

Renewed Need for Strategy and Direction

But while we may be reassured about the book's survival, we must still ask what its role will be in a pluralistic media marketplace. In the midst of these surging forces—changing definitions, blurring industry boundaries, new players, new process technologies, new media formats, changing user habits—most publishers are now aware that to stick to their customary turf is somehow not enough, that they must not only be aware of the changes, both threats and opportunities, but be able to respond to them in an appropriate fashion. Even if incremental steps are taken into unfamiliar territory, they must still be based on some vision of the future, some notion of where those steps are heading.

The changing industry environment points to the need for planning on the part of publishers as well as the need for a new set of managerial skills with which to analyze the situation, assess the options, and decide in which directions to move. Proactive, not reactive, decisions must be made, for as publisher Austin Kiplinger points out, "The leeway for adjusting to change is shrinking year by year as the speed of technological development picks up and product cycles shorten."[7] Not only is new content quickly made obsolete, in both print and non-print forms, but new media technologies themselves are in danger of increasingly rapid obsolescence as they are displaced or joined by even newer media. This raises legitimate concerns about how to cope with such changes, how to create a differential advantage that lengthens the product cycle, or how to roll with the shortened product life cycles and exploit their earlier and shorter profit and revenue bulges.

These and related questions and choices require well-grounded strategic thinking, for those print publishers gathered together to consider their collective doom must also live with Sigel's observation that "both publishing and libraries have a mission that is not synonymous with the future of the book. To publish is to make available information for every human need—education, inspiration, entertainment, commerce, science. There is no way such a mission can be limited to issuing books; if today's publishers do not seize the opportunity presented by electronic media, new publishers will inevitably arise to do so."[8]

SCOPE OF THE STUDY

My concern in this book, then, is for a collection of businesses that perform a vital role in our culture—that inform, entertain, and enlighten us while operating under the same constraints for revenues and profits with which all businesses must contend. The book I conceived was a concise one volume introduction to the changing publishing environment for those in publishing who must make key decisions for the future of their organizations (and their careers). The premise of the study is that it is difficult to move forward confidently without some vision of the future, and the goal of the book is to bring that vision into focus, to provide a context of understanding, and a framework within which publishers can comprehend and consider the range of changes and events.

While trying to put together such a context may seem a worthy endeavor, it is also a highly frustrating one, for the field is fluid, not fixed. Indeed, it is undeniable that many of the specifics discussed herein are subject to change, as the entire environment is marked by perpetual evolution. This makes a hazardous business of attempting to make meaningful statements of lasting value.

A second goal of the study is to stimulate discussion on the development and uses of new publishing media. Those who develop publishing products and services have some understanding of how the various media forms interact in the marketplace. But with the continuing introduction of new forms presenting new opportunities and challenges, publishers need to continually re-evaluate the strengths and weaknesses of these formats and how they interact with each other in a pluralistic media environment.[9]

A third goal is to point to areas where further research, beyond the resources of this study to undertake, may be of benefit. A study such as this cannot delve too deeply into any one medium or market. While a great deal has been published and continues to be on all these specific areas, more research and greater understanding are required in a number of areas, not only in the changing communications and information technologies but in mass and interpersonal communications; in the social effects—on individuals, home life, work, education—of communications media; in cognitive psychology and epistemology; in seemingly unrelated fields such as neuroanatomy, which is just now beginning to reveal to us how the human brain perceives, records, and synthesizes different types of information; in business strategy; and in other areas. In many ways we are just at the beginning of our understanding in many of these areas, and our understanding must increasingly draw upon interdisciplinary studies.

Focus of the Study

I am interested here in the world of *published* or commercial information—information created by an organization specifically for outside sale or use, which by definition moves from a source or sources to a population of outside users—in contrast to the generation and distribution of information for internal use in organizations. My focus is also primarily on *content* businesses, information or "software" firms versus hardware firms, the makers and providers of facilities and equipment for the creation, manipulation, and storage of information. However, the increasing involvement of consumer electronic, computer, and telecommunications firms in the content business will also be addressed throughout the study.

AUDIENCE

Despite tremors and rumblings and ubiquitous signs of broadscale change in the publishing world, I still believe there is a gulf of understanding between this core group and the industry as a whole about the nature, depth, and significance of the transformations in this world. From the time that I began working on this book in the mid-1980s, the industry has continued to change dramatically, and more people in publishing have been exposed to and dealt with the types of issues addressed here, heightening their awareness of the issues and in many cases improving their understanding of them. Still, it has always been my intent to reach beyond the core group of senior level managers and executives, consultants, and researchers—many of whom served as sources for this study—to the broader audience of practitioners and stakeholders in the world of publishing.

Print publishers are still the largest component of the publishing industry and the component with the greatest vested interests and the most firmly established positions of power. But the book is also intended for new publishers, the current or future publisher—e.g., video publishers, software publishers, multimedia publishers, online publishers—whose operations are born of the Information Age and its opportunities, as well as for a variety of other current and future publishing stakeholders.[10]

CAVEATS

The study draws upon my own observations and experiences from time spent in different arenas of the information industry, mainly books, cable television, and software. It also reflects my experience and training in marketing and planning and thus exhibits a more strategic, market-based perspective than a technology-based one. I am not a technologist, and this is not a technical book, although given its heavy concern with technology I often drew upon technical material and technologically-proficient individuals to inform my argument. Technologists and media experts should not seek to learn here anything new about their specialties, although it is my hope that the book will allow them to see their specialties in the context of the broader media universe and the industry forces at work. Neither am I an academic, nor an intellectual property attorney. I am a publishing and media manager, a practitioner talking to other current and future practitioners about where the business is headed.

The study does not consider a range of related and vital social and cultural issues, including ethical implications of new information and communications technologies, political and legal issues, issues of access and equity, issues of social impact, and issues of aesthetics. The study also does not address, except in passing, government or international markets. This does not indicate any lack of importance in these areas, only that the scope of the study had to be constrained for the sake of manageability. Indeed, government markets often present real opportunities for new growth and understanding in information technologies due to heavy government investment in development projects, while global markets represent major arenas for expansion.

The organizing rubrics in the book are designed to be of aid in grasping a complex, multi-faceted, ever-evolving environment. However, none of the boundaries in these frameworks is rigid. For example, to speak of the education market is no longer strictly accurate as structured, curricular education takes place not just in schools but in the workplace as well. There is convergence in almost all areas, convergence among the modes and media of communication, convergence among the distribution cycles, convergence between information and entertainment, convergence between publishing and broadcasting, and convergence between print and electronic firms as well as forms. The best rule of thumb to adopt is that all boundaries are fluid, not fixed.[11]

Throughout the book I frequently refer to publishers as "he" while in other places I refer to both genders. While I use the male pronouns to simplify construction, in almost all instances, except those where a specific individual is referred to, the reader may infer either a male or female referent.

Although there is no objective court of determination on the matter, I have chosen to use disk with a "k" when referring to magnetic media—e.g., floppy and hard disks—and disc with a "c" when referring to optical media, such as CD-ROM, CD audio, and laserdiscs, as well as magneto-optical discs.

There is great frustration in doing a broad-brush study such as this and not being able to delve too deeply into any one area. What we gain in surveying the entire scene we lose in closer scrutiny of any one area. Similarly a book cannot be as up-to-date as periodical or online sources as the swift pace of change easily overtakes the normal gestation process of a book's preparation and publication. New media products will have been introduced since the book's writing, and the markets are growing and producers, developers, and users are learning more every day. Still, while these players and their products and organizations change, it is my hope that the basic tenets of this book will hold, and for their expression, a book is their best (but perhaps not only) repository.

In the final analysis the development of media products and services in any form must be undertaken on a case-by-case basis. While this book takes an analytical approach to its subject—what might be termed a left-brained, managerial perspective—an equally critical part of the success of any publishing venture rests on cultivating the right brain, on nurturing creativity and craft, the wholistic, intuitive, non-quantitative aspects of mind which also shape publishing's products and services. Successful publishing enterprises require both in order to thrive.

PLAN OF THE BOOK

The book is divided into six parts, with introductory and concluding parts framing the consideration of the 7M's in the central four parts.

Part I, "The Paradigm Shift to Publishing in the Information Age," provides a perspective on how the publishing world is changing and introduces the 7M's framework. Chapter 1, "Information, the Information Age, and the New Meta-Industry," looks at how the definition of information has changed and what the designations Information Age and information industry mean. Chapter 2, "Rethinking Publishing: The Paradigm Shift," looks at publishing within the context of the changing industry environment and presents the paradigm shift from traditional publishing to publishing in the Information Age. The concluding chapter of Part I, Chapter 3, "The 7M's of Publishing," introduces the seven key value chain elements that both constitute the publishing enterprise and serve as the structural backbone of the book.

Part II, "Material and Modes," looks at the first two of the 7M's. Chapter 4, "The Material Essence," examines the central role in the publishing construct of the first M, *Material,* and presents the first of the study's *Core Concepts* of publishing in the Information Age (Core Concepts are introduced and highlighted for each of the 7M's throughout Parts II–V). Chapter 5, "Modes of Communication," describes the second value-added M, *Mode.* It focuses on the three major modes of communication and explains why a consideration of mode is increasingly critical in publishing product development.

Part III, "Media and Means," looks at the next two M's of the value chain. Chapter 6, "The Media Matrix: Modes and Means," presents a framework that encompasses and relates the full range of *Media,* the third value-added M, and also discusses the centrality of the *Means* of distribution, the fourth M, to this framework. Chapter 7, "The Media: Profiles and Attributes," provides a summary profile of the range of media formats and a discussion of media format attributes. Chapter 8, "The Media: Life Cycles and the Dynamic Equilibrium," introduces the notion of the media life cycle and the dynamic equilibrium of media formats.

The book then moves to the fifth M, *Markets,* in Part IV. Chapter 9, "Market Environments: Common Characteristics and Trends," looks at the broader market environment from the customer perspective. Chapter 10, "The Media Universe: Profiling the Markets," introduces the Media Universe, profiles the three major markets—consumer, business and professional, and educational—and introduces the six global supermarkets. Chapter 11, "Marketing Tasks," delineates several key marketing issues for Information Age publishers.

Part V, "Management and Money," addresses the last two of the 7M's. Chapter 12, "Strategic Vision and Integrative Management," lays out the Core Concepts in *Management,* the sixth M. Chapter 13, "Maximizing Return: Organizational Strategy and Structure," is the first of two chapters on *Money,* the seventh M, and considers corporate level strategic and structural issues, especially those relating to diversification into new media. Chapter 14, "Maximizing Return: The Intellectual Property Management Program," provides an approach to maximizing return on investment at the product level.

The concluding section of the book, Part VI, reconsiders four major themes of the study in Chapter 15, "The Digital Enterprise and the Paradigm of Promise."

NOTES

1. *See* Ithiel de Sola Pool, *Technologies of Freedom* (Cambridge, Mass.: Harvard University Press, 1983), 23. Pool's chief concern in this work is the potential curtailment of freedom of speech through a failure of the courts and regulators to understand the true nature and role of the new media technologies: "Electronic publishing may start by using computers to bypass the costs of union composition of physical end products that are conventional newspapers and books. But at later stages it may look much more like a telephone or cable system, which the courts are used to regulating, even though it incidentally but importantly prints out words" (*Technologies of Freedom*), 197.

2. *See* Kenneth Andrews, et al., *Business Policy: Text and Cases,* 5th ed. (Homewood, Ill.: Richard D. Irwin, 1982), 554. Business historian Robert Sobel addresses this issue when discussing the nascent computer industry in his book *IBM—Colossus in Transition:* "When a new technology or major innovation appears in an established field, old lines are dissolved, and new perceptions come into being. . . . In the nature of things the conception of an industry—be it 'transportation' or 'railroads,' 'business machines' or 'computers'—will be accepted by the informed public even while their precise natures are debated by lawyers, economists, and scholars. . . . Is there a computer industry? If so, is it unique or a subdivision of business machines? . . . On the surface these may appear academic questions with only marginal application and of little interest to practical men and women. In fact, they are vital ones, and their answers have serious implications in the application of human and financial resources and development of technology and organization." *IBM—Colossus in Transition* (New York: Times Books, 1981), 138–9. *See also* Philip Kotler, *Marketing Management* (Englewood Cliffs, NJ: Prentice Hall, 1980), 64–69, on business definition.

3. Marshall McLuhan, *Understanding Media.* Signet reprint edition. (New York: New American Library, 1964), 255.

4. Benjamin Compaine, *Understanding New Media* (Cambridge, Mass.: Balinger Publishing Company, 1984), 330.

5. Other significant articulators of the new thinking include Harvard's Daniel Bell, information consultant Christopher Burns, communications researcher and analyst Efrem Sigel, NEC chairman Koji Kobayashi, scholarly publisher Irving Horowitz, librarian and information technology specialist Oldrich Standera, and others whose works are cited throughout this study.

6. Efrem Sigel, "The Future of the Book," in *Books, Libraries, and Electronics* (White Plains, N.Y.: Knowledge Industry Publications, 1982), 31.

7. Austin H. Kiplinger and the staff of the Kiplinger Washington Letter, *The New American Boom* (Washington, D.C.: The Kiplinger Washington Editors, 1986), 20.

8. Sigel, "The Future of the Book," 31.

9. Walter Baer, former Director of Advanced Technology at Times Mirror, has stated: "We know that the electronic media differ from print and from each other. We know that successful products and services typically combine electronic and print elements. What we do not know is how the elements should be combined, and in what proportion: print, online retrieval, physical distribution of software, downloading, optical disc storage, and so on. The possible combinations are truly astounding. Determining which combinations provide the greatest value to our customers is perhaps the most interesting part of the electronic publishing story." From "Defining a New Business" in *Electronic Publishing Plus* (White Plains, N.Y.: Knowledge Industry Publications, 1985), 123.

10. These other publishing stakeholders include (but are not limited to) authors and content creators; manufacturers of media products; manufacturers of electronic devices, from computers to VCR's to compact disc players to satellite earth dishes; distributors, network operators, and any and all deliverers of published goods, in print and electronic forms; third parties and intermediaries, such as literary agents and consultants; advertisers; investors, financiers, and shareholders; users, including consumers, managers and professionals, teachers and administrators, and librarians; executives in non-publishing media; executives in non-media companies contemplating movement into the publishing field; government regulators, who must oversee and create the proper conditions for healthy development of the publishing industry for suppliers and buyers alike, domestically and internationally, in print and electronic forms; students of the field and those considering embarking upon a career in publishing; and analysts, observers, cultural watchdogs, and social critics.

11. Cf. Harvey Poppel and Bernard Goldstein, *Information Technology* (New York: McGraw-Hill, 1987), who list convergence as the single dominant trend of their five "infotrends."

PART I

The Paradigm Shift to Publishing in the Information Age

This opening part of the book looks at the changing industry environment in which publishing firms operate. We will look first at how the definition of information has changed and what the Information Age and the information industry mean for publishers. We will then reevaluate publishing in the light of this changing socio-economic and industry environment and consider the fundamental shift taking place in publishing—the shift to publishing in the Information Age. At the conclusion of this opening part, and as prelude to the core of the study, we will introduce the theoretical and structural backbone of the book, the 7M's of publishing.

CHAPTER 1

Information, the Information Age, and the New Meta-Industry

In order to grasp the depth and magnitude of the changes occurring in the publishing world, we must first understand what has happened to information, both the word and its connotations. Issuing from the changing notion of information are several broad and powerful metaphors, such as the information society, the information revolution, the Information Age, and the information industry. This chapter looks at these metaphors, as an understanding of them provides the necessary backdrop for our consideration in Chapter 2 of how, as a consequence of how information has changed, publishing has changed.

INFORMATION, THEN AND NOW

No longer is information a simple word with simple connotations—a phone number, a measurement, the contents of a brochure. Information has taken on a variety of meanings. To an economist "the meaning of information is precisely a reduction in uncertainty,"[1] whereas to a vendor in the commercial marketplace "information is an economic entity because it costs something to produce and because people are willing to pay for it."[2] The word seems to appear almost everywhere in every conceivable context. As communications consultant Christopher Burns has stated,

Information is content, stored and distributed over sometimes unique technologies ("information technologies"), and managed with sometimes unique procedures ("information systems"). When the results are exchanged in commerce they are called "information products" (manufactured before sale) and "information services" (manufactured after sale). The study of the integrity of the content as it is transported is called "information theory" while the practice of storing and retrieving information is called "information science."[3]

In the midst of it all the formerly dry and dull word "information" has assumed a sexy luster, especially as it is touted in magazine and television advertisements. Young professionals who work in prototypical Information Age organizations, such as computer and telecommunications firms, are portrayed as executive heroes on the cutting edge of the latest technology. How has this come about?

Much of the literature points to the period immediately after World War II as the starting point of the new information. The word was used in a new way at that time by a group of mathematicians and scientists, among them Norbert Wiener at MIT, Claude Shannon at Bell Labs, and Warren Weaver at Rockefeller University.[4] Wiener's 1948 book *Cybernetics,* which formulated communication as a statistical problem, was one of several key influences on the work Shannon did at roughly the same time. Shannon published his first paper in 1948 and published a book, co-authored with Weaver, in 1949 by the name *The Mathematical Theory of Communication,* which grew out of Shannon's work in the transmission and reception of clear telephone signals. The book describes information quantitatively, transmitted in bits (short for binary digits), as part of a new model of communication.

The approach was attractive to scientists in the field for a number of reasons. As Everett Rogers points out, "the timing of Shannon's theory was crucially related to electronics, mass communication, and computers," coming just at the time of the introduction of both television and the first digital computer, ENIAC (1946). The new theory was immediately seized upon for it fit hand in glove with the new machines, and a new field of study was born: information theory. Soon it attracted a large group of adherents who co-opted the word information to designate the discrete electric impulses transmitted in computer systems. Thus "information" met a fate similar to many other words appropriated by scientists and technicians. As social scientist Theodore Roszak has stated, "A word that has a long-standing, common-sense meaning is lifted from the public vocabulary and then skewed toward a new, perhaps highly esoteric definition by the scientists. The result can be a great deal of unfortunate confusion, even among the scientists themselves, who may then forget what the word meant before they appropriated it."[5]

The exponential rate of development in the computer field and the explosion in communications technologies over the four decades since the birth of information theory thrust the information theorists and their wares onto center stage. The electrical engineers' definition of information has been adopted, popularized and glorified, and by expanding it to encompass any type of communication, visual or aural, print or electronic, that can be encoded, processed, transmitted, and received, it has ultimately become an umbrella term for the content of any communication. Many react against this broad application of the word because of its lack of specificity and inappropriateness to so many different types of material beyond the scientists' words and numbers, such as graphic material (pictures, charts, etc.), moving visual material in film or video formats, and audio material, including music, sound, and the spoken voice, much of which would fit more comfortably under the rubric of knowledge, art, or entertainment than as information. Nonetheless, information has become the de facto catch-all term.

THE INFORMATION SOCIETY

Evolving somewhat later and in a separate academic camp was the concept of the information society. This idea came from a group of economists and social scientists, among them Harvard University sociologist Daniel Bell. In his influential 1973 book *The Coming of Post-Industrial Society,* Bell hypothesized that modern Western civilization had moved into its third major economic phase, what he calls the post-industrial society, following the first phase agricultural society and the second phase industrial society. In Bell's post-industrial economy, service occupations become the dominant forces of economic activity versus the "extractive" agricultural, mining, and fishing activities of pre-industrial society and the "fabrication" activities of manufacturing, industrial economies. Information replaces natural power—wind, water, and muscle—of the first era and electric power—oil, gas, coal, and nuclear-generated—of the industrial era as the transforming resource.[6]

For the first society, Bell states, the infrastructure for the necessary discourse between people, to facilitate the exchange of goods, was the transportation networks—roads, railroads, seaways, and canals. For the industrial era, the power utilities of steam, gas, electricity, and oil were the new infrastructure. Now, in Bell's post-industrial era, communications networks have emerged as the new infrastructure, from the mail service to newspapers, telephones, radio, television, and computerized data networks. In Bell's characterization the media, especially the newer electronic media, are fundamental to this infrastructure and thus a crucial force in the information society.[7] That is because for Bell, if information is the key "transforming" resource, knowledge is the key "strategic" resource of the era, the chief element that powers the entire economy. He cites the growth in human services—e.g., teaching and health-related services—and professional services, such as analysis, design, and programming, as supporting his "axial principle of the post-industrial society . . . the centrality of theoretical knowledge and its new role, when codified, as the director of social change."[8]

Bell's characterizations of a post-industrial information society were based upon several key studies, chief among them being Fritz Machlup's 1962 study *The Production and Distribution of Knowledge in the United States* and later Marc Porat's study of the National Income Accounts for 1967.[9] Both works, now recognized as benchmark studies, assessed the proportion of information-related job activity in the national economy. Machlup reported that for 1958, 29% of the GNP was spent for knowledge processing and distribution, in five major classes: (1) education, (2) research and development, (3) communications media, (4) information machines, and (5) information services. That year, Machlup found, 31% of the labor force was employed in those knowledge industries.[10]

Porat's study divided the economy into six sectors; the first three are the private manufacturing sector, the public manufacturing sector—public works such as roads and bridges—and the household sector. The other three sectors are all devoted to information work: the *primary information sector,* which includes companies that manufacture and market information machines and services, and the *secondary information sector,* which includes the two other sectors, the private and public bureaucracies which handle planning, scheduling, marketing, and related support services for all the other sectors. Porat's figures show that in 1967 just over 25% of the GNP originated in the primary information sector, and just over 21% in the secondary sector, for a total of 46%, which meant that "nearly 50% of GNP and more than 50% of wages and salaries derived from the production, processing, and distribution of information goods and services." As Bell states, "It is in this sense that we have become an information economy."

Bell also points out that the real rise in employment has come in Porat's secondary information sector, where the increasing complexity of organizations and their operations has fostered an immense need for planning, marketing, control, and related support services. The rise in this sector has propelled the overall shift in the employment base out of manufacturing and into the information-intensive service economy. From the Civil War to just after the turn of the century, farm workers dominated the economy. Likewise, through the first half of the 20th century, industrial manufacturing workers predominated. But in 1975 the number of information workers surpassed all non-information workers combined, and as early as 1967 information workers were already out-earning non-information workers, amassing more than 53% of the nation's total earned income.[11]

While other theorists have characterized the information society in different terms, none of the characterizations is inconsistent with Bell, Machlup, and Porat's characterization of an information-based economy. Management expert and social theorist Peter Drucker, for instance, believes that since World War II our technological society has shifted from a mechanical model to a biological one, where "in an organism, processes . . . are organized around information."[12] The exchange of information, in this view, is fundamental to all existence, and is also, by extension, essential among humans and higher level societies for proper functioning. Technologically we have mastered the development and distribution of food, clothing, and shelter on a mass scale, but now we must exchange massive amounts of information to fulfill these lower level needs in a complex, interdependent society. Hence the rise of information workers and the information-intensive sector of the economy.

A more market-driven view of the information society is posited by Koji Kobayashi, chairman of the Japanese computer and consumer electronics giant NEC: "As the value of information rises progressively and the cost of information falls, the economic equilibrium point will come down to a level where enormous amounts of information can flow. The so-called information society is nothing but a society that has reached this point."[13] Again, the flow of "enormous amounts of information" is the response to the need for communication in order for a complex society to function, and information technology provides the vehicle and the system for that communication.

THE INFORMATION AGE

If information in its newly expanded definition has come to encompass all forms of content in communications, and the information society is one in which the majority of the workforce is engaged in information-handling activities, what, then, is the Information Age?[14]

There are three major changes taking place that, in their combined effect, have created the Information Age. We have seen the first two—the changed and expanded definition of information and the shift to an information-based economy. But these two changes grew out of and are dependent upon the third major change, the revolution in communications technologies.

While some would designate it the media age or the electronic age, the Information Age has become the dominant metaphor as, since World War II, digital processing via computers has emerged as the ascendant information technology. In essence, computer information technology is the driving force behind the convergence of the formerly disparate forms of communication technology, as this simplified overview of the history of communications technologies shows (*see* Figure 1-1).

For over 400 years, until the mid-19th century, mass communication's only vehicle was print, first in the form of books, later in newspapers, and still later in magazines. Largely textual (i.e., words) with some line drawing and other graphic images, these printed materials would eventually incorporate natural images—photographs—after the invention of photography in the mid-19th century. We can refer to this 400-year period as the Age of Print.

Also in the mid-19th century, after 400 years of print-only communication, the telegraph initiated the birth of the electronic era of communications. With the invention of the telegraph in the 1830s by Samuel Morse, for the first time in history a message could travel long distances without a messenger. The power of electronics transcended the reliance upon physical means of distribution for long-distance communications. Moreover, the telegraph permitted a single message to be communicated from one specific point to another. Later in the 19th century the telephone permitted aural point-to-point telecommunication.

With the turn of the century came other new communications technologies, hybrid mechanical-electronic technologies for sound recording and moving

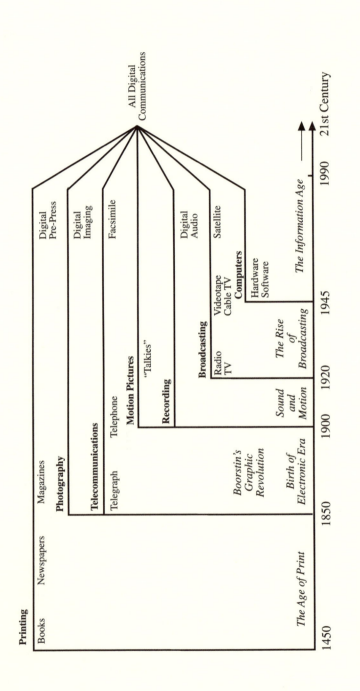

Figure 1-1
The Major Communications Technologies in the Information Age

pictures (the two would not converge for another 30 years). Meanwhile, via yet another electronic technology which had been in the experimental stages for some years, broadcasting was born, first radio (sound) in the 1920s and later television (sound and moving images) in the 1940s. Though electronic technologies, they were also akin to the print technologies in that they were blanket communication technologies, one-way mass media that allowed no point-to-point interchange, or interactivity, as did the electronic technologies of telecommunication.

Meanwhile, as television was just beginning to achieve commercial success, yet another basic technology was under development, the technology that was eventually to serve as the driving force behind the convergence not only of all the mass and interpersonal communications technologies but of the communications industries as well: electronic digital technology, or computers, whose roots as a mechanical device stretched back to the early 19th century. Although the other technologies have not been standing still, since World War II the computer has been the centripetal technology, pulling the other communication technologies together. With the rise of the computer has come the Information Age, an era which will, by the turn of the millennium, witness the digital embodiment of all the major communications technologies.

Viewed in another way, the century-long evolution of electronic communications technologies, from the advent of the telegraph in the mid-19th century, has developed along two parallel lines, creating a business-driven information economy as well as a consumer-driven entertainment economy. The interactive, point-to-point, processing technologies of the managerial, information-oriented world—telecommunications and computers—have arisen alongside the mass media, one-to-many broadcast technologies—radio and television—in the entertainment-oriented consumer world. Up to now, these technologies have evolved along relatively independent tracks (with telephones being perhaps the greatest single exception in the consumer market). But with digital processing technology now infusing all aspects of content preparation and dissemination, from text-based to visual to aural material, mass media communications technologies are converging with interactive information technologies to create entirely new media, thereby providing completely new challenges, opportunities—and dislocations—for both hardware and content firms in the information industry.

Significantly, there have been no displacements among the major categories of communications. All the core underlying technologies—printing, photography, telecommunications, motion pictures, recording, broadcasting, and computing—continue to coexist, as does the demand for the products and services produced by them. This is the popular conception of the Information Age, and one that is no less true: the proliferation of media and communications technologies that has made mass and interpersonal communications both instant and pervasive, flooding us with messages on an unprecedented scale.

A NEW META-INDUSTRY: THE INFORMATION INDUSTRY

The Information Age, then, is nothing less than a new socio-economic-technological paradigm that says not only how the economy is structured but tells us how we work, how we play, and how we communicate. We are witnessing not only the convergence of existing communications technologies but the proliferation of new media for the processing, storage, transmission, retrieval, and display of information in all forms—textual, visual, and aural—and in all markets—consumer, business and professional, and educational. And while we are witnessing this convergence, we are also witnessing the birth of a new meta-industry from the convergence of these separate component industries: the information industry.

The Information Business Map

The new meta-industry is captured in the Information Business Map, created by researchers at the Harvard University Program in Information Resources Policy (*see* Figure 1-2). The original map, first published in 1980, is credited as the brainchild of John McLaughlin.[15] The common denominator for all products and services on the map is information—"news, historical statistics, financial transactions, reference materials, advertising, entertainment"—even the information contained in private communiqués in the mail. Although they experimented with different axes for the map, McLaughlin and his colleagues at the Program eventually settled on the distinctions shown here: Form and Substance horizontally, Products and Services vertically.

The chief contribution of the map lies in its visual schema for displaying on one grid entire industries that are commonly thought to be in distinct and different fields. The version of the Information Business Map shown here highlights the media arena. In this arena we can see that book publishing (lower right) and cable television (upper center), for instance, though not close neighbors, are not only both part of the information industry but are also colleagues in the media business. Books, along with films, video, audio, magazines, and newspapers, are depicted in the Products-Substance corner of the map, while cable is depicted closer to the delivery or Form end of the spectrum.

As noted above, the media industries—publishing (books, magazines, and newspapers), broadcasting (radio, television, cable), recording, and motion pictures—have historically evolved apart from one another, with their own cultures, norms, support systems, specialized production and technical skills, and distribution channels. But the map reveals that despite differences in format and delivery systems, these industries are indeed related: they all develop *content* (Substance). The map further suggests that over time content firms will tend to converge, due to the infusion of information technology (e.g.,

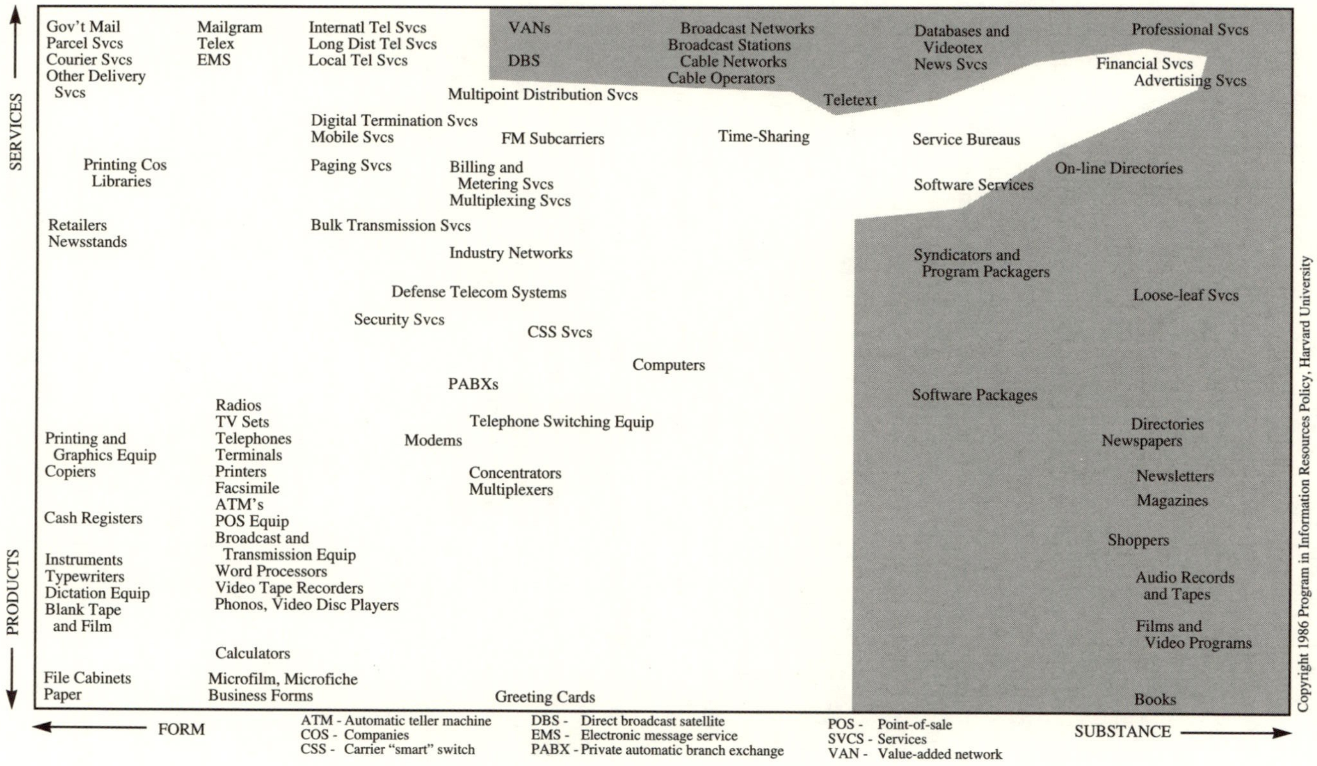
SERVICES
PRODUCTS
FORM
SUBSTANCE
Gov't Mail
Parcel Svcs
Courier Svcs
Other Delivery Svcs
Mailgram
Telex
EMS
Internatl Tel Svcs
Long Dist Tel Svcs
Local Tel Svcs
VANs
DBS
Broadcast Networks
Broadcast Stations
Cable Networks
Cable Operators
Databases and Videotex
News Svcs
Professional Svcs
Financial Svcs
Advertising Svcs
Multipoint Distribution Svcs
Teletext
Digital Termination Svcs
Mobile Svcs
FM Subcarriers
Time-Sharing
Service Bureaus
Printing Cos
Libraries
Paging Svcs
Billing and Metering Svcs
Multiplexing Svcs
On-line Directories
Software Services
Retailers
Newsstands
Bulk Transmission Svcs
Industry Networks
Syndicators and Program Packagers
Defense Telecom Systems
Loose-leaf Svcs
Security Svcs
CSS Svcs
Computers
PABXs
Software Packages
Radios
TV Sets
Telephones
Terminals
Printers
Facsimile
ATM's
POS Equip
Broadcast and Transmission Equip
Word Processors
Video Tape Recorders
Phonos, Video Disc Players
Telephone Switching Equip
Modems
Printing and Graphics Equip
Copiers
Directories
Newspapers
Concentrators
Multiplexers
Newsletters
Magazines
Cash Registers
Shoppers
Instruments
Typewriters
Dictation Equip
Blank Tape and Film
Audio Records and Tapes
Films and Video Programs
Calculators
File Cabinets
Paper
Microfilm, Microfiche
Business Forms
Greeting Cards
Books
ATM - Automatic teller machine
COS - Companies
CSS - Carrier "smart" switch
DBS - Direct broadcast satellite
EMS - Electronic message service
PABX - Private automatic branch exchange
POS - Point-of-sale
SVCS - Services
VAN - Value-added network
Copyright 1986 Program in Information Resources Policy, Harvard University

Figure 1-2
The Information Business Map (Highlighting the Media Arena)

digital computer technology, located at the center of the map) throughout content development and distribution.

If information technology underlies the entire grid, then publishing and the media, in the content-oriented arm of the information business, are as affected by the changes in new information technologies as any business in any sector of the map. As McLaughlin points out, "Growth, turmoil, and conflict are not limited to the electronics-based companies in the middle of the map. Broadcasters, publishers, and other media companies have been repositioning themselves to deal with new ways of collecting, packaging, and distributing information." Global mega-corporations, such as Australian Rupert Murdoch's News Corporation, France's Hachette, Germany's Bertelsmann, and the U.S.'s Time Warner, have arisen to cover the entire media map. Their vision of themselves is simple. They see themselves in the information business, the creation and distribution of content in all media forms. Print and electronic forms become packaging and delivery options at the output end of totally electronic content development systems that in turn feed global, all-media distribution systems.

Non-content information firms have also gained entry into the information business, echoing the moves in the 1960s and 1970s made by Xerox, RCA, ITT, Raytheon, and other technology firms. In the 1990's, consumer electronics companies, notably the two Japanese giants Sony and Matsushita, have acquired content firms, seeking to fuel sales of their hardware through control of software as well as gain entry into the content business as their hardware products are increasingly viewed as non-differentiable commodities.

At the opposite end of the spectrum from the mega-corporations are entrepreneurial firms created around the new technologies. There are some genuinely new areas, such as video publishing, multimedia, and online services, that do not clearly fall within one traditional media segment or another (e.g., broadcasting or periodical publishing) and thus are open, unclaimed territory.[16] There is no inertia in new technology publishers as they have no vested interest in past technologies. Even the established giants in the major media are vulnerable. The major broadcast television networks, all the targets of takeovers and the scene of major shake-ups in the 1980s, no longer rule the airwaves and are faced with "multitudes of competitors. Movie and sports networks, independent stations, program syndicators, and videocassette players all beckon viewers who once had a choice only of the three networks. Advertisers are discovering new choices too."[17] To these media choices we can add CD-ROM, video games, online services, and a variety of other delivery media yet to come.

THE INFORMATION AGE METAPHOR IN PERSPECTIVE

Once the flag of the Information Age has been planted, some caveats are in order, for we would be doing ourselves a disservice if we failed to keep the metaphor in perspective.

Publishers and other key players in the information industry are susceptible to the metaphor's powerful and often indiscriminate application. At its extreme, as social analyst Theodore Roszak comments, "seemingly, there are no longer any fields to till, any ores to mine, any heavy industrial goods to manufacture; at most these continuing necessities of life are mentioned in passing and then lost in the sizzle of pure electronic energy somehow meeting all human needs painlessly and instantaneously."[18] The information society is indeed a reality, but the technology which makes it possible, Roszak feels, must be seen as "an outgrowth of the existing industrial system, which has always been dependent on the 'knowledge' that undergirds invention, management, and marketing. Like the electrical, automotive, or chemical technologies that came before it, high tech arises as another stage in the ongoing industrial process. These technologies do not displace one another; they overlap, compound, and must be coordinated."[19] James Beniger believes that the foundations of the information society were laid in the 19th century through a matching of market needs and technological capabilities. Beniger depicts a "crisis of control"—lost railroad cars, for instance—creating the need for detailed, complex management systems. Computer technology had its roots in this era, and today's automated systems have evolved to meet these needs throughout the industrial and organizational world.[20]

Economists Stephen Cohen and John Zysman also argue against what they see as the "myth of the post-industrial economy:" "We must reorganize production, not abandon it; automate, not emigrate. . . . A substantial core of the service employment is tightly tied to manufacturing. It is a complement, not a substitute or successor, to manufacturing."[21] They cite the statistic that 25% of the GNP consists of services purchased by manufacturers:

Of course things have changed. Production work has changed. People go home cleaner; more and more of them leave offices rather than factories. Service activities have proliferated. The division of labor has become infinitely more elaborate. But the key generator of wealth for this vastly expanded and differentiated division of labor remains mastery and control of production. We are not experiencing a transition to a post-industrial society, but from one kind of industrial society to another.[22]

We are physical beings in a physical world and can no more survive on a diet of information than we can make clothing or shelter out of it. Just as agricultural production and food are still essential in industrial societies (despite the decline of the U.S. workforce involved in that sector to its current 3%), so manufacturing and the output of goods continue to remain crucial in an information society. The shift that has taken place is in the proportion of the workforce engaged in the different sectors. We still produce agricultural and industrial goods in vast quantities, but the bulk of the population is increasingly employed in handling information, hence the information society. We have become a three-tier economy to supply our essential needs: food from the agricultural sector, clothing and shelter from the industrial sector, and information from the information sector. Some societies still survive on agricultural output alone, but they are simpler societies with fewer interconnections and transactions and consequently less need for communication between individuals and organizations. But highly organized, industrialized interdependent societies such as those in the west and the Pacific rim require massive information exchange so that transactions can be processed and daily life can proceed.

It is true that each transition to a so-called new society marks a shift in productive resources, in the labor force, and in the flow of capital and other resources. Efficiency in agricultural production emerged from the advances of the industrial revolution. Now efficiencies in industrial production have resulted from the technological gains of automation—robotics, computers, and many others—of the information revolution. Yet it is important to note that many of the high technology firms that make this possible are *themselves* industrial firms, manufacturers of computers, wire and fiber optic networks, and other goods and equipment for business and industrial use. Many information industry occupations—a telephone repairman, a cable television technician, a fabricator of silicon chips—are in fact industrial, manual labor occupations, despite their inclusion in the information industry sector. We should not delude ourselves into believing that all information industry jobs are white-collar, knowledge-worker, administrative-managerial positions, for despite tremendous strides in automating many facets of business operations, certain physical realities of life still prevail.

SUMMARY AND CONCLUSION

With the rise of information theory and the advent of computer technology in the post–World War II era, the meaning of the word information has expanded to encompass the substance of any communication, ultimately referring to all content digitized into bits and bytes—electronic, fluid, storable, transmittable, and manipulable material. Moreover, the rise of information technology, whether propelled by industrial control needs or seen as a part of the broader technological development of the 20th century, has made the bulk of the workforce into information handlers.

Whether we adopt an economic model, in which our society's productive resources have shifted into an information-intensive mode by replacing industrial society's dependence on machine-power with a dependence on applied knowledge; a biological model, in which the exchange of information is essential to all life and living systems; or a market-based model, in which suppliers arise to meet the burgeoning demand for information, the ascendant digital information technologies are the centripetal force of the Information Age.

In the second half of the 20th century this new socio-economic-technological paradigm has brought the rise of a new meta-industry, the information industry, which includes all organizations involved in the development and distribution of content as well as those firms that manufacture the machines and facilities on which the content is created, stored, and delivered. Industries which historically have developed their own technologies, cultures, and institutions—telecommunications, computers, broadcasting, recording, printing, and publishing—can now be seen on the same map as part of the new meta-industry.

As developers and distributors of all types of information, publishers are placed squarely in the midst of this new meta-industry. Thus it is not surprising that as the new socio-economic paradigm of the Information Age has arisen, so too has a new publishing paradigm arisen, the subject of the next chapter.

NOTES

1. Kenneth Arrow, "The Economics of Information," in Michael Dertouzos and Joel Moses, eds., *The Computer Age: A Twenty-Year View* (Cambridge, Mass.: MIT Press, 1980), 306.

2. John Naisbitt, *Megatrends* (New York: Warner Books, 1984), 31.

3. Christopher Burns and Patricia Martin, "The Economics of Information" (Washington, D.C.: U.S. Department of Commerce, 1985), I-11.

4. For an introductory discussion of Shannon and Wiener's contributions to information theory, *see* Everett M. Rogers, *Communication Technology—The New Media In Society* (New York: The Free Press, 1986), 82–96.

5. Theodore Roszak, *The Cult of Information* (New York: Pantheon Books, 1986), 13.

6. Bell's characterization, which has been grossly simplfed here, is drawn from his "The Social Framework of the Information Society" in Michael Dertouzos and Joel Moses, eds., *The Computer Age: A Twenty-Year View* (Cambridge, Mass.: MIT Press, 1980), 163–211.

7. Bell wrote in 1979:

The really major social change of the next two decades will come in the third major infrastructure, as the merging technologies of telephone, computer, facsimile, cable television, and videodiscs lead to a vast reorganization in the modes of communication between persons; the transmission of data; the reduction if not the elimination of paper in transactions and exchanges; new modes of transmitting news, entertainment, and knowledge; and the reorganization of learning that may follow the expansion of computer-assisted instruction and the spread of videodiscs.

Bell, "The Social Framework of the Information Society," 195.

8. Ibid., 164.

9. Machlup's study was published under that title by Princeton University Press in 1962, and Porat's work was done for his Stanford University Ph.D. dissertation entitled "The Information Economy," presented in 1976 and subsequently issued by the U.S. Department of Commerce Office of Telecommunications in May, 1977 under the title *Information Economy: Definition and Measurement.*

10. In 1963, a year after the publication of Machlup's study, *Fortune* magazine editor

Gilbert Burck calculated that, based on Machlup's categories, 1963 showed 33% of the GNP generated by the knowledge sector. Five years later economist Jacob Marschak predicted that the same economic sector would approach 40% of the GNP in the next decade (the 1970s). Bell, "The Social Framework of the Information Society," 179. Burck's figures were published in his *Fortune* article "Knowledge, The Biggest Growth Industry of Them All."

11. Bell, "The Social Framework of the Information Society," 183. Bell's and Porat's work were the key inspiration for the first of social forecaster John Naisbitt's mega-trends, "From An Industrial Society to an Information Society." Naisbitt's book *Megatrends,* which rode high up on the hardcover and paperback bestseller lists for more than two years after its publication in 1982, brought the notion of the information society to the attention of millions of readers. For Naisbitt the key aspect of Porat's study was how he painstakingly separated and counted the information jobs in the secondary information sectors, those workers who "produce information goods and services for internal consumption within goods-producing and other companies." Naisbitt also includes statistics from MIT's David Birch that show that "only 5% of the almost 20 million new jobs created in the 1970s were in manufacturing (almost 90% were in information, knowledge, or service jobs). . . . While the total labor force grew only 18% between 1970–1978, the number of administrators and managers grew at more than three times that rate—58%." John Naisbitt, *Megatrends* (New York: Warner Books, 1982), 1–33.

12. From Drucker's *Innovation and Entrepreneurship* (New York: Harper and Row, 1985), as quoted in Stewart Brand, *The Media Lab: Inventing the Future at MIT* (New York: Viking Penguin, 1987), xiv.

13. Koji Kobayashi, *Computers and Communications* (Cambridge, Mass.: MIT Press, 1986), 177.

14. The National Museum of American History at the Smithsonian Institution devotes an entire hall to the Information Age. The new exhibition hall "traces the 'information revolution' from its beginning in the 19th century to today's sophisticated computers, and . . . tracks new developments in communications." Smithsonian Secretary Robert Adams stated that the "information revolution was [sic] comparable only to such things as the industrial revolution and Gutenberg's invention of movable type. Such events . . . occur only once in several centuries." Irvin Molotsky, "Information Age Enters Smithsonian," *The New York Times,* 3 November 1985.

15. Founded in 1972 by program director Anthony Oettinger, the Program first published the map and other material for general readership in *Understanding New Media* (Cambridge, Mass.: Balinger Press, 1984), a collection of their most important papers to that time, edited by then executive director of the Program, Benjamin Compaine. The map and aspects of this discussion are drawn from "Mapping the Information Business" by John F. McLaughlin with Anne E. Birinyi, 19–67.

Other maps of the information business have been created, usually variations on the PIRP map. These include the map created by the Information Industry Association (widely published with their material) as well as the map created by the information technology group at Booz Allen Hamilton and published in Harvey Poppel and Bernard Goldstein's *Information Technology: The Trillion-Dollar Opportunity* (New York: McGraw-Hill, 1987). Poppel refers to the new information business as the information technology industry and defines it as the collection of businesses which "produce content and the facilities that deliver content to end users . . . [it] is the fusion of numerous business sectors—entertainment, publishing, office and computer equipment, telecommunications, consumer electronics, and others—that have been related casually, if at all, until very recently."

16. MIT's Negroponte launched the Media Lab in the late 1970s with the proposition that three major industries—broadcasting and motion pictures, printing and publishing, and computers—were on a collision course. "The three industries all have separate professional associations, separate journals, and separate heroes . . . [and] separate languages," says Negroponte in Stewart Brand's *The Media Lab*. "We saw the richest and most promising areas of research and development at their intersections." Brand summarizes: "Negroponte's vision: all communication technologies are suffering a joint metamorphosis, which can only be understood properly if treated as a single subject, and only advanced properly if treated as a single craft. The way to figure out what needs to be done is through exploring the human sensory and cognitive system and the ways that humans naturally interact. Join this and you grasp the future" (*The Media Lab*, 10–11). Pool, Poppel, and others also speak of the institutionalization of the various segments of the communications industry and the inevitable dissolution of these barriers as convergence of the various media accelerates.

Similarly, Daniel Bell cites Canadian historian Harold Innis, McLuhan's mentor, who believed that communications technologies were "the extensions of perception and knowledge, the enlargement of consciousness. He [Innis] argued that each stage of Western civilization was dominated by a particular medium of communications but that the rise of a new mode was invariably followed by cultural disturbances" (Bell, "The Social Framework of the Information Society," 169).

17. Peter J. Boyer, "Chairman Paley Returns to a Different World," *The New York Times*, 14 September 1986. *See also* Ken Auletta's *Three Blind Mice: How the Networks Lost Their Way* (New York: Random House, 1991).

18. Roszak, *The Cult of Information*, 22.

19. Ibid., 29.

20. As discussed in Rogers, *Communication Technology*, 14. Beniger's book, *The Control Revolution,* was published by Harvard University Press in 1986.

21. Stephen S. Cohen and John Zysman, "The Myth of a Post-Industrial Economy," *The New York Times,* 17 May, 1987. *See also* Lester C. Thurow, "The Post-Industrial Era Is Over," *The New York Times,* 4 September, 1989.

22. Cohen and Zysman, "The Myth of a Post-Industrial Economy." *See also* Robert Reich's characterization of information workers as "symbolic processors" in *The Work of Nations: Preparing Ourselves for 21st Century Capitalism* (New York: Knopf, 1991).

CHAPTER 2

Rethinking Publishing: The Paradigm Shift

As we saw in Chapter 1, a new socio-economic–technological paradigm, the Information Age, and a new meta-industry, the information industry, have arisen. As key players in the information industry, publishers are working within a new paradigm as well. This chapter reconsiders the enterprise of publishing in the light of this changing environment and introduces the new publishing paradigm, the paradigm of publishing in the Information Age.

COMMUNICATION AND PUBLISHING: DEFINING THE CRITERIA

We must first distinguish publishing's traditional role in the context of human communication, which we can do by placing it on a space-time matrix, two of the essential criteria which define the act of publishing (*see* Figure 2-1). Coexistence in space but not time (lower left quadrant) requires the physical presence of both the message and the receiver, and thus includes cave drawings, sculpture and other works of art, buildings, and other tangible physical objects. Coexistence in both space and time (lower right quadrant) implies a live interaction, such as a face-to-face conversation, a lecture, or a performance. Neither time nor space are transcended, and no medium is involved.

While broadcasting (upper right quadrant) can transcend both time and space, its chief distinguishing feature and benefit is the transcendence of space—mass, ubiquitous, instant communication. Phone and computer networks (as well as cable television) also fall into this category, though unlike

TIME

		Not Co-Exist	Co-Exist
SPACE	**Not Co-Exist**	Publishing Film Letters Computer Network	Broadcasting Telephone Computer Network
	Co-Exist	Cave Drawing Sculpture Buildings Exhibits Kiosks	Face-To-Face Conversation Lecture Performance

Figure 2-1
The Space-Time Communication Matrix

broadcasting's point-to-multi-point mass communication, telecommunications networks provide point-to-point interpersonal communication.

Publishing is the communications enterprise which by definition transcends both time and space (upper left quadrant). (Significantly, computer networks also fall into this category.) With published products and services, the user also has control, the ability to either physically handle or manipulate the received information in some way, impossible with an evanescent broadcast unless a capture device is used. Publishing also suggests an active choice on the part of the buyer or user, the purchase of individual discrete products or services that the user controls as he or she chooses.

Published products and services are distinguished from the rest of communication, then, through the following criteria. They must be:

- recorded or captured in some form for relay;
- reproduced in some form for circulation;
- susceptible to dissemination over distance, i.e., able to transcend space;
- susceptible to storage for retrieval and use at some future time, i.e., able to transcend time.

But while we can isolate and define the role of traditional publishing in human communication, the significant shift is that it is now blurring with other media and forms of communication, such as broadcasting and computer networks, to create the new publishing paradigm discussed below and throughout this study.

THE TOOLS FOR CONVERSATION: CHANGING PUBLISHING TECHNOLOGIES

Before we address the specifics of that shift, we must also recognize that to be captured and reproduced for broad circulation means, by definition, that a message must have a medium. We can adopt professor Neil Postman's use of the metaphor of conversation "to refer not only to speech but to all techniques and technologies that permit people of a particular culture to exchange messages." Communications media, then, including those media used in publishing, can be characterized as our society's tools for conversation.[1]

Originally, to "publish" or declare a message was to speak from a soap box or to shout out as the town crier. With the advent of technologies to record writing, statements could be recorded and reproduced for dissemination, or at least nailed to the church door. The most radical transformation was brought by the printing press, which allowed mass replication of an expression so that many people could receive it at different times and in different places. Printing was the first mass technology that decoupled the physical presence of the creator from his message. (Even smoke signals and jungle drums have physical constraints, requiring the message's receiver to be within eyesight or earshot of the sender.) With the origin of printing, publishing was born.

From its earliest days, then, publishing has been synonymous with the embodiment of text and image, beginning with the duplication of hand-lettered illuminated manuscripts from medieval scriptoria. The early fixed-type presses were eventually to be replaced by Gutenberg's movable type in the mid-15th century. Not until electronic typesetting came into being over 500 years later were an author's words able to be viewed on an electronic screen.[2] Now publishers can convey both word and image on the screen as well as in ink on paper, and most recently—and of equal significance as the move from paper to screen—sound and moving images have been added to the publisher's symbolic repertoire.[3]

The metaphor of conversation takes on new meaning and immediacy in an electronically interconnected world. Online systems connect groups of scattered users in conversational exchanges. Nicholas Negroponte, founder and director of the MIT Media Laboratory, has said that "Monologues will become conversations, the impersonal will become personal, the traditional mass media will essentially disappear."[4] While we may have some reservations about this characterization—Poppel and Goldstein, for instance, make the significant distinction between *performance* and *participative* media—Negroponte's vision cannot be denied. The new electronic technologies create a two-way conversational model for mass communications that heretofore existed only in the realm of interpersonal, one-to-one, point-to-point communications, via such means as the telephone or telegraph.

The traditional conception of publishing, then, as a paper-based, print-only activity, is expanding to include other forms. Shifts in the major vehicles or methods of human discourse—from oral to written and written to print, and now from print to electronic—have all involved major industrial, economic, and social dislocations and adjustments. As Stewart Brand has observed, the new electronic media have created a "personal renaissance," creating new personal activities versus passivities: "Each violates what is known about audiences . . . Each makes audiences into something else—less 'a group of spectators, listeners, or readers' and more a society of selectors, changers, makers."[5]

THE PARADIGM SHIFT TO PUBLISHING IN THE INFORMATION AGE

Thus publishing is a media-neutral activity. Its forms and techniques have responded to the media technologies—the culture's conversational tools—of the time, and as the interests, tastes and communication habits of the culture change, so publishers have wielded the appropriate media forms to meet those changing interests, tastes, and habits. The most recent changes in the culture's tools for conversation have brought about a shift within the publishing industry, the type of shift characterized by Thomas Kuhn in his pivotal 1962 work *The Structure of Scientific Revolutions* as a *paradigm shift*, a change in one's view of the world that answers persistent, perplexing questions, realigns adherents in a redefined community, and provides a new framework of understanding within which the community of practitioners can move forward.

THE KUHNIAN PARADIGM SHIFT

For Kuhn, business-as-usual, the guiding paradigm of a community of professional scientists at work, is known as normal science. The community of practitioners works together on certain problems and with a shared worldview and understanding. To maintain that community, normal science "often suppresses fundamental novelties because they are necessarily subversive of its basic commitments." These challenges, or anomalies, are "seldom just an increment to what is already known. [Their] assimilation requires the reconstruction of prior theory and the re-evaluation of prior fact." The anomaly "appears only against the background provided by the paradigm," creating what Kuhn calls the "incommensurability of competing paradigms." Kuhn notes "what scientists never do when confronted by even several and prolonged anomalies. Though they may begin to lose faith and then to consider alternatives, they do not renounce the paradigm that has led them into crisis." The transition to crisis happens when "an anomaly comes to seem more than just another puzzle of normal science" and the community moves into "extraordinary science." If the community continues to resist the anomaly-engendered crisis "many of them may come to view its resolution as *the* subject matter of their discipline." It is important to note, too, that, for Kuhn, "crises need not be generated by the work of the community that experiences them . . . new instruments may develop in one specialty and their assimilation create crisis in another."

The community then fragments, some aligning themselves with the new school of thought, others refusing to relinquish the prevailing paradigm. The two groups begin to practice in different worlds, "seeing different things when they look from the same point in the same direction." Attacks on the proposed anomalous theory involve "articulations of the [new] paradigm," none of which is precisely accurate and only serve in aggregate to blur the rules of the current guiding paradigm. The real issue is "which paradigm should in the future guide research . . . that decision must be based less on past achievement than on future promise," and for individual practitioners that shift amounts to a leap of faith: "Rather than a single group conversion, what occurs is an increasing shift in the distribution of professional allegiances."

The paradigm shift, then, is "a transfer of allegiance from paradigm to paradigm [that] is a conversion experience that cannot be forced" and is accomplished through a "relatively sudden and unstructured event" akin to a gestalt switch. It involves a leap to a new way of viewing the same thing: "looking at a contour map, the student sees lines on paper, the cartographer a picture of terrain. Only after a number of such transformations of vision does the student become an inhabitant of the scientist's world, seeing what the scientist sees and responding as the scientist does." Finally, "when the transition is complete" to the new paradigm, says Kuhn, "the profession will have changed its view of the field, its methods, and its goals."

Even though he sees something new and views the world and his task entirely differently, the scientist working within the new paradigm is "still looking at the same world" and much of his language and instruments are still the same: "Since new paradigms are born from old ones, they ordinarily incorporate much of the vocabulary and apparatus, both conceptual and manipulative, that the traditional paradigm had employed," but they fall into a new relationship with one another. In the end, says Kuhn, "the conversion experience . . . remains at the heart of the revolutionary process. Good reasons for choice provide motives for conversion and a climate in which it is more likely to occur."

Kuhn's theory is supported by major examples of such revolutionary shifts in science—Ptolemy to Copernicus, Newton to Einstein, the creationists to Darwin. Kuhn sees his thesis as "undoubtedly of wide applicability . . . for [it is] borrowed from literature, music, the arts, political development, and many other human activities." He also notes that "particularly in periods of acknowledged crisis . . . scientists have turned to philosophical analysis as a device for unlocking the riddles of their field," precisely the type of analysis that has been undertaken in the information industry over the past several years.

If we look at Kuhn's model of paradigm change, all the earmarks are there for a fundamental shift in the world of publishing: philosophical analysis and the study of underlying issues; perplexing anomalies besetting the community of practitioners; different communities seeing the same thing differently; shifting allegiances; and a paradigm of future promise versus one of past achievement. These things all define the current state of the publishing world, which we can illustrate by considering the contrast in the two worldviews across several key dimensions (*see* Table 2-1).

The paradigm shift from traditional publishing to Information Age publishing embraces a new view of the publishing business, a view that is based on

	TRADITIONAL PUBLISHING	INFORMATION AGE PUBLISHING
VIEW OF BUSINESS	Format-based	Content-based
VIEW OF OFFERING	Product: Book, Magazine, etc.	Products and Services: Ideas, Information
MEDIA FORMATS	Print	Print and Electronic
TECHNOLOGY ORIENTATION	Technology-bound	Technology-inspired
PROCESS TECHNOLOGIES	Mechanical	Electronic
MESSAGING SYMBOLS	Words, Numbers, Still Images	Words, Numbers, Still Images, plus Moving Images, Voice, Sound
VIEW OF CUSTOMER	Reader	Reader-Viewer-Listener-User
MARKETING ORIENTATION	Product-focused	Market-focused
COMMUNICATIONS FLOW	One-way: Point-to-multi-point, Disconnected	One-way and Two-way: Disconnected plus Networked
DISTRIBUTION METHOD	Physical	Physical and Electronic
DISTRIBUTION CYCLE	List, Periodical	List, Periodical, Open Channel
MANAGEMENT	Format-specific	Integrative

Table 2-1
The Paradigm Shift to Publishing in the Information Age

the *content* of the communication, not the format. The Information Age publisher conceives of his chief offering—services as well as products—as ideas and information, not the physical products which embody them (e.g., books, magazines, or videocassettes). It is the content, often of a proprietary nature, that is the publisher's chief asset, and value is added to it in new ways by packaging in different media formats, both print and electronic. Thus the definition of publishing expands as the print publishing paradigm yields to the new paradigm that includes both print and electronic formats.[6]

Information Age publishers are inspired by the opportunities offered by the new media technologies and are not bound to offering customers information only in the traditional print formats. Whereas process technologies for traditional publishers include many mechanical aspects, Information Age publishers develop and process content in integrated electronic systems, both for pre-press print output as well as electronically embodied products and services. Traditional publishing uses words, numbers, and still images to communicate, while Information Age publishers expand the range of symbolic languages at their disposal to include moving images and sound as well.

The traditional publishers' customers are readers of books, magazines, and newspapers. The Information Age publisher's customers are also readers, but they are viewers (e.g., of videocassettes), listeners (to audio cassettes), and users (of software and online services) as well. The marketing orientation of the Information Age publisher is toward serving customers' needs in whatever media format best serves the purpose, not pushing product in one format only if superior or complementary alternatives exist.

While in traditional publishing the flow of information is always one-way, from one source to many receivers, in Information Age publishing the flow can be two-way over networked systems, for dialogue and on-demand publications in interactive systems. Thus the paradigm accommodates both passive, performance, broadcast-type media as well as participative, interactive media. Traditional publishing products are distributed physically. The products and services of Information Age publishers are distributed both physically and electronically. Traditional publishers hew to either list or periodical publishing, while Information Age publishers also distribute their information through electronic open channel systems. Finally, to orchestrate the multiple offerings of the firm, the Information Age publisher requires not just individuals skilled and knowledgeable in specific media formats, but managers with the breadth of vision and ability—integrative management—to integrate the various constituencies of the firm into a single whole.

The paradigm shift to Information Age publishing is a mainstream development, part of the historical evolution of the publishing industry which has adapted to changes in technology over time to achieve its broader mission: to inform, to inspire, and to educate. As mentioned earlier there are many compelling reasons for this shift—changing technologies, changing user habits, new processes and products, new competitive threats, and the renewed need for strategy in an industry beset by many changes.

The new paradigm takes account of the perplexing changes, explains them, and bases itself on future promise, not past achievement. In this worldview the new media formats are embraced as opportunities, not feared as external threats. Information Age publishers do not exclude the new publishing media, but instead see publishing as inclusive of all media. Once this paradigm shift has been made, publishers are free to approach strategic business decisions of resource deployment and media diversification as legitimate, everyday business issues.

Significantly, Information Age publishing also means an inclusion not only of different media formats but the organizations that create, manufacture, and distribute—or publish—in these media: videocassette and disc publishers, audio publishers, software publishers, CD-ROM publishers, all developers and publishers of new information formats that are also part of the information industry. The traditional print formats such as books and magazines still exist and have their distinct uses, but as successful new formats are adopted and used on a wide scale, they engender a new equilibrium of media formats and firms. In this manner, institutional change is wrought and industry power shifts, just as the communications industries have accommodated previous shifts in power over time.

SUMMARY AND CONCLUSION

The technologies employed by publishers and media firms to embody their messages are the culture's tools for conversation. With the continual advent of new media technologies, these tools change, and publishing changes, too. The community of publishers is now in transition, each individual looking at the new publishing paradigm and deciding whether to embrace the new or stay with the old. Every individual must decide on his or her own.

The new paradigm of Information Age publishing defines future tasks and directions. It opens up legitimate, revenue-producing publishing activities where choices of product format and delivery are derivative, based on the content to be delivered and the audience for whom that content is intended. The array of format choices and delivery alternatives are at the disposal of the publisher, who must wield the new technological resources in service of his mission: to inform, entertain, and inspire.

The changes in technology and user habits will continue to affect all areas of publishing and all markets, gradually forcing traditional print-based publishers to embrace the new paradigm and adopt innovative approaches in response to the changing environment or face decline. Once publishers assess their place in this dynamic environment, they must plot their strategic courses for tomorrow.

NOTES

1. Neil Postman, *Amusing Ourselves to Death* (New York: Viking Penguin, 1986), 6–8. The term is actually Marshall McLuhan's. Postman cites McLuhan's observation that "the clearest way to see through a culture is to attend to its tools for conversation."

2. As David Backer has summarized it: "Technological innovation in communications media has been occurring at a rapidly accelerating pace. Roughly speaking, it took over 5 million years to get from spoken language to writing, about 5,000 years from writing to printing, and 500 years from printing to radio, telephone, film and television. It took only fifty years from the formative period of television to the demonstration of video discs, and now [1985] it is about five years since the advent of personal computers." David S. Backer, "Prototype for the Electronic Book" in *Electronic Publishing Plus* (White Plains, N.Y.: Knowledge Industry Publications, 1985), 131.

3. In 1961, Daniel Boorstin subsumed sound and moving images under the rubric of publishing when speaking of the various media forms in his now classic work, *The Image:* "Each way is a path to millions of viewers or readers or hearers. . . . Modern publishing [is] books, movies, or television shows or music" (*The Image,* 180). In the thirty years since this was written, the disparate tentacles of the media industry have converged even more, increasing the frequency of transmutability of Boorstin's "dissolving forms." Scholarly publisher Irving Horowitz has stated: "Now that the concept of publishing need no longer be restricted to print, the publisher must rethink what value can be added to the work an author creates. Publishers are uniquely positioned to perceive that work presented in one format could be packaged and sold in another; perhaps they can provide the means for transferring the material into other formats or offer to combine the material with others in a collection in which it would have different applications and could be reformatted." *Communicating Ideas* (New York: Oxford University Press, 1987), 33.

4. As quoted in Stewart Brand, *The Media Lab* (New York: Viking Penguin, 1987), 5.

5. Ibid., 252.

6. Bill Zoellick, co-editor of *CD-ROM—Optical Publishing*, also speaks of the changing publishing paradigm in relation to the development of database material for CD-ROM:

The most revolutionary changes taking place in publishing are not related to hardware, but to *ideas*. People are *thinking* about publishing in a new way. . . . When we speak of the publishing revolution as one driven by ideas rather than solely by technology, this notion of reversing the publishing paradigm stands out as an archetypical example of this revolutionary power. Information that is stored electronically and organized logically is a transportable and searchable commodity. You can repackage, subdivide, and rearrange it to suit a variety of purposes.

From "Changing the Publishing Paradigm" in *CD-ROM—Optical Publishing* (Redmond, Wash.: Microsoft Press, 1987), 1–2.

CHAPTER 3

The 7M's of Publishing

To help analyze the changes taking place in the world of publishing in the Information Age, we can break down the publisher's decision mix to its basic elements and take a closer look at each. These basic elements are the 7M's of publishing, the five value-added M's—*Material, Mode, Medium, Means,* and *Market*—plus the two M's which form the essential infrastructure of all businesses, *Management* and *Money* (*see* Figure 3-1):

Core Concept #1: The 7M's of Publishing

Within each of these five elements are the key processes that add value to the components at any point in the chain. The arrows in Figure 3-1 indicate that the flow is generally clockwise, though the elements must not always be created and enacted in this sequence. *Material* is expressed in one or more *Modes* and is packaged in one or more *Media.* The product or service is distributed via the appropriate *Means* to a *Market,* whose revenues, along with other sources, provide the necessary *Money* to fund the enterprise and keep the cycle in motion for additional new products. The *Management* of the publishing firm decides upon and orchestrates these components for each of its products and services, employing its human, technological, financial, and other resources to achieve its desired ends.[1]

THE FIVE VALUE-ADDED M'S

Table 3-1 details the five value-added M's of the information construct. The five columns represent the 5M's, and the three rows within each column

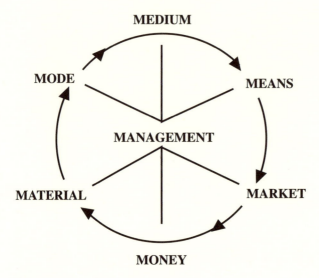

Figure 3-1
The 7M's of Publishing

define the components, processes, and participants which comprise the elements.

The First M: Material—What It Is

The first of the five value-added M's is *Material*—the content, the substance, the subject matter of each published product or service, be it an author's words, a newscast, a bibliographic database, a set of corporate financial statements, or a word processing program. Although material knows only the limits of the human mind and endeavors, for the purposes of our analysis we can class it into five basic categories, each of which will be addressed in Chapter 4: information, knowledge, entertainment, art, and tools.

The processes which *Create* and *Process* these components include everything from researching and seeking out raw material to its refinement and processing in a given mode (the second M), the symbolic languages of expression which capture the material. It is important to note, as does NEC's Koji Kobayashi, that "information processing and conversion are an intrinsic part of information generation."[2]

Participants in the creation and processing of material include all *Originators* and *Creators* of information, from researchers and artists, to writers, photographers, software programmers, knowledge experts (both individual and institutional), creative teams, and performers. Working closely with these cre-

	MATERIAL	MODE	MEDIUM	MEANS	MARKET
	(Content)	(Symbolic Language)	(Storage/Display)	(Transfer Conduit)	(Customers/Buyers)
COMPONENTS	Information Knowledge Entertainment Art Tools	Textual - Words, Numbers, Notations Visual (Images) - Still, Moving, Graphic, Animated Aural (Sound) - Music, Human Voice, Noise, Natural Sound Other - Gustatory, Olfactory, Haptic	Book, Magazine, Newspaper, Newsletter, Magnetic Disk, Optical Disc, Online Film, Videocassette, Videodisc, Broadcast Television, Cable Television Vinyl Disc, CD Audio, Audio Cassette, Radio IMS, PDA's	List/Periodical Physical - Mail, Retail Outlet, Direct Delivery, Kiosk, Theater Electronic - Broadcast, Microwave, Satellite, Telephone, Cable Periodical/Open Channel Other Face-to-Face - Conference, Classroom	Customers - Consumer, Business/Professional, Educational, Government, International Buyers - Advertisers Third Parties
PROCESSES	Creating Researching Writing Drawing Photographing Programming Compiling Gathering Performing Analyzing	Processing Capturing Storing Displaying Editing Converting Structuring Programming	Designing Producing Typesetting Printing Mastering Manufacturing	Transmitting Disseminating Delivering Presenting Responding (Two-Way Systems)	Customers - Reading, Viewing, Listening, Using, Requesting Publishers - Selecting, Identifying, Targeting, Positioning, Packaging, Pricing, Promoting, Publicizing, Selling, Licensing, Supporting, Servicing, Responding
PARTICIPANTS	Originators/Creators Researchers Artists Writers Photographers Programmers Author Teams Performers Knowledge Experts	Processors Editors Film-Video Producers Audio Producers Directors Multimedia Designers- Developers Programmers	Designers Producers Printers Packagers Manufacturers	Physical - Mail Services, Private Carriers, Wholesalers, Distributors, Retailers, Book Clubs Electronic - Broadcasters, Vendors, Network Operators Face-to-Face - Conference Producers, Schools	Customers- End-users, OEM's Publishers- Market Researchers, Market Strategists-Planners, Advertisers, Promoters-Publicists, Salespeople. Customer Support, Space Salespeople, Artists, Photographers, Designers, Copywriters, Licensers

MANAGEMENT AND MONEY

Table 3-1
The Five Value-Added M's

ators are the *Processors* of the material—text, film, video, and sound editors, producers, directors—any individual who takes a hand in shaping the expression and presentation of the material. This includes those individuals who are technically skilled in a given medium as well as those closer to the idea, the substance, and its initial creation. Those creators not proficient in at least one mode must ally themselves with someone skilled in the chosen mode of material capture. Otherwise they will have no expressive form in which to render their creations.[3]

The Second M: Mode—How It's Expressed

The second M, *Mode,* is the set of symbols or language elements in which the material is embodied, expressed, and presented. The three major modes for communications media are the *Textual* mode—words, numbers, and notational systems (e.g., music); the *Visual* mode—images, still or moving, natural, artificial, or graphic; and the *Aural* mode—sounds, including music, the human voice, noises, and naturally occurring sound (e.g., bird calls). Other modes, though for various reasons less frequently employed by the communications media, include the gustatory mode, corresponding to the sense of taste; the olfactory mode (smell); and the haptic mode (touch).

As material must be rendered in a given mode, the processes and participants are the same for both material and mode (*see* Table 3-1). As stated above, proficiency in at least one mode, or access to such proficiency, is required to embody and express material.

The Third M: Medium—How It's Stored and Displayed

The third M is *Medium,* representing both the form in which the material is stored and the manner in which it is displayed, which therefore determines how the material will be produced and manufactured.

The media are blank slates, each capable of handling one or more modes, onto which the material can be written for storage and subsequent retrieval. We thus group the media formats in the major modes as they determine how the material will be rendered and perceived by the end user. Each medium is classified not just according to its modal capabilities but according to its *distinguishing* mode of expression without which it would lose its definition, lifeblood, and primary communicative value. Thus *Textual* media include the familiar print formats of books, magazines, and newspapers, and also magnetic and optical media. *Visual* media include the print media, capable of handling still images, as well as the moving image media of film, video cassettes, interactive video, and broadcast and cable television. *Aural* media—those for which sound is the distinguishing feature—include phonograph records, audio cassettes, compact audio discs, and radio. Multimodal media are those media repositories capable of handling all three major modes. These include magnetic and optical media and integrated media systems, or IMS, my term for combinations of existing media, e.g., a book and a compact disc, developed and intended for use in conjunction with one another.

Processes, therefore, include designing and producing in these media and require technical skills in each format. Participants include designers, producers, printers, packagers and manufacturers, those primarily concerned with embodying the material in some physical form for storage and retrieval.

The media can be either a product—material packaged before distribution—or a service—material packaged for display after distribution, as we will discuss below.

The Fourth M: Means—How It's Delivered

The fourth M is *Means,* the channel or conduit by which the product or service is distributed, how the material is transferred and delivered to the end user. The means of distribution are grouped according to the three distribution cycles: List, Periodical, and Open Channel. *List* products are those physical packages that are created, kept in inventory, and distributed over time at no particular frequency or interval. They are distributed via physical means, such as the mail and private carriers, retail outlets, direct delivery to the user (e.g., door-to-door), or via special means such as kiosk displays. *Periodical* products are those whose distribution cycle is regular—e.g., daily, weekly, monthly—and can be either physically distributed (newspapers and magazines) or electronically distributed—e.g., a daily or weekly television program. The *Open Channel* cycle is electronic distribution only and includes information services (versus products) delivered via the airwaves—broadcast, microwave, satellite transmissions—or connected hardwire, such as telephone lines, coaxial cable, and optical fiber. As the designation suggests, open channel distribution systems require support to supply users with material. Open channel systems also encompass two-way communication, such as online systems, as well as one-way, such as broadcast.

Although technically not a part of the publishing equation as defined here (*see* Figure 2-1), we also include *Face-to-Face,* such as the conference or classroom, as a means of distribution.[4]

Processes involved in transferring information products and services include transmitting, disseminating, delivering, and presenting, and in two-way systems, responding to user requests, demands, or any information sent upstream. Value-added networks (VAN's), a more recent development involving processing and storage of electronically transmitted signals, require additional activities.[5]

Participants for *Physical Distribution* means include mail services, private carriers, wholesalers, and retailers, while *Electronic Distribution* participants include all network operators, broadcasters, and system operators (e.g., cable television system operators). Face-to-face participants include conference producers, theme park operators, and school teachers, as well as facilitators in non-traditional learning environments such as corporations.

The Fifth M: Market—Who It's For

The fifth value-added M, *Market*, includes both the *Customers*—the end-users who receive and use the material—and other *Buyers* who are not end-users of the material, such as advertisers. The three major markets are consumer, business and professional, and educational, with countless ways to segment or sub-divide these markets. The other major markets are government and international markets, where the other four M's are found in new settings.

Customer processes in the market element include reading, viewing, listening, and using, as well as requesting and manipulating material. Publisher processes include selecting, identifying, and targeting the customer or group of customers, positioning the product, packaging, pricing, deciding how customers are to be made aware of the product or service via promotion and publicity, selling, and supporting and servicing customers, where necessary, after they have purchased the product. In two-way systems, responding to customers is also required. Publisher marketing processes also include the licensing of rights to other parties.

Participants include customers, both end-users and others in the customer chain, such as OEM's (original equipment manufacturers). On the supplier side, participants include market researchers, strategists and planners, advertisers, promoters and publicists, salespeople, customer support and service staff, advertising space salespeople, artists, photographers, designers, copywriters, and licensers of property rights.

THE TWO M'S OF THE PUBLISHING INFRASTRUCTURE

The Sixth M: Management—Who Makes It Happen

The sixth M and the first element of the organizational infrastructure is *Management*, the people who run the publishing enterprise and make the decisions regarding deployment of all the other six M's. Hence management's placement in the center of the 7M's construct (Figure 3-1).

Management includes not only those involved in the mainstream operations of the business, the development and marketing of the products and services, but all those engaged in support activities, including general management, human resources, planning, finance, accounting, technology management, and legal and government affairs, some of whom will be at the corporate level and some at the business unit level.

The Seventh M: Money—How It's Paid For

The seventh and final M is *Money,* the essential grease on the wheels that makes it possible for the entire machine to operate. The management of money is critical to the success of any enterprise. For the purposes of our study and the 7M's framework, we will focus on revenues versus expenses, specifically on the firm's effort to maximize return on investment on two different levels: (1) the corporate level, involving issues of strategy and structure—what businesses are we in and how? What options do we have in organizing and diversifying to take advantage of publishing opportunities in the Information Age? and (2) the product level—what strategies are appropriate for managing specific intellectual properties to extract their maximum value?

UNDERSTANDING AND USING THE 7M'S FRAMEWORK

Although we will be looking at each of the 7M's throughout the remainder of the book, a number of observations about the framework as a whole should be made here.

Intellectual Property Development

Readers will note that the 7M's framework applies equally well to any media or information firm in addition to publishing firms. As seen in Chapter 1, publishing and media firms are content or software organizations versus facilities or hardware organizations and are all engaged in the development of intellectual properties. Their operations and interests are increasingly convergent, and the management of these firms should thus be viewed from the most advantageous strategic standpoint—the standpoint that emphasizes the links, relations, and commonalities among the enterprises while remaining properly mindful of the differences.

Wholistic Conception

It should not be inferred that the five value-added M's are necessarily decided upon in linear fashion for a given information product or service. The best products and services are often marked by a wholistic conception that includes a continual interchange between all value-added elements. While the conjunction of the elements defines the given media product or service, arriving at the total construct is done in many different ways, from market-driven, media-driven, or content-driven perspectives. In the end the determining variable will be the salability of the product in the marketplace, which must achieve the necessary advertiser support, buyer support, or both, in order to succeed. Thus end-users and other customers in the market chain

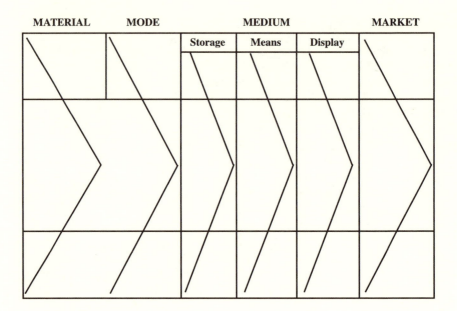

Figure 3-2
The 5M's Reconfigured: Display After Distribution

are integral components of the conception and design of the product or service, as market behaviors, needs, and wants inform the product development loop of material, mode, and medium.

Nor are the 5M's necessarily enacted in a linear fashion, or at least in the single linear fashion depicted in Table 3-1. The penetration of increasingly powerful information technology at both the creator and user ends of the 5M's spectrum have allowed a disintermediation of the publisher's traditional role. The rise of information services, wherein the means of distribution are typically incorporated in the medium, demonstrate how the conventional product-centered conception of publishing does not always hold. The emergence of custom and on-demand publishing, whereby users can select information from remote databases and assemble customized sets of information on-site, in print as well as electronic formats, also indicates the necessity for a flexible conception of the five value-added M's sequence.

In referring to the 500-year period of successful intellectual property law protection based on the delivery of physical, packaged goods, Christopher Burns has stated: "Today the product compromise is coming unglued. Technology makes it easier to separate the expression from the package in which it was first offered—to copy an article without buying the magazine, to record a TV program while zapping the commercial, to download portions of a database."[6] In this sense, we can recast the 5M's to reveal that material may be created, stored, and distributed *before* it is "manufactured," i.e., displayed for use (*see* Figure 3-2). This separation of the storage and display characteristics of a packaged medium, such as a book or newspaper, by the means of distribution is an example of the continued convergence between information products and information services brought about by the penetration of information technology throughout the 5M's framework (*see* Figure 3-3, below).

The Importance of Modes

Many current analyses of publishing dwell on the distinction between print and electronic media formats. The 7M's framework, by placing the primary emphasis on the formats' modal capabilities, seeks to minimize this distinction and reveal affinities hidden by segregation on the basis of print or electronic format only. The mode in which content is rendered is critical, not only for perception and use but for the purposes of media conversion in an all-electronic environment. Moreover, as electronics and automated components continue to invade the process end of publishing, the distinctions between

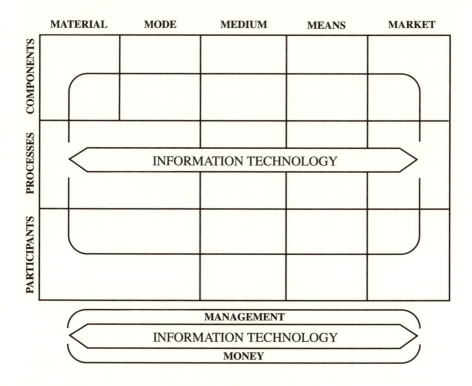

Figure 3-3
Information Technology and the 7M's Framework

print and electronic formats will blur even more. All publishing firms will become electronic publishers, and print output will be but one of many media format choices for publishers, just as it is one of many media format choices for customers.

Another beneficial aspect of viewing the media in modal groups is that new media yet to be developed can be better assessed according to their modal processing, storage, and display capabilities. From a strategic standpoint this is a distinction as useful as print versus electronic forms. Print and electronic forms have continually been shown to coexist and complement each other, whereas competitive electronic formats in the same mode are more likely to displace one another, such as compact audio discs' virtual annihilation of vinyl phonograph records. (The question of complementarity and displacement is addressed in further detail in Chapter 8.)

Total Value

Awareness of where and how value can be added raises a publisher's chances of success, including understanding past successes, whether his own or others. Value can be found and created in each of the 5M's as well as the 2M's of the infrastructure. Each can be used to gain competitive advantage over other firm's offerings or to enhance customer value. Firms can seek opportunities by purposefully studying each value-added element: "How can I add value in each? Where am I weak? Where am I strong? What resources do I have and where am I lacking? What partners might I seek for potential alliance? Where are my competitors weak and strong?" Publishing firms should recognize that content is not the only differentiable component of their products, for while the material itself is certainly critical, the 7M's chain reveals the other critical areas where value can be added, including the processes and participants within each of the elements.

There are also other sources of value beyond the 7M's. There is critical marketing value in intangibles at the corporate level—the goodwill of the company name or presence, brand names, or even an individual manager's reputation. The wise firm seeks out and uses value wherever it can be found.[7]

Information Technology and the 7M's Framework

A key aspect of the value chain not portrayed above is the pervasiveness of digital information technology. Just as the Harvard Information Business Map (*see* Figure 1-2) places computers at its center, so we can show the penetration of digital information technology throughout the Information Age publishing enterprise (*see* Figure 3-3).

Core Concept #2: Information Technology and the 7M's Framework

Information technologies—i.e., digital computer-based technologies versus analog communications technologies—penetrate the entire enterprise, and significant value can be added through them in both process and support functions. Moreover, as the technology for the creation, retrieval, and manipulation of text, images, and sound becomes increasingly powerful at the individual user site, end-users are becoming more powerful, subsuming functions previously controlled by suppliers. Publishing organizations will also harness these technologies with their vast resources. Conversely, autonomous smaller publishing and packaging outfits will increasingly seek competitive advantage through the new technologies and will perhaps outperform the machinery of the larger firms, especially in the creative arena. Publishing firms will continue to provide needed services to authors, producers, developers, and creative teams seeking established distribution channels, marketing clout, and an imprimatur, but in increasingly decentralized organizations (both physically and organizationally) and through alliances made possible by information technologies.

Outside Parties and Shifting Shares

Although the enterprise of publishing encompasses all five value-added M's, the publishing firm itself does not necessarily engage directly in all the elements but may instead choose to manage outside parties in their fulfillment of them. The publisher's task is to orchestrate the parties in achieving his goals. Material, for instance, can be provided by an author for books, a production team for video, a development team for software, a researcher for a database publisher, or an institutional information provider. As for medium and means, the same database publisher may choose to publish his material electronically via a vendor on an online system and via a value-added reseller (VAR) on optical disc. The publisher still makes the choice and controls the total product development and marketing, even though he may subcontract any given activity or element to an outside supplier.

Each of these components adds something different to the total construct, and each must be rewarded. Negotiating these remunerations is difficult—is the data worth 25% or 75%? Is the front-end software worth 75% or 10%? Is distribution worth 40% or 50%? Publishers constantly make these compensation decisions. But now the capabilities of new information technologies are shifting the balance of power among the various parties in the publishing process. If publishers engage in more of these value-added activities they will reap a correspondingly larger return. If they do less, they will get less in return. How these shares are shifting and the corresponding shifts in balance of power is a central issue of publishing in the Information Age.

SUMMARY AND CONCLUSION

In this chapter we have introduced the first two core concepts of publishing in the Information Age:

- *Core Concept #1: The 7M's of Publishing*
- *Core Concept #2: Information Technology and the 7M's*

For the purposes of analysis, the publishing enterprise can be broken into seven basic components, the 7M's. The 7M's include the five value-added elements of the published product or service and the two basic components of the publishing enterprise:

1. *Material*—What It Is
2. *Mode*—How It's Expressed
3. *Medium*—How It's Stored and Displayed
4. *Means*—How It's Delivered
5. *Market*—Who It's For
6. *Management*—Who Makes It Happen
7. *Money*—How It's Paid For

Publishers who understand the 7M's framework can use it to analyze and improve their company's performance in many different areas. The next four parts of the book will take a closer look at each of the 7M's, the changes and trends within each, and how Information Age publishers add value in each area, thereby adding value to their enterprises.

NOTES

1. I have created the 7M's as a simple, alliterative and easy-to-remember presentation of these central elements. The 5M's that represent the core value-added elements of all information constructs have been identified, under different names, in previous theoretical constructs of the activities of publishing and media enterprises. While a close examination of each of these theories reveals slight variations in definition, the general approach to the value-added chain and the key components are roughly the same.

Harvard's Program in Information Resources Policy first published its Content-Process-Format framework in 1980 and later in a collection of the Program's key papers, *Understanding New Media* (Cambridge, Mass.: Balinger Press, 1984), edited by Benjamin Compaine. Booz Allen Hamilton, a technology and management consulting firm, first published its Development-Synthesis-Distribution framework of value-added steps for content media firms in 1984, authored by BAH senior associate Jennifer Bater in their client newsletter, *Information Industry Insights,* Issue 9. It was subsequently reproduced in Poppel and Goldstein's *Information Technology: The Trillion Dollar Opportunity* (New York: McGraw-Hill, 1987). Communications consultant Christopher Burns co-authored the tripartite Creation-Conversion-Distribution taxonomy with Patricia Martin in Chapter III, "The Origins of Value," of their 1985 report "The Economics of Information," prepared under contract for the U.S. Congress Office of Technology Assessment. McGraw-Hill depicted a six-step value-added chain—Collect, Store, Process, Transform, Disseminate, and Sell—based on work done by Michael Porter, in their *1983 Annual Report.* Finally NEC Chairman Koji Kobayashi, in his book *Computers and Communications* (Cambridge, Mass.: MIT Press, 1986), uses the three stages of information generation, storage, and transfer as one of his central constructs. None of these schema have an equivalent element to my Mode, but Kobayashi's "information media" and Burns and Martin's four media classes come closest. *See* note 6, Chapter 5.

I have added the additional two M's, Management and Money, to give a complete picture of the publishing enterprise beyond the published product or service, for they are the two requisites for any business organization. As Peter Drucker says: "Only two key activities are always present in any organization: there is always the management of people and there is always the management of money" (*Innovation and Entrepreneurship* [New York: Harper and Row, 1985], 199).

The central notion of the value chain, as depicted in Michael Porter's book *Competitive Advantage* (New York: The Free Press, 1985), is also represented here. Porter lays out the basic value chain structure and states: "To diagnose competitive advantage, it is necessary to define a firm's value chain for competing in a particular industry. Starting with the generic chain, individual value activities are identified in the particular firm" (45). In this study I use the terms "value chain" and "value-added" interchangeably, whereas Porter makes a distinction between the value chain construct and value-added, defining the latter as simply "selling price less the cost of purchased raw materials" and therefore inadequate for the purposes of broader business analysis (*see Competitive Advantage,* 39).

2. Kobayashi, *Computers and Communications,* 98.

3. "As told to" books, for instance, such as certain sports star and celebrity biographies, provide a good example of material created by one minimally skilled in a mode—in this case, written text—with the assistance of a more proficient "processor"—i.e., a co-author or ghost writer. Similarly, capturing a primitive tribe's native dance would require either choreographic notation, still or moving images, or some other mode.

4. Face-to-face communication dates back to speech and orality, prior to the development of publishing technologies which allowed material to be reproduced and disseminated, and are thus the oldest and most natural part of the entire spectrum of human communications. Face-to-face material and live events can be stored and later retrieved for presentation. Examples include everything from performances (e.g., theater, dance, sports) to theme parks, museum displays, lectures, and conferences. Publishers are aware of and increasingly engaged in face-to-face communications as part of their overall product mix. In the consumer market examples include theme parks such as Disney's Magic Kingdom and sports teams such as Paramount's New York Knickerbockers. In the business market many vertical market publishers have moved into trade show and conference production. In the education market, the classroom is the principal setting for live presentations.

5. Kobayashi classifies a VAN as a "network that provides some added value, not simply information transfer. . . . Information processing and storage can be regarded as the basic functions of producing added value." *See Computers and Communications,* 146–53.

6. Christopher Burns and Patricia Martin, "The Economics of Information" (Washington, D.C.: Library of Congress, 1981), I-7. Burns continues: "The idea of an information 'package' which solved so many of our problems several centuries ago may not be the best intellectual model for the newest and fastest growing aspect of information. In business, science, health care, and government—and prospectively in future home information systems—the role of the author and the publisher, even the role of the printer, is being disintermediated by technology, and the package has become increasingly a 'connection.' "

7. See marketing consultant Regis McKenna's *The Regis Touch* (Reading, Mass.: Addison-Wesley, 1985), specifically his notion of dynamic positioning at the product, market, and corporate levels.

PART II

Material and Modes

In this part we will look at the first of the 7M's, *Material,* the substance of the published communication—the message itself. We will look at the five broad classes of material and discuss how Information Age publishers view material as manipulable into any of a variety of appropriate media forms. Next we will look at the *Modes* of communication, how the material is expressed, defining the three major modes—textual, visual, and aural. We will also consider the increasing importance of mode as a value-added element for Information Age publishers.

CHAPTER 4

The Material Essence

As discussed in Chapter 1, publishing and media firms are the content side of the new meta-industry, the information industry. Thus they are dependent upon the creative process and all the associated activities which provide the material, the content, that is the essence of the publishing enterprise. This chapter looks at the varieties of *Material*, the first M, as well as its role among the five value-added M's.

MATERIAL TYPES AND TRENDS

The third core concept delineates the five basic types of material or content:

Core Concept #3: Information, Knowledge, Entertainment, Art, and Tools

These five categories are convenient classes to help us assess the different types of content and their development, embodiment, and use, but as we shall see, there are not rigid barriers between them.[1]

Information and Knowledge

I address these two content types together not only because they are related but because of the confusion which seems to have arisen regarding the distinction between them. I use the word information here not as the umbrella term which encompasses all types of content, as in the designations information industry and Information Age, but in the prior and more broadly accepted sense of the term, denoting facts or data. Information in this sense is usually compiled and or published for instrumental purposes. Knowledge, on the other hand, is not necessarily intended for a specific purpose and can be appreciated for its own sake. It implies an integration of information, a synthesis. Also, while information is inert, knowledge is kinetic. Information requires the spark of life—a human mind—to transform its inertness into knowledge by endowing it with meaning.[2]

As former Librarian of Congress Daniel Boorstin points out, the different communications media use information and knowledge in different ways. In Boorstin's view the vehicle of the "instant-everywhere" is broadcasting, while publishing is the provider of the "everywhere-past." Boorstin says that "while knowledge is orderly and cumulative, information is random and miscellaneous. We are flooded by messages from the instant-everywhere in excruciating profusion. In our ironic 20th century version of Gresham's Law, information tends to drive knowledge out of circulation." Praising books in particular as the carriers of the everywhere-past, and pointedly critiquing machine-readable formats (e.g., floppy disks and videocassettes), Boorstin says: "The full stock of all past books is available to all of us without special programming or the use of artificially energized, obsolescing machinery."[3]

Television, radio, and online information services are the media which create the instant-everywhere. They are pipelines that provide continuous 24-hour updates to our information stock. The content's electronic embodiment and screen display heighten its ephemerality, disposability, and susceptibility to displacement or alteration. Only when it is stored—not broadcast—is there some admission made of its potential future value.

Contrast the *informed* person, the rote reciter of facts, with the *knowledgable* person, who can place the information in its proper context and understand the significance (or lack of it) of the information given. Knowledge is that which provides the fabric of comprehension, endowing information with meaning. Publisher and author Irving Horowitz observes that knowledge implies "a sense of working to create an integrated framework that permits the production of judgment or insight. . . . Information has always been on a fast track, since it yields data of an ephemeral or immediate need. Knowledge, likewise, tends to be on a slow track, since it yields ideas at a level of abstraction."[4]

One can have information but not knowledge. The printed instructions to assemble a model airplane are information, but only when they are studied, internalized, and understood do they become knowledge, which then empowers the knower to engage in the task of building the airplane. Information is the exposed rings on the stump of a tree, knowledge the understanding of the tree's age arrived at through an interpretation of that information. Knowledge is thus a property of the mind, requiring an active, perceptive intelligence to make the synaptic leap from an inert commodity, information, to apprehension and understanding. Heinz Pagels has said "Information is just signs and numbers, while knowledge involves their meaning. . . . It is a sign of the times that many people cannot tell the difference between information and knowledge, not to mention wisdom, which even knowledge tends to drive out."[5]

I belabor this point because the enterprise of publishing straddles both worlds, producing and disseminating both information and knowledge. The rise and swift penetration of information technologies has tended to dominate the slower pace and gestation of knowledge publishing. But publishing, in its many guises, must meet *all* information and knowledge needs. The information-producing segments have more readily gravitated to technologies which aid in the collection and dissemination of information for immediate, utilitarian purpose, while the knowledge-producing segments have tended to hew to the proven print formats (e.g., books, journals) that continue to meet their needs for lengthier statements, sustained discussions, synthesis, and understanding.[6] Recently, however, the knowledge segments, particularly in scholarly and academic environments, have also begun to recognize the benefits of information technology for their purposes—not speed and rapid dissemination, but vast storage and powerful search, retrieval, and access capabilities ideal for larger bodies of material. In this sense computer technology is bridging the gap between Boorstin's two worlds, creating the *instant-everywhere-past*.[7]

Horowitz points to the inherent nature of the duality between the information and knowledge sectors of the publishing community: "The new absorption by the publication world of a theory of information, predicated on a doctrine of pure service to a market, in effect limits [publishers'] traditional role, abdicating the search for knowledge in favor of commercial criteria of success as measured by profitability or sheer longevity." He views the emergence of such information firms as Dow Jones, Quotron, A.C. Nielsen, and Dun and Bradstreet as "an add-on to the world of publishing" whose traditional role is "the search for knowledge." He concludes that "the co-existence between information and knowledge is not, and need not, always be peaceful. But a world of positive data only would be flat, unimaginative; whereas a world of critical theory, uninformed by data, would be vague, abstract, and ultimately a huge step backward." He calls for an end to the "dualistic warfare" between the purveyors of information and knowledge publishers.[8]

Knowledge publishers would say that our culture's worship of the great god information is a sacrilege, that information is the body and knowledge the holy spirit, that we need a value above market value in our knowledge-producing and presenting institutions. Our culture values the hard, the concrete, the quantitative, the rational, the known. Our desire to know, to be certain, drives us toward information and its manageability and away from the perplexities and mysteries of knowledge, its qualitative nature, and its annoying defiance of neat packages and statistical characterization.

But in fact many publishers straddle the fence between information and knowledge, and thus between "pure service to a market" and "the search for knowledge." Market orientation serves the executive in the publisher, while product, author, producer and content-orientation serve the educator, the communicator, the evangelist, that also lurk in the breast of the publisher. For publishers have a social role as well as an economic role, a commitment to lead, not just follow, an obligation to make known the new, not just provide the expected or wanted. Different segments will make their peace with this duality in different ways, with information providers generally delivering more predictable profits at lower levels of risk, while knowledge publishers, pursuing greater risks and less certain profits, will continue to fulfill a cultural obligation to seek out and promote new statements of value.

Entertainment

It would not be inaccurate to say that if information has found a "happy medium" (*see* Core Concept #20) in computers, then entertainment has found a happy medium in television. The sound and moving images of the video screen—the audio-visual versus the textual-numeric environment of the computer—has in the decades since World War II established itself as the predominant entertainment medium. Preceded by motion pictures in the first half of the century, broadcast and more recently cable television, videocassettes, DBS, and other video media have proven consumers' seemingly insatiable hunger for entertainment delivered in this form.

Even before the sound and image media, including the music recording industry and radio, the print media offered vast entertainment, from pulp fiction and more high-brow novels to serializations in magazines and the comics in newspapers. A consumer-market phenomenon, the entertainment industry has established itself as distinct from the information-oriented segments, the providers of facts and data primarily to business and professional users. But again, one must caution that the distinctions are not entirely rigid. Television produces news as well as sitcoms and movies, while trade book publishers publish non-fiction—information and knowledge—as well as fiction and illustrated books—entertainment.[9] Still, the alignment of the firms in the industry is trending toward the two poles of information and entertainment. Time Warner, with its emphasis on movies, television, music recording, cable, and consumer magazines, is now, despite its core publishing segments, more an entertainment than an information firm, whereas Dun and Bradstreet, Mc-Graw-Hill, and Dow Jones are prototypical information firms.

The distinctions between information (computer) and entertainment (television) technologies will continue to blur, however, as the interactivity of the computer is married to the audio-visual nature of television in the emerging multimedia technologies. The enormous success of Nintendo video games, to cite but one example, demonstrates that digital computer technologies can be highly effective as entertainment media.

Art

Art includes studio art, such as sculpture and painting, the performing arts, such as dance, music, and theater, and any other work which engages the viewer or listener on an aesthetic plane. Art is not held to the demands of logic or rational argument. In a sense, we can view art as a blend of knowledge and entertainment. If knowledge is the arena of the rational dialogue, art is the arena of the non-rational dialogue, involving the imagination of the creator in the design of works of aesthetic value. Art can be created by one individual or many working collaboratively. It is not necessarily designed to be instrumental. It can be primarily expressive in nature or it can have political overtones or practical aims. But it can also be an end in itself, created for the sheer delight or beauty of its composition—art for art's sake.

Tools

The advent of digital information technology has created a new class of content: tools. Whereas formerly information or knowledge encompassed this area in print form, computer software technology has created applications programs which are enabling tools, such as word processing, spreadsheet, and database programs, which their users can employ to perform given tasks. As Efrem Sigel has said: "The inherent nature of software as a tool rather than a consumable information product entails different patterns of use and requires a different approach to production and marketing."[10]

Software programs can be embedded in hardware, such as ROM chip instruction sets in coffee machines and garage door openers. Increasingly, however, knowledge, information, and tools are coming together in digital form, pointing toward an era of so-called "intelligent tools." NEC chairman Koji Kobayashi points out that computer hardware and software were initially developed independently of each other, but that they are now converging: "In years to come there will be remarkable progress made in upgrading system intelligence through software. . . . When intelligent software is refined, computers and communications will be integrated in the true sense."[11] Not only does this point to the convergence between hardware (form) and software (substance), but it points to the convergence between different types of content, as well—information, entertainment, knowledge, and art—with tools. Lotus Development's *One Source* CD-ROM product line combines utilities and data on the same optical disc, referred to as "infoware."[12]

Thus software tools and the other content types will continue to converge as all become digitized. While they will converge, the process algorithms of the tools will still exist separately from the content upon which they work.

But the critical point is that wholly new types of content products will be created, whether called infoware or intelligent tools, content-rich enabling applications that provide users with new ways of attacking problems and accessing and using content of all kinds. The delivery of static, read-only content in electronic form will be supplemented by a new class of interactive applications, knowledge tools, that combine content with appropriate tools for accessing, sorting, storing, and re-using that content from a variety of sources to create new syntheses, whether new knowledge or new personalized content stores. Content-rich online databases allow users to cull the data they seek and recombine it as they choose at their local processing sites. With the addition of other modes, users become multimedia author-producers. Kodak's Photo CD, for example, uses digitized imaging to allow the user, whether residential or commercial, to store and recombine images, text, and sounds as he or she desires. The provision of vaster visual, aural, and textual databases with the enabling application tools provide users with the fluidity of digital processing to achieve their recombinatorial tasks.

Other Content Types and Trends

While these are the main content types from a publisher's perspective, other types of content flow over information systems, such as transactions. One type of transaction is information shuttled in and out of continually updatable databases, usually for the purpose of buying and selling. The financial markets are examples of such information services, wherein widely shared electronic, real-time data is the basis for global buy-sell decisions in stocks, bonds, foreign exchange, commodities, futures, and other markets. In the travel industry the airlines' reservation systems, such as American Airlines' Easy Sabre, are an example of similar databases remotely up-datable from numerous points. In the consumer market a different type of transaction can be seen on networked services. Hybrid systems—downstream broadcast television and upstream telephone line return—currently exist, such as the *Home Shopping Network*. Information services on videotex systems such as IBM-Sears' Prodigy joint venture provide a single loop for purchase decisions on financial services, merchandise, travel and ticketing, and other areas. Interactive full-video services will offer an even richer multimedia transactional environment.

As a content type, transactions clearly violate the traditional unidirectional, one-to-many publishing paradigm. But in the world of electronic two-way information services, network operators must incorporate the responses in their information processing, further revealing the convergence of traditional mass communications media with point-to-point telecommunications media. Pay-per-view services on cable television systems and on-demand publishing on online and videotex services are other examples of network transaction processing.[13] High compression cable systems and fiber optic systems, with their multi-channel capacity, will make video and audio database publishing a reality. Cellular and cable technologies, known as IVDS for "interactive video and data services," also provide these services. With 500 channels of downloadable information, the television becomes an interactive front end to vast stores of screen-delivered information and entertainment.

Convergence is also taking place among other forms of content. Harvey Poppel, for example, has coined the term "infotainment" to refer to the convergence of information and entertainment, citing the *Home Shopping Network, Sesame Street,* and *60 Minutes* as examples. As cited above, software games—instruction sets used as tools for entertainment purposes—are another example of merged content types.

The culture's bias for the new and willingness to submit to quickened obsolescence means shorter product life cycles for many types of content. Art and knowledge—*Gone with the Wind,* footage of man's first landing on the moon—typically reside at the more durable end of the spectrum and appreciate over time, while many types of information—today's weather, sports scores, and stock quotes—are at the ephemeral end and depreciate over time. For list publishers in particular, then, it is true that, like well-located, well-constructed real estate, the right information product, especially one susceptible to derivative and other media possibilities, can continue to pay back its investment long after its creation.

The rise of digital information technology has also highlighted the distinction between linear and non-linear material. Linear material is narrative in nature, one-way, with a story line or other sequential course of development, such as a lecture. It is performance material and is suited to broadcast, film, and book media, to name three appropriate formats. Non-linear material does not have a narrative thread and is more modular in nature, such as a reference book or a news program. Two-way, interactive computer-based technologies, with random access capability, are appropriate for such material, though the print media—magazines, books, newspapers, and others—are clearly suitable carriers of non-narrative material as well. Where digital information technologies stand to better the print media for non-narrative material is in high-volume storage, search and retrieval capabilities, and multimodal capabilities, as we will examine further in Part III.

CONTENT-BASED PUBLISHING

While we can see that the value added at the various stages of the publishing process combine to create the total offering, the material itself is still the central and primary determining component in the success of any given information construct. No matter how well packaged, presented, or distributed, if the content is not in demand then it will have a poor chance of achieving success in the marketplace. For publishers, whose business it is to orchestrate the mix of the 5M's, it is the selection and preparation of the information, the content, that is the heart of the operation. As Bradford Wiley, chairman of John Wiley and Sons, has stated, the real enterprise of publishing is ideas and information, not books or magazines or online databases or interactive videodiscs or any other product format. These are means to an end, conveyers, embodiers of what the publisher really produces and what the users really use: information. The Information Age publisher sees the media for what they are, vehicles for transporting his messages. Books, magnetic media, videocassettes, optical discs—they are all at his disposal, and he must seek the appropriate modes, media, and means for the content in the interest of best serving his market's information wants and needs. This is the fourth core concept of publishing in the Information Age:

Core Concept #4: Content-Based Publishing

Figure 4-1 depicts this concept as a function of two of the 5M's, material and medium. The Information Age publisher's focus is first on the content, the material, secondarily on the appropriate medium into which the content can flow in its many forms.

If management is at the center of the 7M's structure that represents the publishing enterprise (*see* Figure 3-1), then material, or content, is at the center of the 5M's, as shown in Figure 4-2. Working outward from the center, the choices of mode, medium, means, and market combine with the material to make the total product or service. The rings rotate around each other to yield an infinite variety of combinations of these core elements, material being

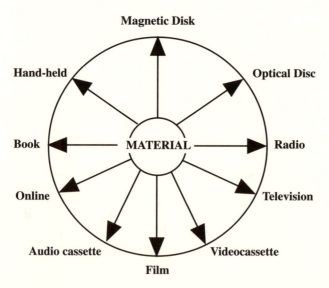

Figure 4-1
Content-Based Publishing: Material and Medium

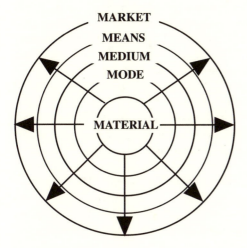

Figure 4-2
The 5M's Wheel

susceptible to embodiment and dissemination in many forms via many channels to many markets. For example, a song (*Material*) could be performed and, thus embodied in the aural *Mode,* could be recorded and packaged as a stand-alone list product—a cassette or optical disc (the *Medium*)—and physically delivered to the user (*Market*) through a retail store or direct mail (*Means*). The same song, though, still embodied in the aural *Mode,* could also be delivered via an open channel broadcast system (*Means*) via radio (*Medium*) to the same user (*Market*).

This is the grand opportunity for publishers in the Information Age—the development of content in a variety of appropriate media forms for a variety of markets. With the paradigm shift, the action is on the margins, the shifting of content from one form to another. As consultant Christopher Burns says: "The vector of change . . . now points toward process. While much of the information landscape will remain familiar, the portion that is changing is that portion devoted to adding value to content through conversion and distribution. . . . and to a great extent that is where the future value is coming from."[14] This has implications at both the product level, the development of specific content in different media forms, as well as at the corporate level: which media businesses are we in? Where do we invest? What is our operating expertise?

The 25th anniversary *Sports Illustrated* swimsuit issue, published in 1989, illustrates how product-level and strategic corporate-level issues interact. The weekly sports magazine's parent company, Time Inc. (prior to its merger with Warner Communications) had developed over the course of twenty-five years a highly successful (though not uncontroversial) mid-winter issue devoted to women's swimwear. Concurrent with the steady twenty-five year rise in prominence of the *SI* swimsuit issue, the company was busy building extensive operations in both cable programming, via Home Box Office, and later video publishing, through HBO Video, principally used for theatrical releases on cassette. The first spin-off, from an earlier swimsuit issue, was a large, full-color, pin-up style wall calendar, published and distributed through the company's book subsidiary, Little, Brown. But in 1989, to mark the 25th anniversary of the issue, Time decided to make a videocassette of the issue's creation, showing the models being shot on location. Because they owned the contents of the magazine, the parent company thus made the decision to capitalize on it by providing it to their audience in a new and different form, adding sound and motion to a subject with innate visual appeal. The estimated revenue on the property was approximately $50 million, with over 600,000 videocassettes sold at $20 each, 118 advertising pages sold in the magazine contributing $18 million, and a special anniversary calendar estimated to sell 750,000 copies.[15]

Not only did Time Inc. own the content in this case, they owned the print and video publishing organizations to develop and market it, and they owned some of the distribution channels as well, such as their own cable systems which delivered the hour-long special program—in essence, an advertisement for the magazine and calendar—on HBO. Cross-media strategies such as this often involve several different parties working under specially negotiated collaborative arrangements. In this case, though, the value added was almost all recaptured by the parent corporation because it not only controlled but owned so many stages of the entire process. By converting and distributing the material in all appropriate modes and media, Time sought and achieved maximum return on a single information asset: pictures of women in swimsuits.

The other major content supplier to mass communications media, advertisers, have used cross-media strategies for some time. The large agencies have been evaluating and exploiting print and electronic forms for as long as they have been available, since their role has been to gain maximum awareness for their clients' products to generate maximum sales. It is doubtful the agencies could achieve that awareness if they restricted their efforts to but one medium—e.g., magazines—while ignoring radio, television, newspapers, and billboards.

As creators, packagers, and transmitters of messages, like the agencies, Information Age publishers know and make use of the strengths of the various media forms and distribution channels to put their messages across to maximum effect. While there are clearly differences in the length and duration of commercial messages versus published content, both share a desire for maximum exposure and awareness, whether in mass or niche markets. Thus questions of mode, media, and means are germane to both advertisers and publishers.

Typically, however, established publishing and media firms have implicit, format-specific agendas. Their number one priority is to fill the distribution pipeline. Book publishers pump books into the bookstores, television networks and cable services fill the airwaves and cables with programming, and movie studios fill the screens with films. There is a ceaseless scanning for the right idea. A good television program may be timely, have innate visual appeal, and be susceptible to compression into program-length time slots. The material has to be fit to the medium, and this vested interest in the medium format and distribution apparatus drives the product development. This is the essence of the product-driven approach, in which the medium is the master, not the market.[16]

But in the new publishing paradigm upper management adopts a supra-format perspective, orienting its thinking *away* from product-driven needs and *toward* serving customers' information needs, in whatever media format is appropriate to those needs and the material. Opportunities are seen in the new formats to add value to the content, to communicate in new and different and sometimes more effective ways. Oftentimes publishers can seek synergies with existing products. They can wrap software around an accounting textbook or package audio tapes with travel or language books. Each adds value to the original print-only construct by communicating to the customer in different modes, combining their effectiveness in a total communication package. Poppel uses the phrase "technology-inspired, market-driven" to stress that while a given media technology may inspire development of content in a certain form, the market will be the ultimate judge of its effectiveness in that form. It must be noted, however, that many products, simply by the nature of their content, will resist conversion into other media as their best and most useful expression is its original form. Many books, due to the nature of their expression and intended audience size, are best expressed in that form. Cost and return on investment are also considerations, for unless the requisite financial resources can be marshalled to fund the project and adequate returns projected from either direct purchase or third party (e.g., advertiser) revenues, then even the most inspired media conversions will remain on the drawing board.

CONTROLLING THE CONTENT

Successful content-based publishing is dependent upon at least two other initiatives on the part of Information Age publishers: ownership of the content, and development of the material, whenever possible, in electronic form. The first of these leads to our fifth core concept:

Core Concept #5: Proprietary Content

In order to maximize return on their information assets, publishers must seek to own or at least acquire through licensing all exploitable rights to their material. If a publisher does not have proprietary content then he does not have a protectable information franchise and has therefore lost a key differential advantage. For list publishers, such as book publishers, these information assets are in the form of backlist properties under license and future properties developed or licensed by the company. If they own the appropriate rights to a given property—a cookbook, an exercise program, a body of research material, a formula—then they alone can exploit its derivative publishing possibilities, such as packaging and distribution in other media forms. Like well-constructed real estate, a premium information product—an Olivier performance, a Mark Twain tale—will continue to pay back its investment long after its initial creation.

While Information Age publishers seek properties appropriate for development in multiple forms, in order to obtain the full rights to such properties, the original proprietor of the content, if other than the publisher, must be willing to license these rights. Content proprietors will only do this, however, if they feel the publisher can develop the property to its fullest potential in all appropriate media. Thus from the standpoint of remaining a viable competitor for content and creators, media firms dependent upon outside sources for their content must be able to demonstrate their capability in total media development, whether through internal development, joint venture, or other means. Sub-licensing by acquiring publishers may be an inadequate or unattractive solution to content proprietors. They will choose not to share licensing income with publishers unless the publisher can demonstrate clear superiority in content development or licensing capability or a willingness to compromise on income shares. If they cannot offer these capabilities, the content creator will retain the rights to be developed by himself or licensed via a third party, such as an agent, who will place them in the hands of a qualified developer. However in that case the original licensing publisher not only loses control over the development and marketing of the content in other forms, he forfeits a return on its conversion and distribution. Just as important, he loses the ability to plan and implement a sustained, sequenced development of the property over its life cycle. Full-service publishers, capable of content development in all modes and media, will thus have greater leverage in attracting those knowledge experts and that talent seeking full media development. Moreover, full-service publishers will be able to protect their valuable information assets by controlling their development and distribution how and when they see fit (*see* Core Concept #43, Chapter 13).

Book publishers currently develop life extension strategies for their properties, typically publishing first in hardcover, then in trade or mass market paperback. Other lives are given such properties through book clubs, translated foreign editions, and ultimately, as they near the end of their first life (the books may be reprinted later, either on their own or in an anthology) on the remainder table. Of course the publisher's ideal is that each product's life never ends, in which case he has a backlist title in perpetual demand as a source of continuing revenue. Still, marketing strategies must be implemented to maintain products even at later stages of their lives if publishers seek to gain the most from their valuable assets.[17]

In an evolving media environment, Information Age publishers manage through the *media cycle,* not just the life cycle in a single mode or medium. If publishing is the selection, financing, packaging, and marketing of intellectual properties, then the life of that content must be extended through a planned, sequenced media roll-out. Because there is no one formula, and as media technologies continue to change, publishers must be willing to experiment and learn through experience which combinations and sequences of media formats perform best. (*See also* Chapter 14.)

MAINTAINING THE DIGITAL LIBRARY

The second key initiative for content-based publishing is keeping the material in its most fluid and manipulable form—i.e., digital:

Core Concept #6: The Digital Library

Though certain material, such as video and audio, is currently created, stored, and distributed in analog form, the clear trend with the penetration of computer processing technologies in all industry segments is toward digital creation, storage, and delivery of all information. The original NeXT computer, the high-powered workstation for the higher education market unveiled by Steve Jobs in late 1988, included what the company termed the *Digital Library,* which included the full text of *William Shakespeare: The Complete Works* (Oxford University Press), *Webster's Ninth New Collegiate Dictionary, Webster's Collegiate Thesaurus, The Oxford Dictionary of Quotations,* and other works, along with illustrations and full text search and retrieval software. If one envisions *all* published text embodied in electronic form and retrievable and manipulable, the digital library is a truly liberating and empowering concept. Some analysts predict that by the turn of the century, this will be the case.

From the originating publisher's standpoint, embodying and maintaining material in digital form means it will be ready to manipulate not only for pre-print purposes but for repackaging as derivative publications, for electronic distribution (e.g., through online systems), electronic packaging (optical disc), and for revision, new editions, and up-dates. As the NeXT product literature also pointed out, the Digital Library can be extended to include non-textual content, such as the digital *image* library (still and moving) or the digital *audio* library, allowing retrieval and manipulation of material in these modes as well.[18]

Information Age publishers thus conceive of their information assets as electronic databases to be manipulated at will. They store text, images, and sounds in digitized form for retrieval, editing, design, formatting, and distribution as required. Pervasive and increasingly sophisticated electronic processes in pre-press, as well as the proliferation of electronic media formats, will eventually make all publishers into electronically literate media firms that develop and distribute products in both print and electronic formats.[19] Digital storage options for text, for instance, include ASCII and SGML (Standard Generalized Mark-up Language) as well as other types of tagged and structured databases. Non-text digital data elements are also susceptible to various tagging and coding schemes. All are evolving along with the tools to manipulate them.

As of this writing, software tools are being developed, such as Frame Technology's FrameBuilder, that yield both laid-out camera ready pages and fully structured SGML tagged databases. In effect, such tools allow text publishers to kill two birds with one stone by inputting data once but yielding multiple format and derivative publishing potential. One industry participant refers to this as the "digital original," the creation and embodiment of the content at all stages of the production process in digital form.[20] Other publishing service suppliers, such as R.R. Donnelly and Toppan in Japan, have developed the necessary tools to assist publishers in all aspects of digital content preparation and development, for both print and electronic products.

With the fluidity and manipulability of structured properties, new product opportunities are also more attractive because of the lower cost of conversion of the material. "Re-purposing" describes the re-use of existing content in other formats. Whatever the modal form of the material, the objective is to capture and store the material for maximum conversion opportunities into specific formats. The existence of that material in structured, retrievable, digital form is the critical first step.

CONTENT FRANCHISES

Publishers can dominate a market niche from a content-based perspective and thus carve out, be identified with, and own content franchises:

Core Concept #7: The Content Franchise

The real estate analogy applies once again. The successful developer of real property may own a vital piece of land in center city or a hotel that is the clear first choice of travelers to that town. So publishers, as developers of intellectual properties, can control a given content area and be the obvious choice, the market leader, for that body of material.

Content franchises usually work best for those publishing and media firms that have a definable, focused body of content, as the publisher becomes closely identified or even synonymous with a given content area, often by virtue of allying himself with the key knowledge experts in the field. The National Geographic Society is a preeminent example of such a firm. Their mission is to explore the world, its geography, and its cultures. To achieve this mission and communicate their findings to their members, the Society's early identity was bound up in publishing a monthly magazine. But since those early days over a century ago they have successfully spread their messages through other media channels, including film, broadcast and cable television, software, and now computer-based multimedia. Their market focus has likewise broadened beyond the initial membership base (e.g., the magazine's subscribers) to encompass formal educational settings and the general populace, the latter reached through television.

To achieve true control of a content franchise, discrete product lines and content continuity, versus stand-alone products, are generally required. Special interest magazines, for instance, provide a focused body of content and direct customer access. A continuity approach such as that used by Time-Life Books creates a focused, extended body of content that can achieve sustained exposure and may thus justify the additional investment. General list publishers, on the other hand, such as trade book publishers, are typically not focused on a single body of content, and thus developing content-based, integrated media strategies around individual properties may be viewed as resource-draining, expensive, and diversionary. If the customer base and product recognition are high for a given list product, though, such as an established application software program or a best-selling book, or if a specific product line or series has established a customer base for the publisher in a content niche, then an integrated media strategy may be viewed as a more worthy investment.

RECOMBINANT PUBLISHING

As high-volume on-site optical storage media and computer-driven networks continue to evolve, the re-use of existing material will continue to grow. This re-use of existing material in new media, combined in new forms and compilations with other existing and new material, is the next core concept:

Core Concept #8: Recombinant Publishing

Recombinant publishing is the Information Age equivalent of anthology publishing, made possible by electronically stored and manipulated content. It is a subset of derivative publishing opportunities that uses content not just in its entire, discrete original form but in segments, as well. An optical disc may combine several whole volumes, such as Microsoft's CD-ROM *Bookshelf,* which carries the *American Heritage Dictionary, Roget's II: The New Thesaurus, Bartlett's Familiar Quotations,* the *Concise Columbia Encyclopedia,* and several other reference works. A multimedia optical disc presentation, on the other hand, may combine selected portions of several text sources with still and moving images and sounds culled from a range of other sources.

Recombinant publishing has a variety of implications for content creators and rights holders alike. Foremost among them are intellectual property rights issues, including the right to use the material for a given purpose as well as compensation to the copyright proprietor or any entity owning rights to the property. As on-demand and customized publishing systems evolve into high-volume multimodal databases feeding online systems that allow recombinations of material for specific user-defined outputs, in both print and electronic forms, it becomes paramount that providers seeking to control authorized use of their material, and obtain appropriate compensation therefor, be equipped to meet these marketplace demands. This will require the development of infrastructure technology which supports the licensing and use of the material, including tracking of compensation. Compressed product development cycles and to-market times will place consistent demands on publishers in this area.

Recombinant publishing also has implications for publishers' product development. Certain types of material, such as reference material, may no longer seek its primary market through pre-packaged formats—e.g., a book—but may be better suited as online database material front-ending on-demand and custom publishing systems. Some format choices will be made in conjunction with content development and acquisition decisions. The shift moves from products (producer-packaged) to services (user-packaged) as user premise equipment increases in power and sophistication. Some question the traditional role of the publisher as content selector, packager, and distributor if users can select and obtain content directly from creators on networked systems, thereby disintermediating the publisher's role. The Information Age publisher's response is to be certain that he continues to add significant and remunerative value in one or more of the 7M's in the value chain.

TALENT, KNOWLEDGE EXPERTS, AND THE NEW CREATIVE POWERS

The final core concept in the first value-added M addresses the rising power of creators and content originators:

Core Concept #9: The New Creative Powers

In an increasingly crowded media marketplace, the quality of the craft and creativity of the information construct will continue to distinguish it from its competitors. In the entertainment industry, key talent is a major source of the value. Just as Michael Jordan draws fans to the basketball arena, so does Stephen King draw readers to the bookstore. (Material, in this instance, is almost *immaterial* with a name author.) The name is the chief selling factor. The more the publisher can lock up the contracts—i.e., "own" the talent— the more he minimizes his risk and can guarantee future success. Thus many publishers will increasingly seek longer term contracts to own their talent—

authors, programmers, performers, directors, producers—as many professional sports teams do with their talent. Assuming a mutually satisfactory
agreement, the security of a contract and certainty of steady income over a
given future period can often create better working conditions for the creative
artist.

However, knowing their market value, and typically dealing through third
party negotiators (i.e., agents), creators are bidding their prices up. As Harvey
Poppel states, "rights owners will continue to demand and probably get spi-
raling prices for compelling entertainment and information content as multiple
media compete for content distribution. Talent—programmers, authors, directors, actors, musicians—will gain a larger share of the revenues generated
by their creative talents. . . . [consequently] participants who heretofore focused mainly on only one value-added stage . . . will seek to enhance returns
by carving turf from other participants."[21]

As authors and knowledge experts increasingly seek coordinated total media
development they will seek full-service publishers, those that are media-
knowledgeable, that are not wed to a single format, that understand and manage the development and distribution of content in all appropriate forms. If
publishers do not offer full media service they will not only lose the full value
of a construction but will lose their ability to compete effectively for those
content-creators seeking multiple media development and multiple channel
distribution. Conversely, those publishers that can fulfill integrated media development and marketing will gain a broader share of the income while controlling the property. Thus for a publisher to commit to one technology or
market means, by definition, that he limits his share of value added, product
control, and growth.

In addition to the demand for high quality content forcing prices upward,
there is also a trend toward increased processing power in the hands of creators. Microcomputers and desktop publishing software have led many content
preparers into the realm of design and production, invading the publishers'
customary turf. The content originator has more power than before via the
microcomputer or workstation, continuing to decentralize publishing even as
the larger firms conglomerate. However, due to their increased technical complexity and the necessity for specialized processing skills, many of the new
media technologies require collaborative efforts. Creative teams often combine knowledge experts and modal processors, such as a finance professor and
a software programmer joining forces to create a software program. Such
technology-skilled creative teams are highly attractive to publishers as they
relieve the publisher of time and cost-intensive processing chores.

Creative product teams are often managed outside the house to preserve
the creativity and autonomy so necessary to those professionals. Just as film
studios have come to be financing, marketing, and distribution mechanisms
for independent producers, so book publishers work with individual authors
and packagers who fulfill a range of creative project aspects, including re-

search, writing, design, layout, and the provision of finished books. Most television programming is produced by independents and sold to broadcast networks or cable programming services. The large metropolitan newspapers buy weather, sports, television listings, comics, columns, horoscopes, and stock market reports from outside information suppliers. As Chris Burns characterizes it, "The complexity of our information constructions have led us to author-teams, and the demands of video and electronic media have raised this to the level of author-companies-program production businesses for whom the word 'author' has no useful meaning. The money does not flow to individuals except in a few rare cases, and neither do attribution or liability. We no longer live in a world where the most important information is created by individuals; information is no longer a business of authors and books."[22] While we may take exception to Burns' last statement, the emergence of content teams is especially true where more complex technologies for either packaging or distribution require technical expertise.

As Terry Deal and Alan Kennedy observe in their book *Corporate Cultures*, changes in communication technologies will both foster and allow new types of decentralized, work-group based organizations to emerge. Information Age publishers typify this kind of organization, for publishing allows the creative group to work independently from the financers, marketing managers, and distributors. It is the appropriate "atomized environment" for the professional knowledge worker who prizes his autonomy and typically looks to peer group reinforcement, not management, for an evaluation of his contribution.

However it is sliced, publishers will still have to disaggregate the final construct as perceived and paid for by the end-user and arrive at rewards for the various inputs. Contractual issues of how to divide the spoils (i.e., revenue sharing) will continue to arise as new media evolve. These issues will be particularly thorny in the area of creator compensation in recombinant publishing. Past practices regarding anthology rights will be only of limited use, while some mix of the concepts of fair use, site licenses, and shareware may be required.[23]

SUMMARY AND CONCLUSION

For the first value-added M, *Material,* we have highlighted seven core concepts:

- *Core Concept #3: Information, Knowledge, Entertainment, Art, and Tools*
- *Core Concept #4: Content-Based Publishing*
- *Core Concept #5: Proprietary Content*
- *Core Concept #6: The Digital Library*
- *Core Concept #7: The Content Franchise*

- *Core Concept #8: Recombinant Publishing*
- *Core Concept #9: The New Creative Powers*

There are five essential content types, though the boundaries between them are not fixed, and much material is a blend of one or more of these types. With the advent of new media forms and digital processing technologies, Information Age publishers are reexamining the potential of content conversion and the opportunity for development of intellectual properties in new modes and media distributed via new means, thereby adding greater value to the construct and generating greater return for both the creator and the publisher. Information Age publishers will increasingly seek to own content and develop and maintain it in digital form for efficient manipulation and media conversion. As a natural outgrowth of content-based publishing strategies, publishers will, when possible, seek to carve out content franchises, owning a content niche in all appropriate media. Many of the new products and services will be combinations of new and existing material made possible by high-volume storage media and high-speed digital networks, creating issues of rights ownership and compensation for publishers and content providers. Content is still one of the chief distinguishing features of any information product, and in an increasingly crowded media marketplace content of true value will continue to demand and receive a premium price. Successful publishers will also seek to work collaboratively with knowledge experts and creators to forestall disintermediation, i.e., direct creator to user contact.

NOTES

1. The U.S. Office of Technology Assessment (OTA) report *Intellectual Property Rights in an Age of Electronics and Information* (April, 1986) creates three classes of "copyrightable works:" works of art, works of fact, and works of function. Works of art correspond to my categories of entertainment and art, works of fact to information and knowledge, and works of function to tools. The OTA report also recognizes the overlap among the categories. *See* Chapter 3, "The Accommodation of Intellectual Property Law to Technological Changes," 66ff.

2. Daniel Bell draws distinctions between data, information, and knowledge: "Information is a pattern or design that rearranges data for instrumental purposes, while knowledge is a set of reasoned judgements that evaluates the adequacy of the pattern for the purposes for which the information is designed. Information is thus pattern recognition, subject to reorganization by the knower, in accordance with specified purposes." From "The Social Framework of the Information Society" in *The Computer Age: A Twenty-Year View,* Dertouzos and Moses, eds. (Cambridge, Mass.: MIT Press, 1979), 171.

3. Daniel Boorstin, *Gresham's Law: Knowledge or Information?* (Washington, D.C.: Library of Congress, 1980), 3.

4. Horowitz, *Communicating Ideas: The Crisis of Publishing in a Post-Industrial Society* (New York: Oxford University Press, 1986), 84 and 96.

5. From "The Computer as Scapegoat," *The New York Times*, 19 February, 1988.

6. Horowitz says:

The speed with which new facts are integrated with or supplemental to [sic] existing data banks requires an increasing use of flexible, non-print media which render such information accurately and quickly. Expense is secondary to speed, aesthetic sensibility is equally secondary to the functional malleability of data. At the same time, the realm of knowledge, the systematic rendering of information in general propositions, will continue to be placed in hard copy form . . . because the print media continue to serve as a relatively inexpensive mechanism for rendering holistic ideas in an aesthetically pleasing form.

Communicating Ideas, 95.

7. For an introductory discussion of the time-sensitive nature of information and the role of high-volume optical publishing media, *see* William Paisley and Mathilda Butler, "The First Wave: CD-ROM Adoptions in Offices and Libraries," *Microcomputers in Information Management*, 4 (June, 1987):109.

8. Horowitz, *Communicating Ideas*, 89.

9. Boorstin has noted that the 18th century viewed "the two delights, 'amusement' and 'instruction,' as inseparable. The book was the prototypical provider of both." He also points out that by moving from amusement to entertainment we have replaced activity with passivity: "While we once had to amuse ourselves, we now expect to be entertained." *Gresham's Law*, 5–6.

10. Efrem Sigel, "The Software Publishing Phenomenon" in *Electronic Publishing Plus* (White Plains, N.Y.: Knowledge Industry Publications, 1985), 110. The *Taxonomy of Educational Objectives* (New York: David McKay Co., Inc., 1956) makes a distinction in the cognitive domain between "Knowledge"—substantive information and ideas that can be recalled—and "Intellectual Abilities and Skills," specific processes which, as aids to performing intellectual tasks, usually involve the manipulation of knowledge and information. The former is equivalent to our classifications of Information and Knowledge, the latter to Tools. See *Taxonomy of Educational Objectives, Volume I: Cognitive Domain*, 201–7.

11. Kobayashi also states that "As its [intelligent software's] forerunner, software in use today for microcomputers and PC's is stored on cassette tapes or floppy disks and sold and circulated separately" (*Computers and Communications: A Vision of C&C* [Cambridge, Mass.: MIT Press, 1986], 63). This physical package model is more readily assimilated into the traditional publishing model and explains the genesis and adoption of the term "software publishing." Although still publishing the same or similar material, the software of embedded and intelligent systems is less easily grasped in the traditional publishing distribution model, another example of technology's necessitating the paradigm shift in publishers' worldview.

12. See the author's interview with Rob Lippincott of the Information Services Group at Lotus, "1-2-3 Goes TV: Interactive Multimedia at Lotus," *BCS Update*, September, 1989, 14.

13. Kobayashi has called hybrid mass media/point-to-point transactional systems "unbalanced bi-directional transmission systems . . . where the downward flow of information . . . is much larger than the upward flow of information to the [information service] centers." An information service center, in Kobayashi's scheme, is the central information storage, processing, and distribution point that anchors the networked system. Kobayashi, *Computers and Communications*, 108.

14. Burns and Martin, "The Economics of Information" (Washington, D.C.: Office of Technology Assessment, 1985), VII-8–9. Burns also states: "If the same information can have more value in one form than it has in another, then the enterprise of conversion is economically legitimate and inevitable. . . . Emerging technologies make new kinds of conversion possible, and our growing reliance on information makes them necessary." "The Economics of Information," III-16. *See also* Boorstin, *The Image* (New York: Atheneum, 1962), 127 ff.

15. *See* "Time Inc. Finds New Ways to Profit on Swimsuit Issue," *The New York Times,* 7 February, 1989.

16. In his discussion of "dissolving forms" in his 1962 work *The Image,* Boorstin wrote: "Every artist marries form to matter: he sees his poem in words, his paint in oils, his statue in stone, his building in some specific material." In referring to the process of adapting motion pictures from novels, he noted that "movie-makers themselves, driven by the needs of the movie form . . . inevitably treat the novel as nothing but the wrapping paper and string of 'literary embellishment.' " (*The Image,* 118 and 148.)

17. For a discussion of trade book marketing strategies incorporating the product life cycle concept and the theory of diffusion of innovation, *see* Leonard Felder, "A Business School Master Plan for Marketing Books," *Publishers Weekly,* 29 January, 1979.

18. The original NeXT brochure states:

With a Digital Library, users can store online versions of complete reference or literary works, plus musical pieces and scores, illustrations and voice recordings. A powerful search and indexing tool, called the Digital Librarian, enables users to "thumb" through memos, mail messages, books and papers, for almost instantaneous access to any textual information, anywhere on the [256 megabyte recordable-erasable magneto-optical] disk. . . . NeXT also expects that third parties will enhance the capabilities of the standard Optical Disk by creating additional Digital Libraries aimed at particular disciplines and areas of interest.

From "The NeXT Computer System: Product Background Information," 1988, 15–16.

19. Information technology author and analyst Oldrich Standera shares this vision:

The ironic conclusion may well be that computerization will help pre-press in doing some things faster than humans and some things that humans could not do, but eventually it will lead to the demise of print-based publishing in its present predominant form and usher in a new era of coalesced print-based and nonprint-based electronic publishing combined with electronic document delivery where the boundaries will be initially difficult, and later on, impossible to draw. This stage might perhaps most befittingly be called "integrated electronic communications". . . . [In this era] paper will not disappear but will become only one of an array of possible output forms of which there will be plenty. . . . There will be both print and nonprint output but no print-based and nonprint-based industry per se in the long view. Both varieties of electronic publishing, which themselves owe so much for their advancement to the convergence of computers and communications with publishing and other more conventional fields such as library and office technology, will merge into the knowledge-based, integrated electronic communications.

The Electronic Era of Publishing (New York: Elsevier Science Publishing, 1987), 268–69.

20. Judith Booth, "The Digital Original," *Publishers Weekly,* 8 November, 1991, 43–44.

21. Poppel and Goldstein, *Information Technology: The Trillion-Dollar Opportunity* (New York: McGraw-Hill, 1987), 32–33.

22. Burns and Martin, "The Economics of Information," IV-14.

23. Horowitz observes: "As publishers yield certain responsibilities, they also yield control; and as authors invest more time and money in the preparation of copy prior to printing and marketing, their share of risks and rewards is likely to increase commensurately. Traditionally authors take a small share of the initial investment, called a royalty. When a larger share of the initial investment is shared with the publisher, the royalty rates should increase." *See* "Technological Impacts on Scholarly Publishing" in *Communicating Ideas* (New York: Oxford University Press, 1986), 30–44.

CHAPTER 5

Modes of Communication

Between Material and Medium stands the second value-added M, *Mode,* the symbolic language in which the material is rendered, such as words, images, or sounds. With the proliferation of new media formats that deploy modes differently from existing media, the importance of the mode of expression takes on new meaning as a value-added component. This chapter will explain how modes of expression directly relate to the body and its sensory abilities. After a consideration of modes as symbolic languages, we will examine the three major modes—textual, visual, and aural—before discussing their role and use in published products and services, including multimodal uses and the strategic importance of mode as a value-added element.

THE SENSES AND COMMUNICATION

In his 1964 work, *Understanding Media: The Extensions of Man,* Canadian sociologist and media philosopher Marshall McLuhan detailed how the communications media are extensions of the body's sensory system. The senses are those functions of our physical apparatus that perceive and interpret the world outside ourselves. Every schoolchild knows the five senses and the associated body parts:

SENSE	BODY PART
Sight	Eyes
Hearing	Ears
Smell	Nose

Taste	Tongue
Touch	Skin

The senses are doorways to perception, to our experience of the world. We can speak of unmediated experience, which is direct observation of and contact with phenomena as they occur, or we can speak of mediated experience, wherein we perceive man-made replications of objects, second-hand representations of the real thing, which extend time and space (*see* Figure 2-1) beyond the limits of our individual physical beings. In order to replicate the original object for reproduction and relay, the media must capture the object or idea and store it in some form, which means creating a second order of that object or idea, an abstraction, something which is not the object itself, but a representation of it—a symbol.

SYMBOLS AND SYSTEMS

Professor Howard Gardner of the Harvard Graduate School of Education has performed pioneering work in the field of cognitive psychology, which studies how we come to know what we know. He has focused considerable attention on how the media interact with the human sensory apparatus in relation to human development and learning. In his 1983 book *Frames of Mind* explicating his theory of multiple intelligences, Gardner states: "The nervous system is so constituted that, provided with certain kinds of experience, the organism is able to learn to apprehend and deal with symbolic entities." Gardner defines a symbol as "any entity, material or abstract, that can denote or refer to any other entity," and cites words, pictures, numbers, and diagrams as classical notational symbols. Significantly, for Gardner symbols can convey not only strict definitional meaning but mood, feeling, and tone, as well: "By including this important expressive function within the armament of a symbol, we are able to talk about the full range of artistic symbols, from symphonies to scientific documents, from sculpture to squiggles, all of which have potential for expressing connotative meanings."[1]

Gardner builds upon these observations to discuss the importance of symbol systems, such as verbal language, mathematics, and dance, seeing such systems not only as the natural outgrowth of individual symbols but as their chief purpose and highest use. Moreover, Gardner says, if symbol-making and symbol-interpreting are among man's defining activities, then specific symbolic products within these symbol systems are among man's greatest achievements: "These symbolic products are the ultimate raison d'etre for symbol systems—the reason they have come to evolve, to the reasons that human individuals go to the trouble of mastering diverse symbol systems." Indeed, says Gardner, the "introduction and mastering of symbolic systems . . . is a major burden of childhood and might even be regarded as the principal mission of modern educational systems." As Gardner sees it, "the challenge . . . is to compose a developmental portrait of each of these forms of symbolic competence and to determine empirically which connections or distinctions might obtain across them."[2]

The picture that emerges from Gardner's studies, then, is of the human individual as a symbol-processing being, whose brain is capable not only of receiving, interpreting, and learning to master complex symbol systems, but of creating higher order symbolic products within these systems. And it is here that we enter the publisher's realm, for, as noted, the communications media employed by publishers capture, store, and relay, in different forms, these symbolic products.

MODES OF COMMUNICATION

We can now add a new column to our sense chart to show the modes of expression and how each relates to the senses:

SENSE	BODY PART	MODE
Sight	Eyes	Visual
Hearing	Ears	Aural
Smell	Nose	Olfactory
Taste	Tongue	Gustatory
Touch	Skin	Haptic

The final mode, the textual mode, is the distinctively human mode of expression which, though sensory in its immediate nature, ultimately relies upon the brain's faculty of reason. We classify it with the other modes, however, as it is the chief abstract symbol system of published communication products:[3]

SENSE	BODY PART	MODE
Sight	Eyes	Textual

Text is language and other human-created notational systems, such as sheet music or mathematical notation, that operate on the brain at a different level of abstraction than the other modes because of their ability to represent ideas versus objects, a notion of the thing rather than a portrayal of the thing itself, an abstract versus a representational portrayal. It defines a separate mode of symbol-making and content capture that is the most distinctively human and thus higher order, while the other concrete symbolic modes of perception we share with all creatures.

As the symbolic element used to communicate a message, the mode is one of its chief distinguishing features. In turn, mode defines the medium. The defining mode of television, for instance, is visual, signifying that even though sound and text are often present, without visual imagery television would not create and display the information in the manner it does. For a unimodal medium such as radio, there is no question that sound is the defining element. Print media—books, magazines, newspapers—are typically bimodal, capturing and displaying both visual (still image) and textual modes.

While the other sensory modes are used to a certain degree by the communications media, they are typically outside what we think of as the normal media channels.[4] The olfactory mode, for instance, is used by cosmetics and pharmaceutical companies: perfume is a medium.[5] The haptic mode is incorporated de facto in many media products simply because they are tangible, but touch is not the primary conveyor of information. Puzzles, for instance, combine visual and tactile sensations, sometimes with textual modes as well (letters and numbers on the pieces). Some video games can be played with a floor-pad input device, with screen moves entered by the feet of players running in place. But these other modes—haptic, olfactory, gustatory—while also based on sensory input, are typically not symbolically mediated but direct sensory modes, less given to symbolization, and thus less susceptible to capture, storage, and relay. They are also relatively information-poor in relation to the symbolic modes. Still, we can expect that as the media technologies evolve, so will their modal capabilities, with capture and relay of haptic, olfactory, and gustatory information a likely prospect in certain future media.

THE THREE MAJOR MODES

Communications media, then, employ the textual, visual, and aural modes as they are the richest carriers of symbolic information, best able to communicate, inform, entertain, enlighten, and perform other information-related tasks:[6]

Core Concept #10: The Three Major Modes: Textual, Visual, and Aural

Textual Mode

Historically, the textual mode has been displayed as pages of written or printed symbols, but with the advent of video display terminals attached to computers in the past twenty-five years we are also increasingly accustomed to viewing electronic screens of text.

In the textual mode the material is typically ingested by the movement of the body—the eye—rather than the movement of the material. That is, the text is static, not moving, and the eye must move across the page or screen to absorb the material. Thus the reader is free to move through the material at his or her own pace. Video (moving images) and audio, by contrast, typically proceed at a predetermined pace. The eye is also faster than the ear and can scan text far more quickly than spoken words can be heard and understood. Even with digital playback enhancements, sped up images or sound lose their meaning and become incomprehensible. In the end, all symbolic communication must be consumed in discrete bites, even in hypertext or hypermedia systems. Each word, sentence, paragraph, image, or sound is a discrete unit, and there is a limit to how far we can go, for the sake of meaningful communication, in deconstructing the individual pieces and recombining them.

Text maintains a unique position among the modes for it is language, as an abstracting mechanism, that is the distinguishing human element, the major symbol-making activity that sets humans apart from all other creatures. To relay precise, sustained, sequential information, we must employ language. Our culture and history are not only founded on language but are an outgrowth of language's abstracting character, allowing us to project into the future, plan, and reason.

If language fades, our humanness fades. As Neil Postman has written: "Speech, of course, is the primal and indispensable medium. It made us human, keeps us human, and in fact defines what human means."[7] The oral tradition became the written tradition, and the focal points of our society and civilization are textual documents, such as the Constitution, whose embodiment could only be in text (even a videotaped version of the Constitution would have to rely on words, whether spoken or displayed visually). In text is the permanent record, the documents that form the foundation and core of our human knowledge and heritage. And it is written language that still conveys the most complex, the most sustained, the most distinctively human communications: "Writing makes it possible and convenient to subject thought to a continuous and concentrated scrutiny."[8]

Visual Mode

In the visual mode information is conveyed by the symbolic language of images. The imagery can be still, as in photographs, charts, or drawings, or it can be moving, as in motion picture photography or animation. To decode these symbols requires not linguistic literacy skills—learned symbol sets—but visual literacy, and usually some literacy in the given medium as well. Moving images are typically displayed on screens and most always in machine-readable formats, while still images can be viewed either on a screen or in printed form, as in the page of a book or magazine, on a billboard or poster, or even projected, as in film or a hologram.

The significant distinction between the textual and visual modes is their effect. As Postman says, "A photograph represents the world as object; language the world as idea. . . . The image and the word have different functions, work at different levels of abstraction."[9] It is impossible to show "tree," the concept, for instance, in an image. Only a specific tree can be represented, whether drawn, photographed, or depicted in any other visual fashion.

In the visual mode the perceiver of information is a viewer. The power and both pre- and extra-literate characteristics of imagery often make it the mode of choice for the dramatic and the emotional. We grow up as visual literates first and only later attach language to things. Moreover we share visual imagery with all sentient beings. Thus imagery operates on a more fundamental cognitive plane than text and can move and motivate at a visceral level. In several successful media formats the visual mode is accompanied by sound, producing a powerful synaesthetic combination. As a result of this power and its blanket reach, television has emerged as the predominant visual medium in the second half of the 20th century. In the business and educational markets new media are fostering new and widespread uses of imagery, providing spatial and relational maps and representing concepts and statistics in graphic and other visual forms. These images can have the power of immediacy and explanation, sometimes of revelation, and often of resonance and retention.

Aural Mode

The third major mode is the aural mode, which employs sound as the primary defining symbolic element. Sound can include the spoken word as well as music, naturally occurring sounds (e.g., bird songs), and noises. In the aural mode, the perceiver is a listener, and the eye is replaced by the ear. The ear's predominance in this mode is important for several reasons, not least because, when material is presented strictly in the aural mode, the thing heard is not seen. This activates the brain to create an image of the thing heard, hence *imag*ination. If it is music or other sounds, versus language, aural input tends to work on the right side of the brain, stimulating the affective versus the rational and cognitive intellectual functions of the left brain stimulated by language.

MEDIA AND MODES

As mentioned above, the textual, visual, and aural modes provide the richest array of symbolic languages and can therefore relay the most fully textured, extended, complex communications. As such, they are the symbolic modes to which the information industry has devoted its greatest attention, developing technologies for capture, storage, and relay. To the extent that it is technologically possible, such as Aldous Huxley's "feelies" in his novel *Brave New World,* information technologies, as noted above, will increasingly engage different senses in mediated experiences. The total sensory experience of virtual reality, for instance, with its re-creation of three-dimensional space, incorporates touch and may eventually incorporate smell and taste.

As the media technologies change, it becomes increasingly clear that the Information Age publisher must remain technology neutral, or "hardware agnostic" in Rob Lippincott's phrase. If the marketplace doesn't push the question, the epistemologists will. As Gardner says, "It is at least an open question, an empirical issue, whether operation of one symbol system, such as language, involves the same abilities and processes as such cognate systems as music, gesture, mathematics, or pictures. It is equally open whether information encountered in one medium (say, film) is the 'same' information when transmitted by another medium (say, books)."[10]

As businesses, publishers do not have the luxury of time to wait for laboratory results demonstrating the manner in which Gardner's "forms of symbolic competence" develop or interact. Thus they will proceed as always, with their instinct and the marketplace as their guides. Without hewing to strict experimental results, we can assert from our own observation and experience that the moving image and sound (film, video) version of material does indeed work differently on the mind than a book that uses text, and perhaps still images, to communicate the same material. We all remember certain images from childhood, whether from television, film, or direct experience. But how many of us remember specific words (unless forced to memorize them through repetition)? Smells and sounds, too, are powerful reminders, capable of triggering a specific recollection of a time and place from years earlier. This combination of modes which affects the different senses, and thus activates different aspects of the brain's information processing capabilities, are the focus of multimodal product developers working with all-digital media. The prospect is of richer environments for the presentation of information, stimulating not just cognitive or affective functions but both, thereby leading to new modes of learning, work, and play.

The impact of the media and the different informational modes on the receiver of information is being studied in the marketplace as well as the laboratory. In a 1987 interactive television study at the MIT Audience Research Facility, Eileen McMahon reported that researchers concluded that "People perform best in conditions that match with their preferred cognitive style and view of the world. . . . The closer the match between the user's internal and the media's external modes of representation, the more conducive the learning environment. . . . It seems likely that successful consumer CD-ROM products of the future will be integrated with 'smart chips,' which will screen and select information from databases according to both the user's interests and cognitive style." Supporting the notion of active involvement by textual media users versus the passivity of the habitual broadcast television viewer, the MIT study also found that "many people were reluctant to use interactive [television] features. In order to switch from an emotional state paralleling 'abandonment' of a TV viewer to an objective decision-making state, an individual must access another part of the brain."[11]

Each medium has different modal capabilities (see Figure 5-1). Because of these different capabilities and the different attributes in presenting these modes (see Chapter 7), we can agree with Postman's assertion, which echoes McLuhan's "the medium is the message," that "Each medium, like language

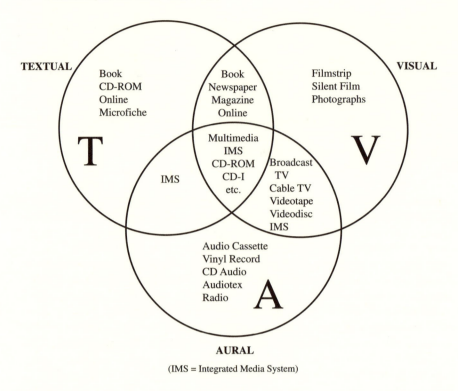

Figure 5-1
The Three Major Modes and Related Media

itself, makes possible a unique mode of discourse by providing a new orientation for thought, for expression, for sensibility. . . . The forms of our media, including the symbols through which they permit conversation. . . . are rather like metaphors, working by unobtrusive but powerful implication to enforce their special definitions of reality." We will continue to have myriad media formats available to us as each presents information and works on the perceiver's mind in different ways: "Every medium of communication has resonance, for resonance is metaphor writ large. Whatever the original and limited context of its use may have been, a medium has the power to fly far beyond that context and into new and unexpected ones. Because of the way it directs us to organize our minds and integrate our experience of the world, it imposes itself on our consciousness and social institutions in myriad forms."[12]

MIXING MODES

The different characteristics of the modes offer many implications for Information Age publishers. Among them are the conversion of existing material from one mode to another and the simultaneous use of information in several different modes.

Cross-Modal Conversion

The conversion of material created in one of the major modes to another mode—for example, a novel (textual mode) into film (visual mode)—is the eleventh core concept:

Core Concept #11: Cross-Modal Conversion

Due to the proliferation of new media forms which capture and manipulate the three major modes in different ways, cross-modal conversion is one of the greatest opportunities presented to Information Age publishers. The advent of video publishing, for example, provides an outlet not only for the publication of existing visual material, such as motion pictures, documentary films, and television programming, but for the conversion of print and audio materials into visual form. The modal conversion as well as the media conversion adds value to the material.

A well-known example is Stuart Karl's adaptation of Jane Fonda's exercise program from the printed page to videotape. The same material in the new mode (moving visual/aural) and new medium (videocassette) was an appropriate choice for the material. The product's success created an entirely new industry segment: special interest or non-theatrical video publishing. Other reasons exist for the program's success, of course, not least among them the appeal of the program's star. But the subsequent success of numerous exercise videos, as well as the extension of the Fonda line, also demonstrated the commercial viability of the new publishing segment. Moreover, it demonstrated that value was lying dormant in certain properties embodied in one mode that were ripe for cross-modal conversion.

Computer-based training provides another example of modal conversion opportunities. Originally rote drill and practice in front of a silent screen, computer training is now adding an entirely new dimension with the inclusion of sound and images. The possibility of interactive language instruction, with text accompanied by an image and then overlaid with the spoken word, is just one evident media replication, if not enhancement, of a face-to-face teaching environment.

Multimodal Publishing

Most existing media formats are bimodal. Books, magazines, and newspapers, although quintessentially textual media, embody both text and images. Even the earliest books, known as illuminated manuscripts, combined text with elaborately hand-crafted images. Most contemporary magazines, except for a handful of literary publications such as *Harper's* and *The New Yorker*, rely just as heavily on their strong visual appeal, usually via photography, as their text, with many women's magazines tipping the balance in favor of visuals. The radical design innovation of the national newspaper *USA Today* was to view the newspaper as a visual medium as much as a textual one, creating colorful, graphic presentation of information throughout the paper. What text is typically provided in the paper is served up in bite-sized chunks for a visually oriented television audience accustomed to consuming information in smaller bits. Though highly controversial for its alleged debasement of the content of the medium, the intuition of the paper's creator, Allen Neuharth, has proven correct. As testament to Neuharth's success, the publishers of competing papers have, in response, been pressed into adopting a more graphic and bite-sized approach in the presentation of the information in their pages, too.

Most non-print media are also bimodal. Television embodies both images and sound. Film ("movies"), though initially only a visual medium, came later to incorporate sound ("talkies"). It is with the rise of digital information technology, which can process material in any of the three major modes, that renewed attention has been paid to how the modes combine with one another to create true multimodal communications:

Core Concept #12: Multimodal Publishing

With digitizing of the material in the three major modes, new methods of presenting information arise. Oldrich Standera's 1987 vision of multimedia publishing is a growing reality: "Joining text [in publishing] are data, voice, sounds, and graphics. . . . With digital encoding being more widely adopted in information technology and with impending new telecommunications links, the impact of images and sound will with certainty be expected to rise. Multimedia electronic publishing is a new phenomenon now in the making, and it is by no means premature to include it in serious research consideration concerning its other aspects in addition to the technical one."[13]

New media often handle different modes in new ways. Moreover, digital media are interactive, giving the user the ability to interrupt the presentation, to redirect its flow, to ask questions, to respond. As certain new computer-based media incorporate these elements, the gulf between today's passive visual viewers (television, films) and active textual readers (books, magazines) will diminish. Standera says: "Writing and reading require an interaction at the cognitive level that makes the reader a less passive recipient of information than, e.g., a habitual TV watcher. Well-applied images and sound as accompaniments to text will strengthen all the positive attributes of text and prove to be useful content enhancers in well-designed applications."[14]

The key here is that mode is a value-added choice on the part of the creator of the material. As noted above, if certain information technologies evolve to process touch (haptic mode), smell (olfactory), and taste (gustatory), then they, too, will be used to enhance communications. It is also important to note that the multiple modes are not strictly additive, as separate components, but are synaesthetic, creating a multilateral impact on the human senses with a concomitant impact on comprehension and retention.

Whether in a single multimodal medium such as computer-based interactive multimedia, or in integrated media systems (IMS) which combine the use of various modes in discrete media such as books, videocassettes, and audio cassettes designed and developed to work in conjunction with one another, new media make possible a total assault on the senses. We can make the analogy to transport via land, sea, or air as the three major modes, the respective media or carriers being cars (trucks, buses, trains), boats, and planes. To extend the metaphor to the military arena, though they may place an emphasis on one mode over the other given the specific circumstances of the conflict, modern militarists would generally not consider waging war in only one mode—land, sea, or air. Effectiveness in reaching objectives is typically achieved through deployment in a combination of modes. Thus in the presentation of information, communications will increasingly refuse to be confined to a single mode and will exploit all appropriate media for their varying degrees of modal strength.

Advertisers, publishers' partners in the media, already wage such "campaigns" and know well that, given the resources, a sequenced, sustained, multimodal, multi-media assault often wins the battle for message awareness and retention. Information Age publishers develop and wage campaigns, too, engaging, where necessary, strategic partners to achieve their objectives. They marshal the full arsenal of weapons, a pentagon of media in a multiplicity of modes. While awareness of the modal possibilities is the publisher's starting point, it is the understanding and effective deployment of the modes and media in the development of individual products and services that determines their successful reception in the marketplace.

Of critical importance is that IMS and multimodal systems, by using all three modes, create experiences that move toward the goal of improved comprehension and retention. As the work of Gardner and others shows, the different modes appeal to different intelligences or "domains" within the individual—text in the cognitive domain (Gardner's linguistic and logical-mathematical intelligences), images and sound in the affective domain (the personal intelligences).[15] The psychomotor domain (bodily-kinesthetic intelligence), for instance, would be activated and engaged by virtual reality systems, just as it is currently engaged by video games (e.g., Nintendo) and other applications such as flight simulators that require eye-hand coordination.

MODAL PROCESSORS

Another important implication of mode as a value-added element is that the material in different modes will be prepared in specialized manners by specially skilled individuals using specialized equipment. The first electronic computers in the 1940s were calculating machines, number processors, which have evolved, among other uses, to include automated spreadsheets and databases at the microcomputer level. Word processing or text processing, the digitization and manipulation of words, did not emerge in the broader marketplace until the 1970s. More recent is image processing, including computer-generated graphics, photographic quality still images, and moving images, including animated and full video images. Digital audio processing, which has been present in analog forms such as phonograph records and motion picture soundtracks, makes possible applications such as voice mail systems, voice recognition, and more sophisticated sound for music, natural sounds, and synthesized sound effects.

As we stand at the threshold of the all-digital era, a new generation of digital multimodal workstations, capable of processing all modes, is being born. This has been the evolution of the desktop computer, from a unifunctional, dedicated terminal to a multifunctional stand-alone processor, to a multifunctional, multimodal, networked machine. An entirely new generation of operating systems, built to process all modes from the ground up, is in development as of this writing by both hardware firms, such as Apple and IBM and Sun Microsystems, and software firms such as Microsoft. Early generation software tools developed for manipulation of digital desktop multimedia include Claris' Hypercard, Asymetrix's Multimedia Toolbook, and Macromind's Director.

Changes in the processing environment wrought by changes in technology are not new to publishers. The flatbed press gave way to the rotary press. Hand typesetting gave way to the linotype machine which in turn gave way to photocomposition. The all-digital processing environment provides ease of storage, retrieval, manipulation, and transmission, speed and accuracy of processing, and cost and time effectiveness, and will eventually make such modal processing systems more attractive than existing, non-digital alternatives, whether the intended output is a print publication or an electronic product or service. While certain computers will continue to specialize in processing selected modes, the trend is toward multimodal processing units.

A corollary of the digital processing environment is the human processing environment. Individuals will develop specialized skills in the development and processing of material in the various modes. New media technologies have always required developer communities as well as user communities, so photographers and typesetters and text editors and video producers will increasingly be joined by multimedia developers, digital image processors, online editors, CD-ROM developers, and others with new skills and outlooks. Some individuals will cross over from existing media—e.g., broadcast television to interactive multimedia—and embody skills in both, while other, younger entrants will cut their teeth in the new media.

While the development end of multimodal processing will continue to evolve with new equipment and new practitioner communities, the user end will also continue to evolve. The new user devices will often be digital out-growths or add-ons of existing mass and interpersonal communications de-vices. Broadcast television, currently a one-way mass medium, will soon be all digital, as will radio. Viewers have growing processing and storage control at the output end, including the availability of non-broadcast material (e.g., vid-eocassettes and discs) and the creation of their own televisual material made on camcorders. Residential telephones, a point-to-point, interpersonal, aural device, will continue to evolve by adding screens for visual and text output and keypads for messaging, as in the French Minitel system, thereby incor-porating all three major modes. They will eventually carry point-to-point full video over enhanced digital fiber optic and global satellite and cellular networks.

In the business environment, on-premise equipment will include document and media processors hooked to intelligent digital electronic information exchange networks that can store, forward, and add other value to multimodal communications. Not far into the next century, a globally interoperable net-work of fully compatible, point-to-point, digital, multimodal, electronic infor-mation highways will connect businesses around the world.

STRATEGIC IMPORTANCE OF MODES

As a result of the expanding modal processing capabilities of new media technologies, Information Age publishers recognize mode as a critical value-added element in the publishing decision mix. This is true at both the product and corporate levels.

Recognizing mode as one of the value-added elements of the publishing construct lessens the distinction between print and electronic formats and instead emphasizes the links in the underlying material. By viewing the ma-terial in its symbolic as well as physical embodiment, Information Age pub-lishers unlock its potential for development in other media formats, regardless of its original embodiment in print, electronic, or other form. In this fashion, content-based publishers see the possibilities for cross-modal conversion or even intramodal, cross-media development of their content in new products and services.

A publisher's awareness of mode is also of strategic value. An assessment of diversification into a new medium—e.g., a book publisher contemplating video publishing—must consider the core aspect of the medium by focusing on its symbol processing capabilities, which in turn suggest the appropriate-ness of the medium for the market and the material. An awareness of mode also reveals connections and continuity intramodally and cross-means as we shall see when we introduce the Media Matrix in the next chapter. For in-stance, a video publisher thinking cross-means will more readily envision broadcast and cable television as competitors, product suppliers, product out-lets, and strategic partners, in addition to seeing himself as a list publisher with links and commonalities with other list (e.g., book and software) publishers.

SUMMARY AND CONCLUSION

In this chapter we have delineated three core concepts for the second value-added M, Mode:

- *Core Concept #10: The Three Major Modes: Textual, Visual, and Aural*
- *Core Concept #11: Cross-Modal Conversion*
- *Core Concept #12: Multimodal Publishing*

The modes are the manner in which material is rendered in symbolic form. Each mode is perceived by different senses and relayed to and interpreted by the brain in different ways. The three modes most susceptible to capture and relay in symbolic form are the textual, visual, and aural modes. The different communications media capture and process these modes with varying degrees of effectiveness, and the proliferation of new media technologies presents new modal opportunities for publishers' material. Cross-modal conversion transforms material from its existing mode to another, while multimodal publishing encompasses several modes at once in a single medium or uses several different media in integrated systems. Information Age publishers use special equipment and specially trained and skilled individuals in the development of material in the different modes. With the changing information technologies the strategic significance of modes, both at the product and corporate levels, has been reemphasized, causing publishers to focus on their material's symbolic as well as physical form. Mode is also an aid in diversification decisions as well as in the analysis of commonalities and competition with other firms and products.

NOTES

1. Howard Gardner, *Frames of Mind: The Theory of Multiple Intelligences* (New York: Basic Books, 1983), 300–301.

2. Ibid., 302 and 26.

3. Although language can in fact be perceived by three different sense organs—the ears hear speech, the eyes read the written word, and the hands read braille—we define text here as written notational symbols read by the eye.

4. Not represented is extra-sensory perception, or ESP, communication which, by definition, occurs outside the five major sensory channels of sight, hearing, smell, taste, and touch. Obviously it is not a feasible mode for publishers as it is not susceptible to capture. It is interesting to note, however, that for ESP to be recognized and effectively used, a "medium" (person) is often employed to provide perceptible sensory output to the messages. For more on ESP in this context, *see* V.V. Raman, "Extra-Scientific

Communication" in *Communication and Civilization* (Rochester, N.Y.: Rochester Institute of Technology, 1986), 107–24.

5. Although limited, olfactory publishing applications have included scratch and sniff advertisements, *Pat the Bunny* ("Now *you* smell the flowers"), and a series of gift books manufactured with perfumed ink (*see* "Words for a Mind, Scents for a Nose, Sales for a Publisher," by Roger Cohen, *The New York Times,* 18 June, 1990).

6. I am aware of two other schema analagous to what I call the three major modes. Koji Kobayashi's "information media" include: Voice/Acoustics; Numerical Data; Text; Still Images, including Graphics, Scanned Images, and Natural Still Images; and Moving Images, including Animation and Natural Moving Pictures. From *Computers and Communications: A Vision of C&C* (Cambridge, Mass.: MIT Press, 1986), 102. Christopher Burns and Patricia Martin group all media into four classes: Literary, for words and numbers; Graphic, for colors, figures, shapes, etc.; Audio-Visual, for sound and motion as well as words; and Non-Literate Notation, for complex symbol sets that have to be learned. From "The Economics of Information" (Washington, D.C.: Office of Technology Assessment, 1985), I-13. Burns and Martin's classification issues out of their definition of information used in the media (as a subset of all information), which they define as "the purposeful construction of symbols."

7. Neil Postman, *Amusing Ourselves to Death* (New York: Penguin, 1985), 9.

8. Postman quotes critic Northrop Frye: "The written word is far more powerful than simply a reminder: it re-creates the past in the present, and gives us, not the familiar remembered thing, but the glittering intensity of the summoned-up hallucination." *Amusing Ourselves to Death,* 12–13.

9. Ibid., 72 and 74.

10. Gardner, *Frames of Mind,* 25.

11. Eileen McMahon, "Scoping Consumer Response to Interactive Programming," *Optical Insights* (Spring, 1987): 7–9. McMahon reports on research done by Diana Gagnon, a post-doctoral fellow at MIT who studied under Howard Gardner at the Harvard Graduate School of Education.

12. Postman, *Amusing Ourselves to Death,* 10 and 18.

13. Oldrich Standera, *The Electronic Era of Publishing* (New York: Elsevier Science Publishing, 1987), 13.

14. Ibid., 13. The author goes on to make an important distinction, based on the modes employed:

Indiscriminately applied imagery and sound, on the other hand, appeal to senses rather than to reason and it appears unrealistic that predominantly image-based information could ever supersede the proven means of linguistic-textual communication. In this respect a potential social and cultural gap could develop between passive media consumers and electronic publishing users, should such polarization occur because of differing predilections in navigating the "electronic seas."

15. Gardner would refer to multiple intelligences. The notion of domains is explicated in the two volume *Taxonomy of Educational Objectives* (New York: David McKay Company, Inc.). The first volume, *Handbook I: Cognitive Domain,* was published in 1956, and the second volume, *Handbook II: Affective Domain,* was published in 1964.

PART III

Media and Means

We have considered the changing industry environment for publishing firms in Part I, and we have looked at the first two of the five value-added components, Material and Mode, in Part II. Now we will look at the next two value-added M's, *Media* and *Means,* and assess their role in the publisher's total offering. We will construct the Media Matrix, the range of media and means of dissemination of information products, before profiling the individual media formats. Part III will close with a consideration of the attributes of these media forms and how we can chart the introduction and growth of the newer, machine-readable electronic media through the market life cycle.

CHAPTER 6

The Media Matrix: Modes and Means

In this chapter we will look at the third value-added M, Medium, the physical form in which the material is stored and displayed, as well as the fourth M, Means, the method of distribution or transmission of material. We will look first at Means, as in our framework media formats are defined by the intersection of Mode and Means. We will then construct the Media Matrix, the grid that displays the entire range of media formats, from the two axes of Modes and Means. Using the matrix as our platform, we will consider how the worlds of publishing, broadcasting, and telecommunications are converging as a result of advances in information technologies. We will also consider the possibilities and problems presented to publishers seeking to own the means of distribution, including the different regulatory environments they will encounter.

MEANS OF DISTRIBUTION

The means of distribution are the conduits through which the material flows to the user. Distribution can be via physical means, electronic means, or even face-to-face, though strictly speaking the last of these is not a publishing or media activity as the material delivered is not recorded, captured, or reproduced for dissemination (*see* Chapter 2).

We can break the distribution of published products and services into three different cycles, as shown in Table 6-1, the next core concept of publishing in the Information Age:

	LIST	PERIODICAL	OPEN CHANNEL
PRODUCT/SERVICE	Long Development Period Durable Content Tangible Product Discrete, Stand-alone Items	Timely Content Short Development Period Tangible Product Series of Items	Timely and Durable Content Short Development Period Voluminous Material Intangible Service Broadcast (One-Way) and Networked (Two-Way)
CUSTOMERS	Mass and Niche Consumer, Business, Professional, Educational	Some Mass Many Targeted, Accessible Consumer, Business, Professional	Targeted/Mass Business, Professional, Consumer
PURCHASE	Individual Items	Subscription/Individual Items	Subscription Free Delivery
MARKETING/DISTRIBUTION	Seasonal, Occasional Physical: Mail, Retail Inventory Maintained	Regular: Daily, Weekly, Monthly, Etc. Physical: Mail, Retail, Direct No Inventory	Continuous, Synchronous Electronic "Live" Inventory
REVENUE SOURCES	User Supported	Advertiser and User Supported	Advertiser and User Supported
MEDIA FORMATS	Print and Electronic Book Videocassette Audio Cassette Software Disk (Magnetic) Optical Disc: CD-ROM, Videodisc, Etc.	Print and Electronic Book Newspaper Magazine Journal Newsletter Optical Disc	Electronic Videotex/Audiotex Teletext Online Services Broadcast (Radio/Television) Cable Television Custom-Published Books Cellular Services

Table 6–1
Means: The Three Distribution Cycles

Core Concept #13: The Three Distribution Cycles: List,
Periodical, and Open Channel

In Table 6-1 we have characterized the key aspects for each cycle: products or services developed; the types of customers; how the product is purchased; how it is marketed and distributed; revenue sources; and the typical media formats for the cycle.

List

List publishers create tangible, stand-alone products. The content is typically more durable than periodical or open channel content, and its development period is usually longer as well. This is partly because the publication of the products is not tied to regular deadlines, and also because, by definition, the storable physical packages are often for durable content. List products are savable, collectible, available for repeated use, referable, and able to cover a subject in depth. They are the repositories of records and archival matter. List publishers can sell to mass markets, though their reach is usually smaller than periodical and open channel products and services. The true strength of list products is in reaching niche markets, though, significantly, little or no direct customer contact is involved in the typical list product, especially in the consumer market, as individual items are typically purchased through third party distributors. (The notable exception to this is software products, which often register users for upgrade purposes.)

Distribution of list products is done seasonally or occasionally, not at any regular time or date. The products are disseminated through physical channels, such as the mail, retail outlets, direct delivery, and special display channels, such as movie theaters and information kiosks. As they are individual package items with some predictable product life, list publications are inventoried. A backlist of continuously-selling items is a staple, for example, of most book publishers. Revenues for list publishers typically come from end-users (often through third party distributors) with advertising revenues minimal, though the reasons for this are more a function of industry custom than format limitations. Advertisers also seek more predictable, identifiable customers than most list products can provide. The media formats available to list publishers have until recently been almost exclusively print-based, such as books, with a major exception being vinyl phonograph disks in the aural mode. In the last 15–20 years, however, a variety of electronic list formats has emerged, including magnetic media for computer software, tape media for the visual and aural modes, and optical discs across all modes.

Periodical

The key distinguishing feature of periodical publications is that they are issued on a regular basis—e.g., daily, weekly, monthly, quarterly—and therefore are typically developed and distributed in a much shorter period than list publications. While for the most part still tangible products like list items, their content is usually more timely. Again, while mass coverage is possible— magazines such as *People, Reader's Digest,* and *TV Guide* come to mind, or large daily metropolitan newspapers—the majority of periodical publications are now niche-oriented in any of the three major markets (the big exception to this is regularly scheduled broadcast television programs). Since periodicals are typically disposable, frequent-issue products, they are sold on a continuity or subscription basis, with subscribers in effect buying on faith in advance based on some good-faith estimate of the product's content and features. This also means that many periodical publishers have direct customer contact, a significant difference from the majority of list publishers.

Periodicals can be distributed through physical means or electronically as in the case of regularly scheduled broadcast programs, but no inventory is maintained for the purpose of ongoing sales. Significant advertising revenues distinguish periodicals from list publications. Media formats such as newspapers, magazines, and scheduled broadcast programs often reap anywhere from one half to all of their revenues from advertising. Other periodical items, such as mail order continuity series books (e.g., Time-Life) or emerging fields such as CD-ROM publications in the business market, rely almost exclusively on subscriber revenues.

Open Channel

The evolution in this century of electronic delivery systems, both one-way and two-way, via both hardwire and the airwaves, has brought a variety of new information distribution alternatives into being, including broadcast radio and television, cable television, teletext, videotex, online systems, and satellite systems. All of these open channel distribution systems are electronic, marked by a continuous transmission or accessibility of signals, and thus the offering is an information or entertainment service versus a tangible product. The material is often timely, but large online databases can carry durable content as well.

Open channel services can be one-way, as in broadcast systems, which are unidirectional, point-to-multi-point media that fit the "performance" model of one-to-many. The two-way open channel services are bi-directional, point-to-point systems, and can be either hardwire (online, cable television) or over-the-air systems (cellular radio, satellite). The two-way systems are a hybrid of interpersonal, point-to-point media and mass point-to-multi-point media, following a "participatory" communications model. Thus open channel systems encompass all the mass and personal communications models: one-to-one systems (telephone); one-to-many (broadcasting); many-to-many (interactive computer network); and many-to-one (feedback, voting, polls, shopping). They also encompass all three major modes—a voice transaction via phone today, for instance, could migrate to a screen-text transaction tomorrow.

Due to their broadcast and connective capabilities, open channel systems can address both mass and niche audiences. While the connectivity of two-way systems implies subscription, one-way services imply advertiser support, hence "free" delivery. The material is delivered to users continuously and both synchronously (broadcast) and asynchronously (online services). There is typically no incremental cost-per-user to the supplier in one-way open channel systems as the material is delivered in a blanket fashion, ubiquitously, instantaneously. No inventory is maintained on broadcast services, while online databases typically maintain "live" inventories available for instant access.

Face-to-Face

As noted above, face-to-face, live, in-person events cannot, by our definition, be classified as a means of publishing distribution in the sense that primary experience cannot be disseminated unless embodied in a medium—e.g., a baseball game over radio—at which point it becomes a media offering. However, such in-person events certainly qualify as forms of communication—indeed, they are the most ancient and often the most powerful—and are important to publishers as another means of presentation of material: a museum exhibit, a play or other dramatic staging, a lecture, a conference. Face-to-face events also allow publishers to create lists of names for direct customer contact.

In the business and professional markets, seminars, trade shows, and conferences have become a big business. Content-based publishing firms such as Cahners and IDG have separate divisions devoted to providing planned gatherings for the communities of specific publications and content areas.

The full variety of media packaged with live events is rich. Non-information products spun off from or tied in to live events fall into the category of merchandising—a T-shirt from a Broadway play, an armadillo mug from a natural history museum. A museum exhibit such as Van Gogh at the Metropolitan Museum of Art can have a book or video tie-in. Each mix of events and materials is different. *Champions of American Sport* was an exhibition in the early 1980s that traveled to three major museums, aired as an HBO special on cable television, and appeared as a full-color illustrated book published by Harry Abrams. In effect, Information Age publishers can extend their content franchise by becoming producers of live events, as well. They envision the broadest possible range of exposures for the material and choose the most appropriate for the subject at hand. Often it means soliciting one or more joint venture partners in the enterprise.

SIGNIFICANCE OF MEANS

Distribution cycles are of significance for many reasons. They highlight product development issues as well as the appropriateness of material for the given means and media, and they distinguish tangible physical products from intangible services.[1] They define the nature of the publishing or media enterprise and suggest the appropriate type of personnel. Just as there is a different "head" or gestalt in the different media technologies—high-tech hackers and the denizens of the literary book world, for instance, have until recently been inhabitants of almost entirely different industry cultures—so is there a different head in the different publishing cycles. Time orientation is critical for the people working in a given organization and plays into all aspects of product development, processing, manufacturing, and marketing of the firm's products. A publishing firm may well be engaged in the different cycles, and many are, in both books and magazines, for instance. But within the company the different cycles define distinct activities. The cycle suggests product development requirements, such as long or short gestation periods and depth or breadth of content. It suggests the types of markets, mass or targeted, consumer or educational, and determines how the product is marketed. List publishers, for example, typically must find their customers anew with the publication of each stand-alone product, meaning an entirely new marketing campaign, while periodical publishers, having sought and won customers, are more concerned with maintaining their established subscriber base. (A notable exception is software publishers, whose customers are typically registered users who seek information regarding technical support, product upgrades, and new releases.)

The distribution cycle also plays into ownership of content. Magazines and newspapers usually maintain a complement of content creators on staff to meet tight deadlines, while book publishers and film studios usually work with independent suppliers, either via license or work-for-hire arrangements, as the creation process and gestation period of list products is of an entirely different nature. Software publishers and reference publishers, however, are in yet another category as list publishers whose material often demands full-time in-house content creators.

The relation between material and means is highlighted by the advent of computer networks, where participation and immediacy displace the one-way, slower gestation period of traditional publications. In a broader social or scholarly sense, the great dialogue of the ages takes time. But we now have the possibility of different metabolisms pulsing within the larger organism, some at a higher rate, others at a slower rate. This is because open channel systems merge aspects of point-to-point interpersonal telecommunications, like the telephone, and one-to-many mass communications, like publishing or broadcasting. Personal messages and packaged messages are now available on the same system, and thus the hybrid technology creates a new medium. One can add value by adding a message on top of somebody else's message or an item from a database, compacting the process of research and synthesis that is the essence of scholarship (leaving aside, for the moment, copyright and rights implications). Computer networks such as the WELL (Whole Earth 'Lectronic

Link) have been described as "as much a step backward to the 19th century literary salon as a step into the future. 'People used to write letters all the time. Now we do again. . . . It's for people who enjoy communicating through the written word,' says one of the system's regular users. . . . In this sense, the medium is doing more than television, a one-way, mass broadcast medium, to create the convivial global village that Mr. McLuhan envisioned in the 1960s . . . [it needed] a more interactive medium, computer networks."[2]

New means of distribution also challenge the view of publishing that has grown up over time as a function organized through certain established channels via certain means of distribution. Electronic networks disintermediate information suppliers and customers, putting them in direct contact with one another. Publishers formerly made the connection through physical distribution. But one information sender can now reach many receivers without a gatekeeper. Soon this will be possible in the visual mode as well—full video transmission from individual sites to any other site over multimodal networks. Video production, thanks to camcorders, is already in the hands of individuals. All these individuals lack is a network to disseminate their video messages, just as computer bulletin boards currently post and send textual messages. The NeXT computer was the first to provide a glimpse of this messaging medium, with imaging and voice capabilities built-in to accompany textual e-mail. In NEC chairman Koji Kobayashi's terms, the publisher of the future will be an Information Service Center, or ISC, a provider of information to physical and electronic delivery systems, allowing for two-way feedback and content selection on demand. Kobayashi's ISC is a fully digitized data source connected to a value-added network, either fiber optic or satellite, while home, business, and educational users receive, store, and transmit information with on-site, multimodal digital terminals.

THE MEDIA MATRIX

With an understanding of both modes and means, we are ready to construct the Media Matrix. The matrix encompasses all media formats, the blank repositories on which information is captured, stored, transmitted, retrieved, and displayed, and it defines the product and service scope of the media. It is derived from the Information Business Map (Figure 1-2), but in the Media Matrix the products-services axis, representing the means of distribution, runs horizontally, while the three major modes define the vertical axis. The Media Matrix is the next core concept of publishing in the Information Age:

Core Concept #14: The Media Matrix: Modes and Means

We can define the individual media formats by placing them in the cells of the matrix. Each medium typically has a defining mode—e.g., books are the quintessential textual medium, broadcast television the quintessential visual

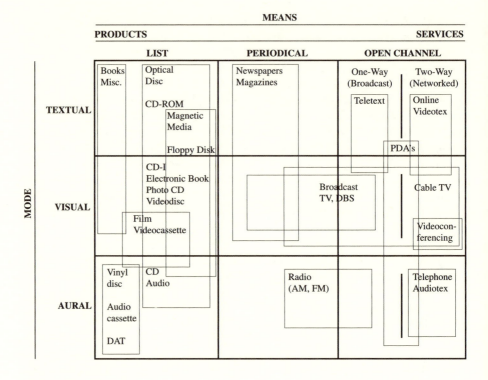

Figure 6-1
The Media Matrix: Modes and Means

medium. But, as noted earlier, most formats are at least bimodal, and thus are portrayed as extending across more than one cell in the matrix. Also, as we will see below, the evolving technologies are blurring the boundaries between the traditional media definitions and roles (*see* Figure 6-2).

To define the media in terms of modes and means decouples information from our understanding of it through current media, a necessary task if we are to see new uses and new ways of thinking about information made possible by the new media. Many publishers familiar with and organizationally invested in existing media formats are not prone to seeing opportunities in new media formats, whereas Information Age publishers take advantage of such opportunities by redefining their businesses around their content and its possibility for packaging and delivery in different media.

The matrix reveals how the new media and information technologies have made possible the development and delivery of content products and services in all modes. For instance, until the introduction and widescale adoption of the VCR in the late 1970s and early 1980s, videocassette publishing did not exist, and the only option for the delivery of television programming was via broadcast airwaves. Now, of course, video programs can be delivered as physical stand-alone products in the form of videocassettes and discs and as services via satellite, microwave, and cable in addition to broadcast airwaves.

New media will continue to evolve, and publishers proficient in the development of one type of material in certain modes (e.g., moving visuals) or delivered via certain means (e.g., list) must learn to assess these new media opportunities for their organizations. The matrix provides some level of predictive value in that the displacement of media formats typically occurs within rather than across cells in the matrix. In the aural/list cell, for example, the survival of vinyl phonograph discs is now severely threatened by cassettes and CD's. (The coexistence of a plurality of media formats throughout the matrix, and their interaction, will be addressed further in Chapter 8.)

It is important to note that in electronic and other machine-readable formats, a compatible player base is critical for published products and services. Television broadcasting is useless without receivers that tune in broadcast signals and reproduce them for viewing. Computer software, CD audio, and online services are of no value without the proper user-premise equipment to capture, decode, and display the material. This is not true for print media, for which storage and display, typically on paper, are one and the same.

The Media Matrix will serve as one of the principal building blocks throughout the remainder of the study. When we add the market dimension in Chapter 10 we will create the Media Universe, and in Part V we will see how both the matrix and the universe can serve as strategic tools for media organizations.

PUBLISHING, BROADCASTING, AND TELECOMMUNICATIONS

The Media Matrix also reveals publishing's historical core—the upper left-hand cell defined by the intersection of the textual mode and the list/periodical cycles' and broadcasting's core—open channel distribution in the visual/aural mode; and telecommunications' core, open channel distribution in the aural mode. This leads to the next core concept:

Core Concept #15: Convergence: Publishing, Broadcasting, and Telecommunications

The core of publishing is list and periodical products in the textual and visual modes. But the former definition of publishing as the selection, processing, and dissemination of discrete print products distributed asynchronously no longer holds. Products can also be services if delivered synchronously in open channel systems. Moreover, electronic list formats have joined print formats in allowing the publication of moving visual as well as aural information. Additionally, broadcasting, the continuous transmission of signals to a mass audience of users who receive the signals simultaneously, now delivers not only visual (television) and aural (radio) information but text (teletext) as well.

The convergence of the three activities of publishing, broadcasting and telecommunications and their technologies has brought an expansion of choices in the media universe, bringing both confusion and opportunities for content firms. As discussed in Chapter 1, for over 500 years, through the mid-20th century, textual information was defined in print form only, ink on paper, as newspapers, magazines, newsletters, and books, periodical and list products. For centuries prior to that, paper and paper-like materials, such as vellum, were used for the capture and display of text. In the 1970s the coupling of digital processing computers with video display terminals made text electronic, readable on screens for the first time. By linking digitally processed text to telecommunications networks, the three technologies allowed publishers to store and transmit text electronically. This is the upper right-hand cell of the Media Matrix, textual/open channel, which includes online information services.

The introduction of videocassette technology in the mid-1970s created another revolution. When videocassette recorders were introduced to the market, for the first time in history individuals could play back and store pre-packaged moving images and sound on their own machines. Moving images and sound could be *published*—not broadcast—in stand-alone (list) pack-

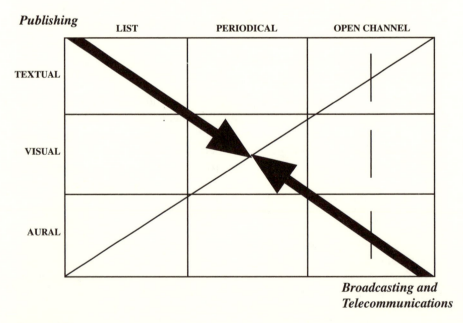

Figure 6-2
The Convergence of Publishing, Broadcasting, and Telecommunications

ages. Theatrical films were an obvious source of material for the new medium, as was other pre-existing filmed and televised material. Soon new content was created specifically for the new medium, opening up special interest categories, the visual equivalent of non-fiction book publishing, as theatrical films are the visual mode equivalent of fiction publishing.

Thus two major communications revolutions took place almost simultaneously: the "broadcast" of text and the "publishing" of moving images. These two developments illustrate how the changing information and media technologies are changing the world of publishing in fundamental ways. And as product and service differences blur, so do the industries which develop and distribute these products and services.

The convergent publishing, broadcasting, and telecommunications technologies have provided increased efficiencies and market coverage at both ends of the mass-niche spectrum. Satellite technology allows global or national blanket coverage via television and pre-press newspaper and magazine production. At the same time the proliferation of different types of machine readout devices for stand-alone list products—computers, VCR's, audio cassette players, optical disc players—allows local, segmented, uses of information. Thus open channel systems are pushing the upper limits of mass communications while list publishing media push the limits of segmented, customized, niche information.

ELECTRONIC HIGHWAYS

The influx of telecommunications into the mass communications arena of publishing and broadcasting brings us to the next core concept:

Core Concept #16: Electronic Highways

As the physical highways of the past and present have carried information products, so electronic highways carry information services. Because these highways combine point-to-point communications with near ubiquitous coverage through telecommunications systems, they are appropriate for both mass and niche applications. The highways are both wired (telephone system, cable television) and wireless (broadcasting, cellular transmission, DBS).

The attractiveness and intuitive logic of a ubiquitous multimodal communications infrastructure makes its reality a matter of manifest destiny. John Sculley sees the personal information device of the future as a knowledge navigator moving along these electronic highways (the Newton personal digital assistant, or PDA, launched by Apple in August 1993 is an example of such a device). He sees the evolution of such interconnected personal digital systems as analogous to the development of the automobile, whose technology and method of functioning had to be "buried" before it became a successful personal device on a mass scale. If personal computer technology is to finally achieve the much vaunted user-friendly status, allowing users to "drive" effortlessly on "electronic highways" with "intuitive interactive access to stored information and entertainment," it must evolve to the same point of invisibility as automobile technology, becoming truly transparent to the user.[3] Moreover, such highways will make possible the seamless flow of externally published content into the user's personal device, so that internal and external information, in all modes, can flow together.

The enormity of the nationwide undertaking to create such an infrastructure—and ultimately the national multimodal network will interoperate globally, as does the current international telephone network—will take a combined effort between government and private enterprise. With the advent of the Clinton administration, the issue of who will build and maintain the public and private portions of these information systems has become the subject of intense debate. Regardless of the outcome, all parties agree that all public and private communications networks must interconnect seamlessly. As information and entertainment content suppliers, publishers will distribute their goods on these national and global electronic highways, while other information and transactional services will coexist on these same highways. An example of one early effort at distribution of commercial content over the current meta-network, the Internet, is the Online BookStore, which began transmitting the full text of selected titles over the service in early 1993. Other commercial online information services, such as CompuServe, have been providing information over the electronic highway for more than a decade.

In such an interconnected distribution network, the communications model shifts from performance to participation, from lecture to conversation.[4] But while the networks comprise a growing segment of the publishing activity, we should also recognize that one-way mass communication will continue to exist for its own reasons. Not all communication fits the model of an informal dialogue or conversation, and often we seek to know from those who know— to be educated or lectured to by the knowledgeable or to be entertained by the talented. In these instances, a sustained one-way flow is appropriate. The multiplicity of media options will allow both types of exchanges to proliferate in the new information environment.

FORWARD INTEGRATION

One option for Information Age publishers is to manage the electronic highways. But forward integration—i.e., controlling the means of distribution—is expensive and requires a different set of technical skills. If content developers do own the means of electronic distribution, they are generally treated as separate businesses within the same enterprise, such as Time Warner's multiple system cable operator (ATC) and Ziff Communications' ZiffNet. Dow Jones has chosen not just to control but to own and operate its electronic information service, Dow Jones News/Retrieval. They retrieve the information, edit and process it, format it for both print and online publication, and maintain the information service that distributes the content to end-users. Outside network operators are used only in the final step of distribution, tying into the phone network for delivery to end-users.

It is also important to note that in most vertically integrated enterprises the initial impetus for capturing more of the value added fades as the distribution business establishes its own agenda. The various component pieces of a vertically integrated operation eventually find it economically prudent to offer their expertise in service of more than just their own parent company's needs. Once a distribution operation is established, for example, outside product suppliers are sought. In some instances, the component parts of the parent enterprise transact business with each other at arms length, and the benefits of capturing the added value only accrue to the organizations involved when profits flow to the parent's consolidated bottom line. In others, the individual units are more tightly integrated (*see* Core Concept #44, The Horizontal Organization).

Different Regulatory Environments

To the extent that publishers as content providers integrate forward into network or system operation, they must not only assume the technological and financial challenge of sustaining an open channel system but be prepared for regulatory environments dissimilar to those of list or periodical publishing. The three major communications spheres of publishing, broadcasting, and telecommunications have historically grown up around different philosophical, technical, and regulatory bases. Publishing has been nurtured by First Amendment protections allowing freedom of expression, as well as protection of ownership of expression through copyright. Broadcasting has seen closer regulation of spectrum space and content. Telecommunications conduits are viewed as common carriers, and thus as point-to-point interpersonal systems have had little or no censorship. The merging of the underlying technologies muddies these distinctions and makes regulation increasingly difficult.

In his landmark study of colliding communications regulatory environments, *Technologies of Freedom,* Ithiel de Sola Pool says: "Whatever the precise situation, electronic information systems are in the same business as the print media and will therefore displace and converge with hard-copy publishing. It would confuse the mechanism with the function to subject data networks and storage devices to legal precedent from the previous electronic media rather than to the law of print, and the consequences would be dire."[5]

There is also the potential for abuse on these networks. Cable franchises, for instance, are currently granted by local municipalities as virtual monopolies. Companies such as Time Warner, noted above, are both program supplier and network operator. The company ran into regulatory difficulty when they were charged with limiting access on one of their cable networks to their own programming, failing to allocate channel space to competitor's services.[6] In a computer network case, IBM and Sears' joint-venture videotex service, Prodigy, provoked controversy in 1990 when they revoked certain subscribers' privileges and refused to carry certain personal messages. Clear answers are not readily apparent, but it is just this type of issue that de Sola Pool anticipated.

What for content providers and publishers is forward integration into information services is backward integration for the network operators. The 1991 ruling allowing the seven regional Bell operating companies (RBOC's) divested by AT&T in 1984 to enter information services demonstrated to all concerned that regulatory changes can bring significant and dramatic shifts in the competitive landscape. Equally significant was the mid-1992 FCC ruling allowing the RBOC's to transmit television programming, providing a major threat to the cable television industry.

SUMMARY AND CONCLUSION

In this chapter we have delineated four more core concepts of publishing in the Information Age, relating to Means, the third value-added M, and Medium, the fourth M:

- *Core Concept #13: The Three Distribution Cycles: List, Periodical, and Open Channel*
- *Core Concept #14: The Media Matrix: Modes and Means*
- *Core Concept #15: Convergence: Publishing, Broadcasting, and Telecommunications*
- *Core Concept #16: Electronic Highways*

The three distribution cycles of list, periodical, and open channel represent the frequency with which media products and services are distributed. The cycles have an impact on the choice of medium and material and also dictate a variety of organizational concerns, such as culture, human resources, and structure. All media formats are derived from the intersection of modes and means, the two axes of the Media Matrix. The matrix lays out the full range of current media and accommodates future possibilities. It also reveals how the formerly separate worlds of publishing, broadcasting, and telecommunications are converging. The electronic highways of the open channel distribution systems bring some of the greatest changes and challenges to the publishing industry, including the potential for significant value-added through forward integration. However, the distinctly different historical development of these three major spheres of communications means that players moving from one realm to another can expect to confront not only different technical and operational demands but different regulatory environments as well.

NOTES

1. Cf. Lynn Shostack, "Breaking Free From Product Marketing," *Journal of Marketing* 1977 as quoted in Davis/Smith, *Marketing in Emerging Companies* (Reading, Mass.: Addison-Wesley, 1984), 26.

2. John Markoff, "Whole Earth State-of-the-Art Rapping," *The New York Times,* 15 April, 1989.

3. John Sculley in "Foreword" to Poppel and Goldstein, *Information Technology: The Trillion-Dollar Opportunity* (New York: McGraw-Hill, 1987), xii–xiii. *See also* Sculley's own book, *Odyssey* (New York: Harper & Row, 1987), as well as Frederick Williams' "Scenarios to the 21st Century" in *The Communications Revolution* (New York: New American Library, Signet reprint edition, 1983), 224–5.

4. *See* Poppel and Goldstein, *Information Technology,* 116. The performance-participation dichotomy was coined by Booz Allen Hamilton principal Joseph Garber and published in *Information Industry Insights, #7.*

5. Ithiel de Sola Pool, *Technologies of Freedom* (Cambridge, Mass.: Harvard University Press, 1983), 199. *See also* the 1986 U.S. Office of Technology Assessment report, *Intellectual Property Rights in an Age of Electronics and Information,* especially Chapter 9, "Federal Role in the Administration of Intellectual Property Rights."

6. *See* Sidney W. Dean, Jr. and Eric Schmuckler, "A Major Victory for Cable Viewers," *The New York Times,* 18 March, 1988. The case concerned Manhattan Cable's carriage of then parent Time Inc.'s pay services HBO and Cinemax and not Bravo and Showtime. Due to a citizens' lobby which applied pressure through the courts, the company agreed to carry the competitive services.

CHAPTER 7

The Media: Profiles and Attributes

A fundamental question for Information Age publishers concerns the relative mix of products and services in the different media forms: what will be the market share for each form? What will be the revenues and profits generated by each? This mix will be dynamic as new media forms are introduced and gain share from established print and other electronic forms. The root publishing question becomes: given the content of the message, what form—or forms—is most appropriate for conveying the content and is best for the user? This chapter considers the attributes of media formats and profiles the current range of media. It also considers interaction among the media forms and takes a glimpse at trends in future media.

ATTRIBUTES OF MEDIA FORMATS

A starting point in the assessment of media formats is an awareness of their attributes. These strengths and weaknesses are relative, not absolute, central to consultant Christine Urban's notion of comparative advantage, which she says "does not reflect what a format can do, or even do well. It is a statement of what the format does *better* than available alternatives."[1] The consideration of the various attributes of each media format aids in determining the appropriateness of the various types of content to the medium and its intended use. The attributes inherent in the medium are indicators of which of the user's information needs will or will not be met.

Information Age publishers also consider the effectiveness of the various formats in fulfilling the goals of third parties. For instance, advertisers will see a trade-off in performance levels and audience targeting capabilities of cable television versus magazines. The media have their uses for the suppliers of information as well as the end-users, and the ultimate commercial viability of a medium may well be tied to its ability to fulfill the needs of these third parties as well.

Typical attributes for media formats include the following:

Timeliness—how dynamic is the information in the medium? The weather forecast is important today, a stock price or a traffic report this minute. Dickens, however, has been around for a century and most likely will be for another (recalling Pound's observation that "Literature is news that stays news").

Durability—how long will the information last in a given format? Books are generally designed to have more staying power than newspapers, for instance.

Breadth of Content—a newspaper's coverage, like an online service, is typically broad.

Depth of Content—a book can have more in depth, however, on any given subject than a newspaper can. A general knowledge encyclopedia combines both breadth and depth (but not timeliness, unless it is updated, as in online services).

Production Quality—newspapers have relatively low-quality printed graphics compared to the color, paper stock, and other production characteristics of magazines or books. Within electronic formats, videotex graphics are still relatively poor, though perhaps useful in other ways, in comparison to the graphics and full motion video on television.

Ease of Use—most print formats are familiar, easy to use, and not machine-readable. They usually require literacy in a given language, however. In electronic formats, television is familiar to most and one of the most accessible of all media: children and foreigners can watch a culture's television before they can read. Computers and their related media still struggle to live up to the designation "user-friendly," but they are getting closer with each generation.

Portability—books go anywhere, videotape viewing does not. Newspapers can be carried on the train or plane, online information services (as of this writing) cannot. Portable hand-held players, such as Electronic Book players, personal organizers, and PDA's (personal digital assistants), add to the mix.

Cost to User—this is dependent on the volume of manufacturing runs, production costs, third-party revenue sources, such as advertising, and other factors.

Interactivity/Manipulability—the degree of control over the information by the user. In real time, NBC is beyond one's control, but a tape of a broadcast is more in one's control, as is a magazine or book. Conversely, books don't "listen," they only "talk." Interactive multimedia both listens and talks.

Connectivity—while interactivity is local manipulation and use of information, connectivity is the ability to communicate with other machines (e.g., online databases) and individuals. Computer networks allow this capability, as do point-to-point interpersonal (versus mass) communication devices, such as the telephone.

Modal Capability—while print formats are bimodal, providing high quality text and still images, they do not provide moving images or sound. A compact audio disc offers high-quality sound, while a videocassette offers both sound and moving images. Multimedia optical discs carry all three major modes.

Appeal to Advertisers—market size, definability, identifiability, and regular, sustained coverage, are among the media attributes that appeal to advertisers. Media formats with such appeal can reap revenues from these third parties as well as end-users.

Of course the individual product or service developed within any given format will exploit the medium's potential differently, and this is at once a publisher's constraint and a challenge to innovation. For instance, *USA Today* raised the level of newspaper's graphic quality through its introduction of four-color charts, maps, and photographs. The success of *Lotus 1-2-3* (and VisiCalc before it) can be directly attributed to the value it added to a formerly static ink on paper medium by electrifying it. At the same time, publishers should bear in mind that performance on such attributes is only of importance in relation to users' expectations and for the purposes they seek the information. For many newspaper readers, the color graphics in *USA Today* may not be of significant value.

At the broadest level—i.e., the medium format as a class versus a specific product or service—the consideration of the capabilities of the various formats yields a truer understanding of the role the different media will play in a world marked by multiple formats and broad user choice. Moreover, as new media are introduced, new and different attributes are created. For example, when Philips' compact disc interactive (CD-I) was first introduced to the market, motion and sound become available on a compact optical disc playable on television, and those formats without interactive moving image and sound capabilities were at risk of being placed at a competitive disadvantage. The introduction of holographic and virtual reality devices will add participatory three dimensionality, a totally new attribute.

The attribute listings presented here should be seen as a conceptual starting point reflecting the array of media format choices open to Information Age publishers. Other attributes include the ubiquity of a broadcast or cable network, the size of the installed base of machines for electronic formats, the nature of the display (a printed page is always viewable, the material on an electronic screen, evanescent), and many others. They should be re-created anew by each publisher seeking competitive format analysis or the appropriateness of a content-format fit, especially in assessing the introduction of a new media format. Publisher David Miller, for instance, summarizes the attributes of CD-ROM as follows: "They let the user possess the information, not just dial it up; they're interactive in real time; they provide hard copy on demand; they can handle images much better than existing online services; they're capable of dense, compact storage; they're durable and permanent; and they offer enormous economies of scale in mass replication."[2]

PROFILES OF MEDIA FORMATS

The following profiles of current media formats are intended not only to highlight the chief attributes of the formats but also their capabilities in relation to other formats in a changing media marketplace.

Books

The key attributes of books relative to other media formats include their durability of content and form, breadth and depth of content, high production quality, tangibility, portability, low cost, familiarity, and ease of use.

Lewis Coser and colleagues, in their insightful study of the book publishing industry, *Books: The Culture and Commerce of Publishing*, state that "Books are carriers and disseminators of ideas. More than any other means of communication, they are the most permanent, reasoned, and extensive repository of the thoughts of civilized man."[3] Like passenger ships or trains in an era of flight, books are slower and more familiar in an era of electronics. And like ships and trains, they will not be displaced but complemented by the new media forms, for they are too versatile and too strong in too many ways, not the least of which is their engrained position in our culture. Their mute, non-obsolescing machine-free operation and tangible presence offer an essential counterpoint to the barrage of ephemeral images we have grown accustomed to living with. As John Cole of the Library of Congress' Center for the Book has phrased it, we are "a culture of the book." Our laws and religions are founded on books and the ideas contained in them. Books are the accepted form for a serious statement on a given topic.

Not only does the book remain the central form for the embodiment of ideas, it is also the guiding metaphor in a media mad world. If someone is an expert in a field, we say he "wrote the book." We describe spoken word audio cassettes as "talking books" and as McLuhan pointed out "film, both in its reel form and in its script or scenario form, is completely involved with book culture. All one need do is to imagine for a moment a film based on newspaper form in order to see how close film is to book."[4] In fact we can view developing a book property as the equivalent of research and development in other industries. It is the creation of the necessary blueprint, the prototype, the fullest expression of the idea. It is often the original book that is converted into other media forms to achieve maximum exposure and maximum return for the creator and originating publisher.

Books are clearly bimodal, with the capacity for high-quality visual as well as textual content. Some books, such as children's books and art books, can be purely visual in their construction and appeal. Moreover, the flexibility of the book medium, as well as the book industry's mature understanding of the integration of textual and visual elements, is not only well established but continually demonstrated anew.

New publishing media will have different impacts on different types of books in different markets, and each publisher must assess his content and his audience and determine whether a book is in fact the best form for the function. If it is not, and if users feel comfortable or prefer the same content packaged and delivered in alternative forms, then the book will either be supplemented by or lose share to the newer forms. For instance, CD-ROM in the reference area combines voluminous yet compact on-site storage with ease of search. Videocassettes and discs in the instructional and how-to area can also subsume some of the functions of a book, as in the example of Jane Fonda's exercise tape cited earlier.

Another issue for book publishers is the cost of resources, specifically the heavy burden undertaken in the production and manufacturing of thousands of bound volumes, with associated inventory and shipping costs, usually with no reliable estimate of sales. As Ithiel de Sola Pool stated, "The costs at almost every stage of electronic publishing and record keeping are becoming lower than those for hard copy. The time is fast approaching when having information on paper rather than by computer will be an extra cost alternative done only for taste or convenience."[5] Such thinking is troubling to book publishers, whose enterprises are structured and staffed to manufacture multiple identical copies of the same content for physical distribution. But as de Sola Pool also points out, "Publishing remains a business devoted to organizing texts and information and offering this material widely. . . . Whether a publisher preprints and warehouses multiple copies or prints on demand is a matter of market strategy, not cultural substance."[6] Whatever the form of production, users will come to appreciate anew, in our computerized, electronic culture, the immense value-added in "hard-copy printout" that is illustrated and of high production value—i.e., a book. Moreover, the attractiveness of books as tangible physical objects, combining craftsmanship with mass production techniques, will undoubtedly persist.

Thus publishers of books will wield technology and other available means to sustain their enterprises. If the production costs of paper and manufacturing *do* become prohibitive and prices cannot be borne by end-users alone, book publishers may turn to advertising support or other third-party project underwriters, in programs such as that pioneered by Whittle Communications' Larger Agenda Series introduced in 1989.

Of equal significance for book publishers is that material originated and stored in electronic form at all stages of its processing will also be susceptible to delivery and formatting as *customers* choose, in addition to how publishers choose. The conventional conception of a book as a pre-packaged item will be supplemented by a different type of book, a user-created book produced on-site, that combines material of the user's choosing from multiple electronic sources. The output may be electronic—i.e., played back on a hand-held or desktop device, in one or more modes—or it may be printed and bound in a bookstore or other site. These customer-created books will be in addition to yet another class of books, on-demand publications, those publications which are centrally produced in response to either bookstore (or another intermediary, such as a university) or end-user demand. McGraw-Hill's Primis system is an example of such an on-demand publishing system.

In short, the attractiveness of the printed page and the bound volume as display formats will persist in a screen-oriented electronic environment. But the path taken to this end point, and the nature of the volumes and their contents, will most likely change, with centrally produced multiple copies of identical texts supplemented by remotely produced units with customized contents.[7]

Magazines

Key attributes for magazines include portability, high production quality—far better than newspapers and rivaling books—relatively low cost, and both broad content and deep content within each publication's given subject area. Magazine content is also relatively timely because of frequency of publication.

Because they excel in so many ways, magazines have proven to be a durable format. Moreover, as demonstrated by the trend from general to special interest publications, the combination of these factors with the magazine's concentrated focus and ease of availability, either through newsstand sales or direct to the home via subscription, define a medium with broad appeal. Perhaps most importantly, advertisers will continue to underwrite more than half the business as long as they can so easily reach targeted, definable, identifiable portions of the population. Not only can magazines target, segment, and continually deliver information to specialized audiences, they can extend their recognized content franchises into selected new media, such as *Business Week* and *National Geographic* on video, Standard & Poor online, and *Newsweek Interactive* on CD-ROM, with a relative degree of assurance of salability based on their established imprints.

In the professional publishing environment, online computer networks have had an impact on journal publishing. The immediacy of information exchange afforded by such networks, linking far-flung colleagues in giant, multilateral colloquia, has put pressure on the slower gestation and distribution cycles of print journals. Still, the issue of peer review and imprimaturs make the print publishers, as guardians of selection criteria and standards, a necessary arbiter in the world of scholarly information. How—or whether—this role will be played in an online environment is still to be determined.

Newspapers

In terms of gross revenues, newspapers are still the largest single media segment, larger than broadcast television. Two-thirds of their revenue is derived from advertising, one-third from circulation. Key attributes include timeliness, broad coverage, portability, and low cost to the consumer.

As with magazines, the convenient and established path newspapers provide for advertisers makes them a likely candidate for survival well into the 21st century. Also, as the largest single revenue component of the entire media industry it will take unprecedentedly major shifts in consumer usage habits and industry norms to displace this giant. Newspapers have thus far withstood the onslaught of both television and radio, astutely capitalizing on what the broadcast media have to offer by devoting coverage to them, adopting some of television's visual approach to the presentation of information, and reaping healthy benefits from television and radio advertising and listings.

Newspapers do, however, face real challenges. As readership continues to decline and as successive generations of TV-bred consumers age, newspapers will be pressed by competitive media. Other challenges are faced in the production end, where process innovations must be harnessed to keep costs low if newspapers are to retain a competitive edge, although as of the beginning of the 1990s, most major metropolitan dailies had dealt with this issue. Resource constraints, such as the cost of newsprint and the cost of physical distribution to millions of end-users, are competitive disadvantages in relation to open channel electronic formats. And as electronic textual (e.g., online) and visual (e.g., broadcast and cable television) media proliferate, there will be even more competition for advertiser dollars. In this context, it is no surprise that newspapers invested heavily in the videotex trials of the 1970s and 1980s, fearing loss of revenue and readership. With the success of Prodigy and the potential reemergence of consumer online services via the local telephone operating companies in the 1990s, newspapers once again face critical decisions in this area. Many are now involved in new efforts to provide information online, whether via national services such as Prodigy, CompuServe, or America Online, or via local services. The wireless personal communicators of the not-too-distant future will create yet another alternative format for the delivery of timely information direct to users. The newspaper model, page layout and all, can conceivably be incorporated into this screen-display medium, with search features akin to current newspapers.[8]

Miscellaneous Print Formats

Other print formats include newsletters, directories (e.g., the yellow pages), loose-leaf forms, catalogs, calendars, maps, post cards, and other print-based forms. Although there are a variety of formats here, most share the key attributes of portability, flexibility (of form to content), low production cost, and low production quality.

The familiarity, ubiquity, and typically low cost solutions to users' information needs of these formats make them extremely useful for the purposes they serve and unlikely to be prone to severe erosion by new media, although each format must be looked at individually. Maps, for instance, face competition from digital mapping schemes, in cars and elsewhere. At least one publisher, Rand McNally, is aggressively pursuing electronic delivery alternatives through the development of such products as InfoMap, RandMap, and Randata in the business market, computer-generated mapping schemes based on census tract data. Similarly, as current shop-at-home channels and online direct-order services take hold, consumer merchandising catalogs may see a shift in their means of delivery. However as complementarity and not displacement of formats is often the rule, we are equally likely to see integrated media systems, hybrid print-electronic systems that take advantage of the relative merits of each format—e.g., a print catalog that supplements an online ordering service.

Magnetic Media

Magnetic media, including semiconductor chips, smart cards, and floppy and hard disks, hold software, the algorithmic codes which determine how a computer functions. They are all machine-readable formats. Their key differential advantages are read and write capabilities and their ability to work with software as an electronic tool to manipulate content. Because of their innate differences from other formats, magnetic media are exemplary of the redefinition of boundaries taking place in the publishing world. Moreover, as digitally encoded media, they represent the future, as the preparation, storage, and often the display of content for all media forms will soon be digitized. As with their higher-volume competitors, optical media, magnetic media can also store both informational content and software tools, content and tools which can either be packaged and delivered by a publisher or licensed for package and delivery by other parties, such as software publishers or OEM's (original equipment manufacturers).

Optical Media

Optical media, specifically optical discs, are a cousin to magnetic media. But while they carry digitally encoded material, they can carry much greater volumes of material than magnetic media and in a less volatile state. The significance of high-volume storage is optical discs' capability to combine both traditional content types—information, knowledge, art, and entertainment—with tools for their manipulation. Moreover, while most early optical disc formats were read-only, successive generations, sometimes in magneto-optical form, are writable as well.

There are a variety of emerging optical disc formats, with CD-ROM, first cousin to CD audio, the current king. The medium is compact yet capable of high-volume storage and superior search capabilities. Its capacity—650 megabytes per 5 1/4" disc, the equivalent of 300,000 pages of information, or hundreds of books—and the fact that it can be physically delivered and controlled as an on-site peripheral, make it an extremely attractive publishing alternative. CD-ROM's are also cheap to mass produce, due to the successful introduction and market acceptance of CD audios.

Proprietary CD-ROM formats are also emerging for hand-held computers with removable discs, such as Sony's Data Discman Electronic Book format introduced in the United States in the 3rd quarter of 1991 after a successful launch in Japan the previous year.

CD audio, or compact disc, is a digital optical medium. Key features include random access, non-deterioration of content, high production quality, and programmability. Such features can add value to both musical and non-musical content. While we can expect CD audio to garner an increasing share of the audio market, at the moment audio cassettes stand in relation to CD audio as videocassettes stand in relation to videodiscs: they are not read-only media, but have both recording and playback capabilities. The technologies continue to evolve, with digital audio cassettes and recordable compact discs blurring the distinction between the two formats. Regardless of the outcome of that battle, compact audio discs have almost completely eliminated the vinyl phonograph record market.

Online Services

Key attributes of these open channel services include timeliness, breadth and depth of content, connectivity, the ability to be downloaded to the user's site, and on-site interactivity and control.

The bulk of today's 500-plus online services and over 3,500 databases are for business and professional information users. Most of these are bibliographic databases, with a growing number carrying full-text of the articles or content sought. The Internet, originally a government-sponsored network, now exists as a meta-network connecting all services, and is tilting toward commercial applications to supplement the academic, scholarly, and professional uses.

The consumer online segment is delivered via phone or cable. It includes such services as CompuServe, one of the original consumer services, and Prodigy, the joint-venture between IBM and Sears that went national in 1990 and has attracted more than a million subscribers. Teletext, one-way information services delivered via the vertical blanking interval of the broadcast television signal, is, to date, far less established, at least in the United States. One notable costly and well-publicized teletext venture failure was Time Inc.'s Timetext in the early 1980s. In Europe, however, the BBC's government-supported Ceefax, to name one example, has been in operation for more than a decade. Consumers obtain a special decoding device from television dealers to obtain the textual information residing in the vertical blanking interval of the broadcast television signal.

Online services can be viewed as both narrowcasting and broadcasting. To obtain the information a subscriber must pay, use specialized software, and have a user ID. Thus it is similar to subscription publishing in that the user must make a purchase decision prior to obtaining the information supplied. Moreover, by their nature online services are two-way, unlike one-way broadcast media. The promise of online services, then, lies in their connectivity, whether wired or wireless. The distinctive attribute becomes its connection, which provides a two-way exchange, instant updatability, searchable access to voluminous data stores, and point-to-point messaging capability, a proven popular feature.

Another hope for online services lies in high-speed, high-volume fiber optic networks that are capable of bringing voice, video, and data together, delivered to computers or interactive set-top television devices. In the business and professional markets such networks, when linked with one another, will provide transparent, interoperable access to massive digital data stores, searchable by users from their own sites, with value added via hyperlinked, cross-database features to propel research beyond confining linear approaches. But in order for such networks to fully develop, a number of technical, financial, and legal obstacles must be surmounted.[9]

Videocassettes

With the introduction of videocassettes in the early–mid-1980s, based on the widespread penetration of the VCR, individual viewers were for the first time able to make their own programming choices. Although successfully adopted by the motion picture studios as a mass market product, videocassettes' attributes can also move them away from the mass market of feature films and broadcast television toward segmented and special interest audiences. Key cassette attributes, in addition to motion and sound, include high production quality, ease of use, user control over content, and their savable, durable quality. If cable television, a broadcast-publishing hybrid, has emerged as a televised magazine rack in the home, with advertising-supported special interest channels paid via bulk subscription and non-ad supported pay channels paid for totally out of subscriptions, videocassettes have emerged as the equivalent of books: discrete packaged items that can be selected and paid for by the purchaser.[10]

Among other things they offer, videocassettes can visually demonstrate a skill with moving, not static, pictures plus narrative voice-over. In this sense videocassettes are a complement to material presented in a book. But they are also typical of new media because they are a hybrid of existing forms that is at the same time something new in and of itself. The strategic implication is that players from both sides, with expertise in publishing and distribution of physical product (medium and means) and expertise in broadcasting and film (material and mode), will converge with competing interests in the same cell of the matrix.

Videodiscs

Videodiscs, a laser-read optical storage medium for analog video, while a growing format have to date failed to penetrate as successfully as cassette tapes. While both are electronic storage media, videocassettes are a recordable, magnetic, linear medium, while videodiscs are a read-only medium that can be viewed either in linear or random access fashion. In many ways they embody more book qualities than videocassettes do, especially for non-narrative, random access purposes, such as reference material.

In her catalog for "Books and Other Machines," an exhibition she designed and mounted for the Library of Congress in 1985, Alice Schreyer stated that Vidmax's 1983 videodisc *National Gallery of Art* was the first "video book." It contains 1,645 still images of paintings and other objects as well as a tour of the gallery with Director J. Carter Brown. The disc was also described as a "book without pages" that would have been prohibitively expensive in hard copy.[11] There are strong signs that the high production quality, random access capability, and zero content degradation of videodiscs will soon bring them to the forefront. The medium's chief drawback in relation to videocassettes is its inability to record programming, though erasable discs and players may well emerge soon. If this were to happen, videocassettes would be in direct competition with the read-write discs and might be relegated to the status of an interim technology.

Higher level videodiscs are known as interactive video, which marries a videodisc with a computer. Interactive video is currently found primarily in the business, professional, and government markets, with training the largest application. In the consumer market, informational touch-screen interactive video kiosks have been placed in shopping malls, museums, and freeway service areas as point-of-purchase displays and providers of information. Educational market applications are generally too costly for widespread use, but some programs have been brought to market.

The modal potential of interactive video is enormous, but the constraints are also great: cost and skill and labor intensity of production, involving a precise blend of computer and video technologies and skills. But perhaps the biggest threat is from the all-digital, computer-based interactive multimedia, such as DVI, CD-I, and Windows on the MPC, which is the real trend in interactive information delivery in multiple modes.

Film

Feature-length motion pictures can be seen as the first format in the studios' multi-window release. After theatrical release, films are then published on videocassette for consumer rental and purchase, then cablecast via pay services, then broadcast or cablecast via network, independent stations, or advertiser-supported cable. Pay-per-view via cable is emerging though not yet established as the second window between theatrical release and cassette distribution. International distribution, through as many of the same windows as possible, duplicates this sequence of steps in globally segmented markets. The combined international revenues often surpass domestic proceeds.

As film is susceptible to publication on cassette or disc for the small screen, the types of films produced and the nature of the theatrical film experience on the big screen will change. Many observers feel that home video technology, with its cost savings, convenience, and bigger screens and higher definition, will continue to make it harder for viewers to find reasons to go to movie theaters. Middle ground films and those that do not make appreciable use of the theatrical large screen format will be viewed at home on cassette, disc, or other media. By 1990, expenditures for the sale and rental of videocassettes had outstripped theatrical box office receipts by 2-to-1.[12]

Some analysts feel that to continue to draw moviegoers into the theaters, films will have to have an epic, spectacular, big screen quality (e.g., *Jurassic Park*) or otherwise take advantage of the group viewing experience. Hollywood studios may not find the big screen investment worthy of the risk if they know cassette sales will eventually recoup costs in any event (although good box office performance is still the best advance indicator of healthy cassette sales). On the other hand, a *Doctor Zhivago* or *Out of Africa*, which offer an undeniable and qualitatively different big screen experience, can also look attractive in terms of gross box office receipts and long-term after market sales. Meanwhile a variety of mega-screen formats has emerged, such as the giant 70 millimeter IMAX, projected on 66 × 40 foot screens (installations at the Smithsonian in Washington and the American Museum of Natural History in New York) and OMNIMAX with its giant wrap-around screen (Boston's Museum of Science). Other large-screen and non-standard theatrical formats include Circle-Vision 360 and Mosaic Screen, currently installed at EPCOT

Center and DisneyWorld.[13] Such theaters represent the ultimate big screen experience, an experience which will be difficult if not impossible to duplicate at home, even on large screens.

Broadcast and Cable Television

Broadcast television's key attributes include blanket coverage, no direct user cost, sound and motion, immediacy, and enormous advertiser appeal.

Until recently television has been confined to the realm of broadcasting, the continual, synchronous dissemination of signals to a mass audience. A number of independent stations grew up as alternatives to the networks. Then in the early 1980s the proliferation of cable systems brought another change in the landscape, and as of this writing cable is in nearly two out of three U.S. homes. The emergence of the videocassette market came next. All changed the way we look at television. The viewer has more program choice and control and is no longer strictly dependent on downstream broadcast fare, though for major, socially significant events—a Presidential inauguration, the World Series, the Persian Gulf War—the networks still provide the connection we all seek.

Broadcast television is both a marketing medium and a programming medium. The fact that American broadcast television relies exclusively on commercial sponsorship for its annual $20 billion plus in revenues dictates to a great degree how programming decisions are made—by and large, for the mass audience. The advent of cable television, which as a medium was initially developed in the mid-1950s for rural signal delivery but began to achieve its current mass scale with the introduction of satellite-delivered programming in the mid-1970s, brought the promise of narrowcast programming and subscription-based television free from advertiser constraints. Indeed, certain pay networks, such as HBO, Showtime, and The Disney Channel, have been able to prosper on straight subscription revenue. But the other basic level programming services have increasingly sought lucrative advertising revenue. In the mid-1980s cable ad revenues surpassed the $1 billion mark, making it the fastest growing of all advertising segments.

Thus cable, with its twin revenue streams of viewer subscriptions and advertising dollars, is also a new media hybrid, between broadcasting and publishing. Moreover, the move toward multichannel—500 or more—interactive fiber optic cable television systems will allow cable operators to offer a vast array of entertainment and information services, many of which will be paid for on a per-usage basis. The multichannel systems will also allow carriage of transactional services such as banking and shopping. How the cable operators will fare in their competition with the local telephone operating companies for such services remains to be seen, with regulators having allowed the phone companies to vend entertainment as well as information services. Southwestern Bell's purchase of two major capital area cable systems in early 1993 could start a new wave of mergers and acquisitions among the two industry segments, intensifying the competition for home-delivered services. Yet another recent development in broadcast television, an interactive return channel for viewer requests made possible by using a portion of the broadcast radio spectrum, may have an impact on the connectivity advantage.[14]

As of this writing, the medium of television is poised for tremendous turmoil and growth. A blizzard of strategic alliances among cable, broadcast, computer, satellite, programming, and telecommunication firms indicates the intense, high-stakes jockeying for positioning in the coming world of digital television. Microsoft, for example, in its alliance with General Instrument and Intel, seeks to provide the operating system standard for the world of digital television— 90-plus million homes—just as they did the de facto standard—MS-DOS— in the personal computer world. The range of resources required to effectively attack these new business opportunities is fostering the alliance building, which bespeaks a transitional phase to a new industry with new firms whose breadth of expertise will span the required range of tasks. The size and prominence of the corporate players involved, plus the size of the sums being wagered, suggest not only the magnitude of these tasks but the magnitude of the expected rewards, as well, when the paradigm shifts to the new medium of computer-based television.

Audio Cassettes

Aural media such as audio cassettes have two characteristics that differentiate them from media in the other two major modes: they are strictly unimodal—i.e., incapable of capturing or displaying other modes—and they are all electronic. Audio cassettes' other key attributes include sound, portability, low cost, and ease of use. Suitable applications of recorded material include the spoken word, such as poetry readings, plays, or novels, and book-cassette combinations.

Since the 1940s there have been sporadic forays by print-based publishers into territory occupied by firms with recording production expertise, such as Caedmon. Now there are numerous audio publishers within major trade houses. The increasing transfer of material from printed form to audio form has also opened market opportunities for the release of radio material, both old (*Amos 'n' Andy*) and new (Garrison Keillor's *Prairie Home Companion*), and other material which originated in aural form.

Audiotex

Audiotex, also known as voice information services, 900 services, and dial-up services, delivers pre-recorded messages on demand over telephone lines. It began as dial-in time, weather, and sports, and has more recently expanded to include advertising, promotional, and informational uses. Beyond consumer applications (notable among these is the plethora of pornographic services), business uses are proliferating, such as Dow Jones' *Dow Phone*. Newspapers and magazines have adopted 900 services not only as supplemental information sources but for customer and subscriber services as well. Barriers to entry are low and the field is fragmented, but with regulations shifting in favor of the local operating systems and away from third-party information suppliers, the arena could change dramatically.

Radio

Like television, its visual counterpart, the aural broadcast medium of radio is a marketing medium as well as a programming medium. Key attributes include currency, ubiquity, low cost to the user, advertising appeal, and ease of use: users need only listen, leaving hands and eyes free to do other tasks.

Radio's migration into audience segmentation is akin to the movement in special interest magazines in print and cable in television, the principle difference being that radio is, with notably few exceptions, solely advertiser supported. The degree of audience segmentation is pronounced, with leading stations in large metropolitan areas typically having no more than 3–5% of the total audience. Broad classes include FM (frequency modulation) and AM (amplitude modulation), with FM's superior signal quality making it ideal for music, while AM has taken over the realm of talk. However, the introduction of stereo AM and digital radio may shift these patterns.

MULTIMODAL MEDIA

Multimodal media are representative of the trend toward the convergence of modes. We can identify three important multimodal media types:

Cross-Media Interaction

The first of these multimodal types is the next core concept:

Core Concept #17: Cross-Media Interaction

Cross-media interaction refers to the interaction of information products and services in separate media formats with one another. We speak of cross-promotions, tie-ins, and spin-offs. Oftentimes this will mean interaction between the same content converted and packaged in different media, such as Ken Burns' *The Civil War*, which was developed for broadcast television, book form, videocassette and disc, and audio formats, among others. The success of the television series created awareness for and drove the sales of all the other products. More recently Daniel Yergin's *The Prize*, a history of the oil industry, started as a Pulitzer Prize-winning best-selling book and was subsequently released as an eight part PBS documentary. An exhibit developed around the same subject and source materials opened at a New York gallery concurrent with the PBS airing. When a motion picture is released, there is often a paperback tie-in of the original book (or a novelization if the film was developed from an original screenplay), a soundtrack, available in several different audio formats, and eventually the film itself on cassette and disc. The studio's publicity department will use radio, television, newspapers, and magazines to garner as much coverage for the film as possible. Advertising will appear in the same media and may extend to include outdoor forms such as subway, bus, and billboard displays. The intent is to catch the potential moviegoer/viewer in a crossfire, a multimedia web wherein the repeated messages ricochet in the mind of the viewer, consciously or subconsciously reinforcing each other with a concomitant increase in awareness and retention.

Integrated Media Systems

About ten years ago, Ernest Boyer, former U.S. Commissioner of Education, wrote: "Television extends human sight, computers extend memory and the ability for calculation. Books extend wisdom. It is now our task to fit together these tools, the new ones with the old, and make learning something truly exciting."[15] Integrated media systems (IMS) represent this convergence among media formats toward the goal of more effective learning, information, and entertainment systems:

Core Concept #18: Integrated Media Systems

Like cross-media interaction, IMS also combine different media, but the distinction is that IMS are developed to work in conjunction with one another, not just the same content adapted cross-modally or across media but two or more media products and/or services designed to work in conjunction with one another. The discrete product and service forms take advantage of their complementary strengths. Typically the publisher adds value to the material by extracting, formulating, and storing significant, savable, reviewable, portions of electronically presented material.

Many publishers are moving in this direction through the establishment and internal coordination of the various media groups. One of the earliest IMS pioneers was SyberVision, the California-based publisher that develops self-teaching units in sports and other areas—*Skiing with Jean Claude Killy, Weight Control, Successful Parenting*—that combine a videocassette with a series of audio cassettes and a print guide. Paramount Publishing is aggressively promoting such combinations. The arrangement through their Prentice-Hall general reference group with Weight Watchers International is emblematic of this effort, procuring rights to a major brand name and seeking to exploit it in multiple media, including books, video, audio, and software products. Calloway Editions' fall 1992 release of Madonna's *Sex* with an audio CD is another example of purposely combined media formats. The company's trademark for such integrated audio-book products is "Boundsound," suggesting the formats' integration. (*See also* Core Concept #32, Building and Extending Brands and Imprints, and Core Concept #43, The Full-Service Publisher.)[16]

Other institutional knowledge experts, authors, and content experts are appropriate for IMS development, and we will see them in video, hear them on audio, read them in books, and use their products on the interactive screen. Early examples include Julia Child on cooking, Jane Fonda on exercise, David Attenborough on nature, and Jacob Bronowski on the history of science. Integrated media systems also offer enormous promise in the educational market, where they are often referred to as integrated learning systems (ILS).

Interactive Multimedia

Whereas the foregoing two multimodal types combine different, distinct media formats, interactive multimedia combines the digital processing capabilities of computers with the audio-visual capabilities of television and the textual content of books all in a single medium. It has attracted a great deal of attention from industry leaders in publishing, computers, entertainment, and consumer electronics over the past several years, and by one industry group's estimate will grow from a $5 billion market in 1992 to a $24 billion market in 1998, a compound annual growth rate of 24%.[17] The applications span the range of markets, from business, to education, and the home:

Core Concept #19: Interactive Multimedia

This all-digital multimedia environment is made possible by a confluence of advances in four technologies: first, the development of increasingly powerful processing in computer chips; second, the digitizing of sound and more recently the digitizing and compression of full-motion video; third, the development of increasingly sophisticated visual displays in personal computers, including color, high resolution, and motion; and fourth, the development of high-volume, on-site, all-digital storage media, such as optical discs.

Some multimedia formats are television peripherals and run on set-top devices, and others are intended for desktop or hand-held computer use, although eventually the distinctions between the two may fade for certain types of applications, such as games. Among the former are Philips' CD-I, Commodore's CDTV, Tandy's VIS (visual information system), and Panasonic's 3DO player. Computer-based multimedia formats include those for Macintosh and for Windows, based on Microsoft's DOS and Windows system software and CD-ROM technology. Portable hand-held players are also emerging, such as Sony's multimedia CD player, which plays CD-ROM XA discs. As of this writing, most of these platforms are incompatible with each other, that is, discs created for one player cannot be played in another. Many analysts feel that, as with most successful media formats, either one player will have to emerge as dominant or standards must be created and agreed upon in order for the market to coalesce and achieve real growth.

The range of applications is almost limitless. One business market product released in early 1992, *Lotus Sound,* allows users to use voice or other sounds to annotate electronic mail and other PC-created documents. Consumer applications developed thus far include reference works, such as *Compton's Interactive Encyclopedia* and Microsoft's *Cinemania, Encarta* and *Musical Instruments;* children's books such as Discis Books' *Peter Rabbit* games and the Multimedia Publishing Studio's *Adventures of Curious George and the ABC's*; and a variety of other works. Educational market applications are under development at a number of major publishing and technology firms, though an impediment to the market's development at this writing is the lack of an installed player base (*see* Chapter 10).

THE HAPPY MEDIUM

Whether unimodal, bimodal, or multimodal, a host of factors play into a publisher's media format choice, subtle and often complex factors which take account not just of content but of the depth or breadth of coverage, convenience or ease of access to the user, cost, interaction with other media, and other attributes discussed above. Such attributes create the values to which customers respond and play a central role in determining which particular product or service a user is likely to choose. Publishers, therefore, must know the media formats well and be aware of their capabilities. All these factors combine to lead to the best media choice for any given product or service, as embodied in the next core concept:

Core Concept #20: The Happy Medium

Information Age publishers see different media forms as part of the value added to the information. Mead Data's LEXIS and West Publishing's WESTLAW, online legal information services, add value over their print counterparts by offering the user powerful search and retrieval capabilities, features not offered by the same content in print form. David O. Selznick's film version of *Gone with the Wind* may not necessarily be better than Margaret Mitchell's book, but its conversion from book to film, from the textual to visual mode, provided not only a rewarding viewing experience for millions of viewers but a lucrative venture for the producers. Sam Tyler and John Nathan's book-to-film and later film-to-video conversion of Tom Peters and Robert Waterman's best-selling management book *In Search of Excellence* added value to the underlying content, created a new product, and took advantage of the attributes of the film, television, and video media in a fashion that addressed users' wants and needs. It also created additional economic value for both the original creators and those who undertook the conversion.

A publisher's media choice is critical not just in the conversion of existing material but in the development of wholly new material, as well. The new publishing paradigm sees the idea first, then its embodiment. By understanding the capabilities of the full range of media technologies, Information Age publishers can be technology-inspired, while product creation and development can be fulfilled by knowledge and media experts working in collaboration with the publisher as the marketplace presence.

TRENDS AND DEVELOPMENTS: FUTURE MEDIA

What does the future hold? We can plug in our crystal balls and watch them glow. Although we cannot possibly foresee all the future media developments, one thing remains relatively certain: that the main force for technological change in the media will continue to come from computers. Digital information technology will continue to penetrate all 7M's of publishing (*see* Core Concept #2).

Hardware

The advances in computer hardware will continue to make computers easier to use, which will mean that their true power can be harnessed by more users. In their extremely short life—the first Apple II was introduced just seventeen years ago in 1977—personal computers have already evolved to an astounding degree. The original character-based interface has largely yielded to the graphical user interface, with multiple windows on screen, pull-down menus, and mouse-based point and click commands, all of which bury command characters and structures and make the computer easier to use. Desktop personal computer equipment, in itself a revolution, has been joined by laptop, notebook, and hand-held processors with as much power as their desktop counterparts.

The clear trend is toward faster processing at cheaper costs and higher volume storage at lower costs. Screen displays will be both larger and smaller, flatter, and higher definition in all sizes, meaning that there will be appropriate screens available for every personal and group display need. Devices will not only be smaller and lighter but portable, too. Scenario's DynaVision PC with a built-in CD-ROM drive is an early example of such portable power, storage, and display, with Sony's multimedia CD-ROM XA player and Data Discman also representing the trend. Hand-held wireless communicators known as personal digital assistants, such as Apple's Newton and Tandy-Casio's Zoomer, combine some or all of the features of a telephone, a radio, a hand-held reader-viewer, and a PC, taking multimodal user input as well as processing multimodal output. They are easy to use, often with pen-based and voice-driven natural language interfaces.

All computers will eventually come to be viewed not only as tools to manipulate data but as information sources as well, in effect becoming new media, or even appliances—everyday items like telephones. Stated another way, the enhanced computer-processing power of existing devices such as the telephone and television will transform them into new types of information and entertainment devices. AT&T announced three new devices in early 1993: the Videophone, which transmits moving images of the callers at either end; the Smart Phone, a chip-based phone with a screen and keyboard allowing transactions, messaging, and other new services; and the Personal Communicator (aka "EO"), a stand-alone, pen-based tablet that functions as a personal organizer as well as communicator. All three devices enable telecommunications services well beyond POTS ("plain old telephone service"), carrying different modes of information and enabling users to perform different tasks. Author George Gilder describes the personal device of the future as the telecomputer, which allows every receiver of information to be a sender, too, in all modes.

The larger trend exemplified by such new devices is toward more and more computing power in the hands of users (*see* Core Concept #26, User Power), providing flexibility, customization of service, and choice. More content will be available through more channels, whether delivered via twisted pair, coaxial cable, fiber optic systems, satellite, cellular, or other means. Such systems will enable individuals, whether in school, at home, or on the job, to perform tasks in new ways by combining personal, user-created information with published information supplied from outside sources. As in Gilder's scenario, the empowered user is also a new creator and information provider, as well, providing either self-created information or new syntheses of personal and commercially available information, in his or her choice of mode.

Another trend at the high end is toward massively parallel processing computers, which harness the power of several CPU's (central processing units) working simultaneously and, in conjunction with each other, will increasingly perform tasks too complex for single processor computers to handle. When Thinking Machines of Cambridge, Massachusetts unveiled the Connection Machine in 1986, with 65,536 CPU's, its makers offered this analogy: "Imagine that you are given the task of searching through 50,000 magazines for articles on a particular topic. If you read through each magazine, this might take you several years. Imagine instead that you could give the magazines to 50,000 people in a football stadium and announce over a loudspeaker that everyone should look through his or her magazine for articles on the desired topic. The search process would be reduced from years to minutes."[18]

As noted above, connectivity, the ability to communicate electronically to remote sites, is another high growth area, whether via hardwire networking or the airwaves. Scientists at the Ultrafast Science Center at the University of Rochester are developing superconductor devices that perform 100 times faster than fiber optics with higher volume capacity, capable of sending the complete contents of the Library of Congress over a phone line in *two minutes.* Fiber optics, they point out, is limited by the need to convert signals from electricity, to light, and back to electricity.[19]

Transmission technologies such as asynchronous transfer mode, or ATM, are closer to implementation and also hold great promise for high-speed, high-volume information delivery in all modes. These information transfer systems will eventually have an impact on the type of material available and how it is accessed. Today's audiotex, online, and pay-per-view cable services are the precursors of these on-demand multimodal databases. In the not-too-distant future, remote access on-demand to massive visual, aural, textual, and multimodal databases on both wired and wireless networks will be the norm.

Software

While advances in information technology will continue, software tools will continue to evolve as well. Authoring tools will become cheaper and easier to use. Hypertext is one automated approach to material that may gain broader use in the years to come. The concept of hypertext (variously known as hypermedia, intertext, augmentation, or non-sequential documents) was first proposed by Franklin Roosevelt's science advisor Vannevar Bush in his now-famous piece published in the July 1945 *Atlantic Monthly,* "As We May Think." In the 1960s Doug Engelbart, working in the lab at Xerox's Palo Alto Research Center (PARC), and iconoclastic programmer and computer visionary Ted Nelson, who published his theory of a system called Xanadu, both advanced hypertext. "In the year 2050," says Nelson, "there will be 13 billion people and very few trees, so virtually all publishing will be electronic."[20] Apple Computer's Hypercard program for the Macintosh, released in 1987, was the first off-the-shelf product incorporating hypertext principles. Since then, a variety of other programs based on non-sequential database techniques have come to market. As Brown University's Andries Van Dam has stated: "Hypermedia is a totally new medium—it's a superset of all the media we've had so far. The trick is to combine these media in a compelling but manageable way."[21]

Other advances in software development include artificial intelligence and its subset expert systems, programs that embody the information content of a given knowledge expert in a decision-making routine—e.g., an accountant's expertise embedded in an audit program or a heart surgeon's knowledge of symptoms and conditions entered into a diagnostics program.

The ultimate user-friendly expert system is the android Data in the television program *Star Trek—The Next Generation.* He provides a human, natural language, voice-interface with all the processing power and information resources of a supercomputer, realizing the who-cares-what's-under-the-hood scenario which made the automobile a mass technology: anybody can drive.

Still, expert systems raise difficult questions of liability and suggest a disturbing Orwellian effect, if taken to its extreme, in which decision-making power is ceded to distant, unknown, centrally programmed, and quickly obsolescent experts.

As noted above, as computing power is the set of functions which enable other processes and uses, many of which will be the extensions of capabilities of existing devices which are already firmly established, the computer itself as a distinct item will disappear, and access to and use of information through various automated enabling devices will become the norm. In such an environment, the key to successful applications will become paramount. Software—tools and knowledge, tools and information, tools and entertainment— that works in the best interest of the user will become central to success. If any content desired is available anytime anywhere on connected systems and devices, then knowing what that content is and obtaining easy access to it becomes the critical first task. Intimate, friendly, and functional user interfaces will also become critical. So-called "intelligent agents" will emerge to access and provide information based on the user's expressed interests.

However it is accomplished, navigation through the vast realms of digital data, Gibson's cyberspace, will be critical if meaningful information is to be extracted. This leads to the next core concept:

Core Concept #21: Information Navigation and Access

Using the navigational tools which provide efficient information access is part of the user's response to the mediated environment (*see* Core Concept #24). These user-friendly navigational tools will become increasingly critical as the trend in the conversion of print and televisual data into digital form, accessible online, continues apace in the Information Age.

Other applications such as three-dimensional imaging and holography will find their uses. Other modes, such as the olfactory, haptic, and the gustatory, are also potential areas of exploration, although as noted above, the textual, visual, and aural modes are the richest symbolic information vehicles. Virtual or artificial reality, such as that being explored at the Virtual Environment Workstation Project at NASA's Ames Research Center, creates multi-sensory interactive electronic simulated environments. Once refined, the power and learning potential of these simulated environments will be exploited for both training and entertainment purposes. "It's like we've just hit the coast of a whole new continent," says virtual reality pioneer Jaron Lanier. "There will be enormous uses that we can't predict now at all. Nobody can. It's a new medium. It will hold an entirely new world . . . [an] emerging universe of alternate electronic realities."[22]

By covering the broad spectrum of new media possibilities, research centers such as the MIT Media Lab push the boundaries of thinking beyond the immediate commercial applications and toward unknown, but discoverable, future directions. That this is true is not lost on the scores of corporate sponsors whose collective multi-million dollar annual investment makes the Media Lab go. As then Time, Inc. CEO Richard Munro stated in the mid-1980s: "Let's face it, we're in a volatile industry. Any way we can protect our flanks is a prudent investment."[23]

For publishers, development of new products for new media formats will typically be an incremental process. Horizon technologies may hold great promise, and some medium unknown today may eventually revolutionize the publishing industry as the automobile, unknown to people in the mid-19th century, revolutionized not only personal transport but the way we live. Publishers' decisions to move in new and different directions will be made from a base of experience in established media formats, and each new medium will have to prove itself in the marketplace.

SUMMARY AND CONCLUSION

In this chapter we have delineated five more core concepts of publishing in the Information Age for the third value-added M, Medium:

- Core Concept #17: Cross-Media Interaction
- Core Concept #18: Integrated Media Systems
- Core Concept #19: Interactive Multimedia
- Core Concept #20: The Happy Medium
- Core Concept #21: Information Navigation and Access

While the strengths and weaknesses of existing formats may be intuitively obvious to both producers and users, attribute assessment allows publishers to evaluate new media as well as reevaluate existing media in relation to new media formats. Many media formats are bimodal, while those media which support all three major modes are multimodal. Multimodal types include cross-media interaction, integrated media systems, and interactive multimedia. Information Age publishers seek the most appropriate medium for the material and the market, the "happy medium," though there is often more than one appropriate format for a given body of content. As future media emerge, some will evolve from existing formats and technologies and others will emerge without familiar reference points or metaphors. For the foreseeable future, digital computer technology will continue to be the principal force driving changes in the media. New content conduits will continue to proliferate, and users will have increasing computing power. A critical task in the new content-rich environment will be efficiently navigating the available information resources to meet users' needs.

NOTES

1. Christine Urban, "The Competitive Advantage of New Publishing Formats," in *Electronic Publishing Plus* (White Plains, N.Y.: Knowledge Industry Publications, 1985), 42.

2. As quoted in Michael Rice, *Toward Enhancing the Social Benefits of Electronic Publishing* (New York: Aspen Institute for Humanistic Studies, 1987), 5.

3. Lewis A. Coser, et al., *Books—The Culture and Commerce of Publishing* (New York: Basic Books, 1982), 362.

4. Marshall McLuhan, *Understanding Media* (New York: New American Library, Signet reprint edition, 1964), 250.

5. Ithiel de Sola Pool, *Technologies of Freedom* (Cambridge, Mass.: Harvard University Press, 1983), 41.

6. Ibid., 193–94. De Sola Pool adds: "Publishing's strategies may change, while it retains in an electronic era as vital a function as ever. It remains the vascular system of science, democracy, and culture."

7. *See,* among other references, Joseph Dionne, "Redefining the Textbook: The Impact of Electronic Custom Publishing," *Logos,* 2 (4), (1991): 190–94.

8. *See* Roger Fidler's prototype electronic newspaper in Mark Walter, "Genres: Applying Technology to Different Applications," in *The Seybold Report on Desktop Publishing,* 7 (1 December, 1992): 16–24.

9. For a discussion of both the possibilities and constraints, *see* Robert Weber, "The Clouded Future of Electronic Publishing," *Publishers Weekly,* 29 June, 1990, 76–80. Weber cites several major constraints, including user-premise technology, the investment in the fiber optic plant, computer standards, display technologies, and intellectual property rights issues.

10. Erik Barnouw foresaw the role of videocassettes in their infancy in 1982:

Ultimately addressing its audience through television screens already in place in hundreds of millions of locations, video tape . . . could be mass-duplicated and marketed like a book via stores, organizations, or mail order. . . . The book analogy is fitting in a number of ways. The ½-inch cassette is comparable in size to a paperback, fits neatly on shelves like a book, is comparable in price to a book. It can be marketed via sale and/or rental. Means for using it are widely available in home, office, school, museum, library, church. . . . The cassette player is becoming one of the most prevalent of utilities. Use requires no special skill or training. . . . A video work can be readily marketed in small or large editions, and can therefore give economical service to specialized groups. . . . In short, it has implications for countless pursuits involving education, persuasion, documentation or inspiration.

Erik Barnouw, "Video and the Printed Word" in *Books, Libraries and Electronics* (White Plains, N.Y.: Knowledge Industry Publications, 1982), 51–52.

11. Alice Schreyer, "Books and Other Machines," Washington, D.C.: Library of Congress, Center for the Book, 1985, 6.

12. Jib Fowles, "The Upheavals in the Media," *The New York Times,* 6 January, 1991. Fowles reports 1990 cassette revenues at $10 billion.

13. Vincent Canby, " 'Big Screen' Takes on New Meaning," *The New York Times,* 19 April, 1987, 18, Arts and Leisure section. Canby quotes George Lucas as saying that "the film industry is operating on the assumption that character is all," indicating Hollywood's lack of interest in the technological advances of film. If this is so, Lucas

and others feel, Hollywood may someday be producing for an exclusively home cassette or disc market.

14. *See* Edmund L. Andrews, "F.C.C. Plans to Set Up Two-way TV," *The New York Times,* 11 January, 1991, and Robert E. Calem, "Coming This Year: Talkback TV," *The New York Times,* 17 January, 1993.

15. Ernest L. Boyer, "The Book in Education" in *The State of the Book World— 1980* (Washington, D.C.: Library of Congress, 1981), 31.

16. *See* Maureen O'Brien, "Weight Watchers Leaves NAL for Prentice Hall Partnership," *Publishers Weekly,* 8 February, 1993, 9, and Eben Shapiro, "Edging into Madonna's Limelight," *The New York Times,* 19 October, 1992.

17. The figures, from independent computer market research firm Market Intelligence, are for all hardware and software revenues, worldwide. The study was cited in "World Multimedia Markets to Quintuple, Approach $25 Billion," in *Microsoft Multimedia Newsletter,* December 1992, 10.

18. From "A Vision of the Future" in "Off the Grapevine," *Computer Update,* July/August 1986.

19. James Gleick, "New Frontiers of Communication Lie in Test Superconductor Device," *The New York Times,* 2 October, 1987.

20. As quoted in Paul Freiberger, "The Dream Machine," *Popular Computing,* April 1985, 65.

21. As quoted in Jeffrey Young, "Hypermedia," *Macworld,* March 1986, 121.

22. Tom Ashbrook, "You are about to enter another reality . . . " *Boston Globe,* 28 July, 1988, 65–66.

23. As quoted in Edward Dolnick, "Inventing the Future," *The New York Times Magazine,* 23 August, 1987, 59.

CHAPTER 8

The Media: Life Cycles and the Dynamic Equilibrium

In this chapter we will look at the introduction and acceptance of new media technologies through the market life cycle. After laying out the characteristics of the typical market evolution, we will introduce the concept of the dynamic equilibrium.

THE LIFE CYCLE OF MEDIA TECHNOLOGIES

The history of the introduction and growth of electronic media technologies suggests a pattern, a six-phase market development life cycle, from the conception and development of the medium prior to birth (market introduction) through growth to maturity and revitalization, which can be depicted as a simple S-shaped curve showing sales over time through the six-phase cycle:[1]

Core Concept #22: Media Technology Life Cycle

Unlike ink-on-paper print products, electronic publishing products are machine-readable only and are thus dependent upon the installed base, features, usage habits, and other characteristics of their respective machine populations. Thus a prerequisite for Information Age publishers intent on developing products for one of the electronic media is an awareness of the medium's market life cycle phase.

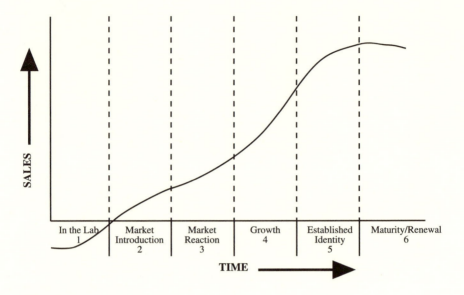

Figure 8-1
Life Cycle of Media Technologies

Phase 1—in the Lab

In discussing the diffusion of technological innovations, Everett Rogers, a seminal figure in the development of diffusion theory, observes: "The ultimate consequences of a new communication technology seldom are known or can be very accurately predicted when the new medium first becomes available. ... But after a period of some years, the new technology and its potential applications gradually become more thoroughly explored."[2] Indeed as Rogers and others have pointed out, some great inventions are greeted quite casually at the time of their introduction, including radio and television.

The impetus for the initial existence of the device more often than not comes from technology, the technological imperative that pushes science and technology forward. In some instances the initial concept is not purposely conceived but comes as a chance revelation or accidental outcome of another effort. Videotape is proof of Rogers' point that technologies can exist for some time before different applications are found for them. It was used in broadcasting for almost 20 years before being placed onto cassettes by Sony in the 1970s. Cable television is another example, first used in rural Pennsylvania in the 1950s but only achieving major industry status with the advent of satellite-delivered programming in the mid-1970s. The scenario for a medium's development, then, is not always as deterministic as one might think.

In this pre-birth gestation phase, the publisher's role is usually minimal,

PHASES

	1. IN THE LAB	2. MARKET INTRODUCTION	3. MARKET REACTION	4. GROWTH	5. ESTABLISHED IDENTITY	6. MATURITY/RENEWAL
MEDIA TECHNOLOGY (Hardware)	In Research and Development; Technology-driven; Heavy R&D Costs; Few Players; Limited Field Testing	Few Features; Low Penetration; Competing, Incompatible Formats; Heavy Manufacturing and Marketing Expenses; Low Quality: "Get It Out"	Accept or Reject; Comparison to Other Media; Learn From Market; Re-development Costs; Attribute Honing	"New and Improved" Add More Features; Many Suppliers In; Rapidly Increasing Penetration; Renewed Marketing Push	Full Status Product; Format Preferences Exhibited; Standards Emerge; Shake Out; High Penetration; Slower Growth Rate; Segmented Markets	Component Systems; Continued Refinement; Consolidation and Market Leaders; Low-Cost Suppliers; Need For Renewal
PUBLISHER ROLE	Options; Ignore; Wait and Watch; Seek Preemptive Participation	Explorers Only; High Risk-High Reward; Search For Applications	Incorporate Feedback; For New Applications; Search for Distinctive Attributes	Fast Followers In; Risks Reduced; More Competition	Slower Market Growth; Segmented Markets: Divide and Conquer; "Me-Too's" In; Brand Names-Positioning	High Barriers To Entry; Mergers and Acquisitions; Niche-Seeking; Boundary-Blurring; Price Competition
PRODUCTS	Joint Venture or Licensing with Hardware Developer; Convert From Existing Media; Time, Cash, Other Resources Required	Few Available; Convert Existing Content; Bundle With Hardware	Learning The Medium; Decentralized Product Development; Seek "Golden Nuggets"- Killer Applications	Product Flood; Broad Segmentation; Less Bundling With Hardware	Need Product Innovation; New, Medium-Specific Applications; Creative Imitation	New Applications; Cross-Media Interaction
CUSTOMERS	Defined But Hypothetical; Some Test Market Data	Media Junkies And Innovators; No Established Habit; Seek Frame Of Reference	Is There Primary Demand?; Can It Be Used? How?; Little Awareness; Early Adopters In	Broadening Base; Segments Developing; Marketing Stepped Up; Early Majority In	Broad Awareness-Familiarity; Established Habit; Late Majority In	Novelty Value Gone; Laggards In; Need Revitalization
INFRASTRUCTURE	No Experienced Suppliers, Manufacturers, or Distributors	Few and Immature Distribution Channels; Manufacturing Farmed Out; Piggyback on Existing Distribution	Need For Distribution; Waiting For Signals	Emphasis on Efficient Distribution; Manufacturing At Capacity; More Producer-Suppliers In	Routinized Manufacturing; Established Distribution; Experienced Suppliers Available; Manufacturing-Distribution Costs Drop	Price-Sensitive Manufacturing; Competition in Distribution Channels; Supplier Bargaining Personnel: Musical Chairs

— MEDIUM —   — MATERIAL —

Table 8-1
Life Cycle of Media Technologies

unless in a more calculated roll-out strategy he is sought out by the hardware developer for participation in the creation of early applications for the machine, the necessary fuel in the engine to make the machine go when it hits the marketplace. Just as the early hardware suppliers seek to create the standard, preempting the competition in order to own the market, Information Age publishers can also lead into the marketplace. The early phases provide opportunities for true innovation, both in hardware and software, while the market-driven phases come later. Almost all other aspects of the new technology, such as customers, distribution systems, and product sources, will be unknown or at best, unclear.

Phase 2—Market Introduction

If the media technology in question is a new-to-the-world technology, even to get to the point of market introduction it has had to go through innumerable layers of screening and testing, from original concept testing to projected profitability, market research, and market testing. By the time the new medium is introduced a launch strategy has been developed which will position it in the market. The choice of launch strategy dictates to a great degree how the market will react in the early phases, but hardware and electronics firms will often try to make the purchase of the new device more intuitive by likening it to existing media, e.g., Sony's positioning of their Data Discman as "the electronic book of the future." Ted Levitt, co-developer of the product life cycle theory, states that complex and new-to-the-world products take longer to get established: "The more unique or distinctive the newness of the product, the longer it generally takes to get it successfully off the ground. . . . The world has to be told, coddled, enticed, romanced, and even bribed . When the product's newness is distinctive and the job it is designed to do is unique, the public will generally be less quick to perceive it as something it clearly needs."[3]

In Phase 2 there will be little content product available as, for many established firms, product development at this early phase will be viewed as a risky diversion of resources for an unproven quantity. Most developers and publishers will prefer to wait and see how the market reacts, though some pioneers, those versed in the technology and its demands, will be first in, often based on development contracts or licensing agreements with the hardware manufacturers. For these pioneers, risk may also bring reward should the new medium prosper, as content niches can often be preempted. Early content product is typically converted from existing sources: online services converted print databases, pay cable services and videocassette publishers turned to Hollywood's movie vaults for their initial program supply, and videodisc publishers "repurpose" existing video footage. As Alice Schreyer points out, this was also true in the early development of printing technology: "Early printing was primarily reprinting—of religious, legal, and classical texts already available in manuscripts—but by the time of the Reformation, less than 100 years after Gutenberg, books were no longer 'mechanical manuscripts.' They had become a force for change and influence unanticipated by the first printers."[4]

The industry infrastructure is limited or non-existent at this point, distribution and manufacturing are jerry-rigged, and producer-suppliers are few. Only true media junkies and innovators are in the market to buy the new technology.

Phase 3—Market Reaction

After the medium is introduced a crucial reaction period takes place, a time when purchasers and users must evaluate the technology and its capabilities and determine how or whether it will be used and how or whether it will be incorporated into their lives and established media habits. Often this phase may last quite some time, especially with more complex and new-to-the-world technologies versus those that are extensions of existing technologies, for example, the VCR as a television peripheral. It takes time for potential buyers to evaluate the options, arrive at purchase decisions, gain experience with the medium, and explore the content product options. Competing incompatible formats will also slow acceptance as they cause confusion and uncertainty among potential buyers.

For producers of hardware and suppliers of software it is also a critical time. They must listen and learn at this stage of the market dialogue and incorporate feedback into new product plans. While hardware manufacturers are focusing on machine features and performance capabilities, pioneering content developers are learning about the new medium and its potential for information presentation. The first real wave of content product development, now decentralized, begins. If the medium is to succeed, innovative content developers will have to create what every other medium has had to put it on the map: its market creator, its golden nugget, its killer application, what MIT's Russell Neumann calls "trigger services," the software, the programming, the content product that establishes an initial purpose for the medium, thereby driving the purchase of the machine-players and creating wide perception of its acceptability. Milton Berle and Howdy Doody gave the American public a reason to buy television sets in the early 1950s, while in Britain it was the coronation of Queen Elizabeth II in 1953. HBO's delivery of first-run uncut movies in the home brought millions of subscribers to cable television. *Lotus 1-2-3* put PC's on financial managers' desks across the country, and *Jane Fonda's Workout* made the purchase of a prerecorded videotape—and thus a VCR—an intuitive act. These golden nuggets are crucial, for despite the capabilities of a given new medium, potential users must see a clear reason to buy. As de Sola Pool put it, "The market, not technology, sets most limits."[5] This is the critical phase at which these limits are tested.

At this early phase, publishers should also beware of fads and novelty value, sometimes difficult to discern in an apparently successful medium. Fads are characterized by big initial use and widely favorable publicity, followed by an abrupt and irreversible drop-off in sales.

While the second wave of content product development is on, the infrastructure still lags. Resource commitment is uncertain in an unproven climate, and most distributors and manufacturers have their hands full with business as usual.

Phase 4—Growth

If market reaction is favorable and other conditions (e.g., regulatory and economic) are favorable, the medium will enter its growth phase. The growth of television, for instance, was largely stalled by the diversion of producer and consumer attention and resources during World War II, though several stations were on the air as early as 1941. The immediate growth potential of the market has been established through Phases 2 and 3, and now a raft of new hardware suppliers comes in. New machines flood the market in addition to the "new and improved" versions of the original brand names. Gold rush is the prevailing attitude and everybody joins in. In the marketplace the early majority of buyers, roughly a third of the eventual buying population, purchase their first machine.

In content products the field also attracts those publishers and producers willing to stake a claim. Much of the territory is unclaimed and the true market builders will be developed in this period, broad-based applications or programs that take advantage of the machine's widening appeal and increasing penetration. Content suppliers will be increasingly decentralized from hardware providers, and hardware-software products are bundled together much less frequently. Manufacturing capacity strains to keep pace, and for the first time distributors begin to jockey for position as everybody seeks a stake.

Phase 5—Established Identity

But the heady growth phase can only last so long. Even the most torrid markets—compact audio disc players, VCR's—cannot sustain the initial rate of growth, and as the late majority of buyers begins to purchase, a more established pattern of sustained but slower growth emerges. Penetration rates achieve high levels—depending on the medium, 40–50% or higher.

Certain hardware formats emerge as superior or preferable (the two are not always the same; witness Sony's Betamax versus VHS) to others, a development necessary for the movement toward standardization that is appealing to content suppliers and users alike. Users have had time to react to the offerings and format preferences have been exhibited—e.g., audio cassettes versus 8-track cartridges, IBM PC's and MS DOS clones in the business environment. This forces a shakeout among machine manufacturers, and content developers and publishers must be aware of those formats which remain and prevail.

Additionally, content suppliers have now had time to become familiar with the medium's true strengths and weaknesses, and new content products are introduced that are uniquely created for the new medium, products that represent a later stage of evolution that could not have been envisioned by the medium's originators. Examples of such Phase 5 products and services include MTV in cable television, hypertext and desktop publishing applications in microcomputer software, call-in shows and all-news formats in radio, home shopping in television. These later generation manifestations represent thinking "within the medium" that expands its originally envisioned capabilities and opens new territory for exploration.

The spur to innovation is also a result of the increasingly jammed product space. Content products are faced with a market glut and duplication. In order to maintain growth, content suppliers must respond to a more mature market which seeks increasingly segmented applications and product innovations to address their specific needs. This forces a movement away from the mass, market-creator type of products—horizontal applications such as database, spreadsheet, and word processing in computer software—and toward more vertical, niche applications, such as those tailored to specific industries in the business and professional market. Such new products also mark the existence of a growing pool of experienced content suppliers who are now familiar with the medium and actively exploiting its undiscovered possibilities.

Eventually the new technology emerges as more appropriate for some applications than others and establishes its own identity in relation to other media. The new medium will have a distinctive bundle of attributes that make it best suited for certain types of information or entertainment, and both producers and users will gravitate toward it for these reasons.

Phase 6—Maturity and Renewal

If Phase 5 represents the content suppliers' search for the best use of each medium, then Phase 6 moves toward the best use of the medium interacting with other media, including hybrids of print and electronic forms. Media developers take a more wholistic or systems view of the media environment. Thus not only is content converted from one form to another as in the earliest phases of the medium's development, but it can be purposely developed for several media forms simultaneously.

For hardware manufacturers Phase 6 is a time of increasing competition. An overcrowded marketplace prompts consolidation. In cable television, systems are clustered as multiple system operators (MSO's) buy out the smaller independent operators. Not only is buying easier than building, it is usually the only way MSO's can achieve the geographic consolidation, and hence regional economies of scale, they seek. By this phase of market development, hardware refinements have reached a third generation and early Phase 3 equipment buyers seek replacements and upgrades. Some hardware is configured with other media devices in component systems. Industry pioneers, especially content providers, can cash in their chips as they too are sought after and purchased for their development expertise, product lines, established imprints, and distribution networks in a mature marketplace.

It is during this phase that one can also see a loop-back effect where the entire market "returns" to Phase 1, what Philip Kotler calls "market reconsolidation" and Poppel terms "renewal." Usually this is the result of the introduction of either a radical hardware innovation or an entirely new media technology that forces a market redefinition and the creation of a new, though still shifting, equilibrium. In aural list media, the introduction of the compact disc player is an example of this effect, as it forced the marketplace and thus producers to reevaluate existing formats, in this case, vinyl phonograph records and audio cassettes. The three audio formats now coexist in a redefined equilibrium, with cassettes and discs the clear winners, vinyl the loser.

OTHER FACTORS IN THE MEDIA TECHNOLOGY LIFE CYCLE

While the sequence of the phases presented here is generally followed, the speed with which a given technology passes through the phases varies widely. Market development can telescope drastically as in CD audio or VCR's, or be slower and far more gradual, then suddenly take off as a result of technological innovation or regulatory change, as with cable television in the mid-1970s. Some media, of course, never make it through the full development cycle if, after introduction, the market reaction is negative or indifferent (e.g., the RCA capacitance videodisc player). Others stall at a certain phase. Consumer videotex, for instance, has until recently been stuck at Phase 3 as lukewarm market reaction forced many suppliers, such as Knight Ridder's Viewtron, out of the market. However the recent market successes of Prodigy and America Online can be viewed as a second generation launch, in essence an entirely new market introduction after the earlier failures. The success of the government-supported Minitel system in France tells a similar story in that market.

Broadcast television provides another illustration. Today 98% of the nation's 92 million households have television, describing a healthy machine population that makes the production of broadcast programming, for either national or regional audiences, an economically viable enterprise. However in the 1940s when the machine population was almost non-existent and advertisers were not involved, content producers were true pioneers, and the bulk of programming was drawn from pre-existing sources, such as the theater, and was presented live. As time went on and the various constituencies—producers, broadcasters, advertisers, viewers—became more familiar with the capabilities and uses of the medium—and with each other—the penetration of televisions in the population grew. This in turn fueled the programming supply. Eventually the Hollywood studios, which initially viewed television suspiciously and as a dangerous competitor to the theatrical box office, broke down, and in the early 1960s they began licensing their libraries of films to the networks and subsequently to the independents through syndication. Broadcast television has since become ubiquitous—more environment than medium, as Fred Williams has put it—and it is now the archetypal mass medium. The majority of programming is now produced specifically for the medium, with some synthetic live events—Daniel Boorstin's "pseudo-events," such as award shows and sports events—staged just for television, totally reversing the initial notion of televised coverage of authentic events.

While this defines the mature broadcast television market we have today, the most recent phase in the evolution of the market is the introduction of several competitive technologies, namely cable television, the VCR and the videodisc player, and direct broadcast from satellite (DBS), each of which has brought significant changes in viewing habits. These new media have embarked upon their own market evolutions and have thereby caused a general redefinition and revitalization of the television market. As of this writing, the next wave of innovations, including digital high definition television (HDTV) and interactive television, are in the wings.

In the mid-1980s, William Paisley and Matilda Butler of Knowledge Access International foresaw a similarly promising course of development for CD-ROM, characterizing its three development phases as feasibility, replacement technology, and new applications: "Like the earlier technologies, CD-ROM leaves the laboratory as a solution in search of problems to solve. . . . Later it will perform new functions that in some cases will be unforeseen consequences of its unique characteristics. It is these new functions, more than the replacement functions, that will make CD-ROM as indispensable in our lives as the telephone, the airplane, and television."[6]

Today all product life cycles are shorter and accelerated. Technologies come and go more quickly, in part because our mature, structured, capitalistic system allows for unprecedented mobilization of resources in pursuit of opportunities. Moreover, the media technologies themselves foster information exchange and a broad awareness in the populace of changes in these technologies, which in turn drives market demand, which in turn speeds up the life cycle process, in effect creating an organism capable of quickening its own metabolic rate. For content firms, faster media life cycles put additional pressure on development and marketing cycles, already compressed by the crowded, competitive product environment.

THE DYNAMIC EQUILIBRIUM

What effect does the introduction of new media have on existing media? A common initial reaction is that print forms will be displaced by electronic media. But the history of the media thus far tells a different story.

While we can anticipate the continuing development of new electronic forms, it seems unlikely that books and magazines and other proven, durable formats will go away. On the contrary, as new media develop, the specific strengths of existing formats are re-examined, re-emphasized, and highlighted anew under the intensified competitive glare of the new formats. Radio found its strength in targeting specific audiences as television became the new mass medium. Books are a superior medium and flexible in countless ways, and the wonders of their high-quality "hard copy" output will come to be appreciated in a new way, even seen as a luxury item, in a screen-oriented society. Moreover, the general effect of more media and more information seems to perpetuate itself, so that information consumers seek to know more in depth about a subject or to extend and deepen a viewing experience by reading more about it.

But while books will survive, they will also watch other media forms take their place alongside them. They will be complemented by a new, broader range of media formats that offer advantages over the traditional formats, and there will be a widening plurality of media forms. As Carol Nemeyer, former Associate Librarian of the Library of Congress, has put it: "There is no reason to ask: 'Is the book dead?' The supposed contest among the media is a myth. Each has its uses and its users. . . . Books will survive, and so will many other forms of communication, some familiar, others yet unimagined."[7]

This is one of traditional print-based publishers' toughest challenges in the Information Age: to learn about other media technologies aside from the established print-based ones; to learn to evaluate them and their capabilities; to learn about their usage by customers and their differential advantages over and complementary attributes with other publishing formats; and to learn to manage them effectively in the creation of new products. This leads to the next core concept:

Core Concept #23: The Dynamic Equilibrium

We made the analogy before between the transportation of goods and people and the transportation of information. John Sculley has spoken and written of a new infrastructure of cable, fiber optic, and satellite data highways, the communications equivalent of automobile roads and railroads, that will connect the "knowledge navigators" of the future. Just as different modes of transportation have arisen and forced new equilibria over the years, so the newly introduced media of communication will create successively new equilibria. As publisher and sociologist Irving Horowitz has stated: "The history of science and technology indicates that the latest and newest modes of communication and transportation do not liquidate the need for earlier forms, but rather become value-added phenomena."[8]

The development of the transportation of ideas and information, then, roughly parallels the development of the transportation of goods and people.

Each sphere has now developed to the point of a coexisting plurality of forms, an array of choices that continues to exist by serving different purposes and needs. In transportation the automobile may rightly be seen as a displacive technology—it put the horse and buggy out of business—but it was only able to do so for two major reasons: the superior set of attributes which met users' (perhaps non-explicit or latent) needs; and the complex infrastructure—the petroleum, rubber, steel, glass and concrete industries, among others—that was built over time in order to make the new machine mode of transportation possible on a mass scale. There was no room for the horse in the new scheme, for not only was it inferior on most all counts (e.g., speed, hauling capacity), it no longer fit the system when the new automobile-centered infrastructure evolved beyond it.

A different equilibrium was created by the introduction of the airplane and later the jet plane, which siphoned off the bulk of long distance passenger train travel but did not preempt local passenger travel nor even a great deal of freight shipment, much of which shifted to trucking. Today the three major modes of transport—land, sea, and air—coexist, with the respective carriers each serving consumer and commercial customers' needs according to their relative capabilities.

So in the transportation of ideas and information, complementarity, rather than displacement, is most often the rule (see following "The Dynamic Equilibrium: A Roundtable of Expert Opinions"). Perhaps the most notable exceptions are within the same cell of the Media Matrix (*see* Figure 6-1). In the same cell new media formats are more likely to displace existing ones—for example, CD-ROM for certain types of reference books, CD audio for vinyl phonograph records—but even in these instances, total displacement is unlikely. Cross-modal media prove, as a rule, more complementary, as do cross-means. In the aural mode, for instance, radio (open channel) and list (CD audio and audio cassettes) coexist and complement each other because one is a tangible, physical, reusable product while the other is an intangible, ephemeral service that provides blanket coverage.

THE DYNAMIC EQUILIBRIUM: A ROUNDTABLE OF EXPERT OPINIONS[9]

Marshall McLuhan, philosopher and media analyst: "A new medium is never an addition to an old one, nor does it leave the old one in peace. It never ceases to oppress the older media until it finds new shapes and positions for them."

Anthony Oettinger, chairman of Harvard's Program on Information Resources Policy: "In the 1950s when television took off everybody predicted that the radio industry would die. . . . The industry has survived. . . . But where radio once was the mass medium of choice, radio is today a specialized medium—fragmented, addressing particular audiences—but profitable doing that. The print media and distribution of information in other forms, such as theatrical film, will experience discomfort . . . if some significant portion of their revenue base is eroded. They will be transformed in some way, but they will survive."

Christopher Burns, information consultant: "The availability of so much free information [e.g., broadcast radio and television] would seem to place pricing pressure on competing media like movies, books, and records. Yet we find no indication that this competition is now a concern; the other media have adapted and survived. People who hear a song on the radio will nonetheless buy the record; people who see a movie on television develop an appetite for more of the same and often rent or buy videotapes of the same programs."

Ron Rice, professor, Rutgers University School of Communication, Information, and Library Studies: "To deal with a new competitor, a medium which is already in place will reestablish its niche by focusing on those things which it does particularly well, on its positive attributes. Before the threat came in, perhaps the audience and the vendors did not really have to think about what those positive attributes were."

Alice Schreyer, museum exhibit curator: "There is strong evidence from libraries and bookstores that successive adaptations stimulate audiences to read the original works, [which] confirms the complementary nature of books and other machines. . . .Vast new audiences are introduced to books through films and television and the screen expands the dimension of reading. Adaptations breathe new life into the works on which they are based, treating us to the printed word to savor, relive, and deepen our experience."

James Billington, Librarian of Congress: "New technologies will take over a lot of things that are going into books that ought to be in the new technologies, and the book will be a form on which there is a greater burden to do the integrative and imaginative things that books can uniquely do rather than be simply inefficient transmitters of a kind of raw information."

Edward Tenner, publisher and technology analyst: "For nearly all [microcomputer] software, documentation and packaging account for the bulk of production costs. . . . Even the Information Industry Association . . . distributes news to its members by a weekly (paper) letter, not an online service. . . . There is every reason to think that electronics will drive, not drive out, print and paper as forcefully in the next decade as it has in the last."

Ithiel de Sola Pool, MIT professor and communications researcher: "Clearly the relationship among media is more complicated than always giving mutual support or always displacing one another. . . . There is no steady state to which the process of unification and differentiation will lead. The trend as far ahead as anyone can see is toward a convergence among media, with great communications institutions working in many modes at once in interconnected ways. Convergence does not mean ultimate stability, or unity. It operates as a constant force for unification but always in dynamic tension with change."

Daniel Boorstin, historian and former Librarian of Congress: "Momentous technological changes . . . are neither displacive nor reversible. Technological innovations, instead of displacing earlier devices, actually tend to create new roles for the devices which at first they might seem to displace."

J. Kendrick Noble, Jr., consultant and media industry analyst: "One of my rules is that no medium ever totally replaces another because each does certain things best."

The dynamic equilibrium refers not only to the effect of new media on existing media, but to the cross-pollinating effect the media forms have on each other. New hybrids find new ways to fit media together (*see* Core Concept #17, Cross-Media Interaction). Call-in radio shows combine a mass medium—broadcasting—with the point-to-point interpersonal medium of the telephone. Printed pages in a book, magazine, or newspaper freeze the image and text that appear on the evanescent computer or television screen. *USA Today* is a newspaper wholly conceived as an adaptation to the television viewer's world, so that we can now "watch" a newspaper. We can now also "read" television (teletext), "listen to" books (audio cassettes), and watch music (MTV). Such effects are the result of a pluralistic media environment.

At the same time, each media format will continue to provide qualitatively different experiences for the user. Each medium provides a different symbolic and sensory experience, with different implications for memory, learning, and pleasure. And each individual item produced in each format creates its own micro-environment, an experience different from any other—listening to Garrison Keillor's *Prairie Home Companion,* for instance, is not the same as reading *Lake Wobegon Days.*

SUMMARY AND CONCLUSION

In this chapter we have introduced the final two core concepts for the third value-added M, Medium:

- *Core Concept #22: The Media Technology Life Cycle*
- *Core Concept #23: The Dynamic Equilibrium*

Publishers can expect that the developmental course of a successful new media technology will follow a series of evolutionary phases from market introduction through growth to maturity and revitalization. Each phase of this evolution has implications for the content products developed, and ultimately each successful new medium takes its place alongside the others in a redefined equilibrium. While the media will continue to converge into a digital electronic whole, the range of forms—print and non-print alike—will continue to exist. As de Sola Pool stated,

> To say that all media are becoming electronic does not deny that paper and ink or film may also continue to be used and may even be sometimes physically carried. What it does mean is that in every medium—be it electric, like the telephone and broadcasting, or historically nonelectrical, like printing—both the manipulation of symbols in computers and the transmission of those symbols electrically are being used at crucial stages in the process of production and distribution.[10]

If the history of the media thus far is any indication, the different media experiences will continue to be valued and will continue to complement rather than displace each other, offering a richer mix of media experiences than was previously available.

NOTES

1. The market development phases discussed here derive from the product life cycle concepts developed by William Cox, Robert Buzzell, Theodore Levitt, and others, as portrayed along with the market evolution concept by Philip Kotler in *Marketing Management* (Englewood Cliffs, N.J.: Prentice-Hall, 1980), Chapter 12, "Product Life-Cycle Strategy." The discussion also derives from Everett Rogers' notions of the diffusion of innovations, specifically as discussed in his book *Communication Technology: The New Media in Society* (New York: The Free Press, 1986), Chapter 4, "Adoption and Implementation of New Communication Technologies."

In their book *Information Technology: The Trillion-Dollar Opportunity*, Harvey Poppel and Bernard Goldstein propose an alternative to the S-shaped life cycle, born out of dissatisfaction with the lack of market dimension in the existing curve. In their U-shaped scheme, the two axes are Supplier Experience (horizontal) and Customer Sophistication (vertical). The cycle flows counterclockwise from the upper left quadrant, through four stages: Emergence, Proliferation, Shake-out, and Renewal. *See Information Technology* (New York: McGraw-Hill, 1987), 190–93.

2. Rogers, *Communication Technology: The New Media in Society*, 23–24.

3. Theodore Levitt, "Exploiting the PLC" in *The Marketing Imagination* (New York: The Free Press, 1986), 180.

4. Alice D. Schreyer, "Books and Other Machines" (Washington, D.C.: Library of Congress, 1985), 2.

5. Ithiel de Sola Pool, *Technologies of Freedom* (Cambridge, Mass.: Harvard University Press, 1983), 6.

6. William Paisley and Matilda Butler, "The First Wave: CD-ROM Adoption in Offices and Libraries," *Microcomputers for Information Management*, 4(2): 109–27, 114.

7. Carol Nemeyer in "Foreword" to *Books, Libraries, and Electronics* (White Plains, N.Y.: Knowledge Industry Publications, 1982), 5. Nemeyer adds: "I am exhilarated by the prospects and the prospecting."

8. Irving Louis Horowitz, *Communicating Ideas* (New York: Oxford University Press, 1986), 20.

9. Marshall McLuhan, *Understanding Media: The Extensions of Man* (New York: New American Library, Signet reprint edition, 1964), 158; Anthony Oettinger in "Foreword" to Compaine, *Understanding New Media* (Cambridge, Mass.: Balinger Publishing Co., 1984), xviii; Burns and Martin, "The Economics of Information" (Washington, D.C.: Office of Technology Assessment, 1985), IV-4; Ronald Rice, unpublished interview, 8 December, 1986; Alice Schreyer, "Books and Other Machines," 84; James Billington, "New Librarian of Congress Looks at Books vs. Technologies," *Publishers Weekly*, 16 October, 1987, 16; Edward Tenner, "The Paradoxical Proliferation of Paper," *Princeton Alumni Weekly*, 9 March, 1988, 17ff; Ithiel de Sola Pool, *Technologies of Freedom*, 39 and 53; Daniel Boorstin, *The Republic of Technology* (New York: Harper and Row, Colophon reprint edition, 1978), 29; J. Kendrick Noble, unpublished interview, 14 October, 1986.

10. Ithiel de Sola Pool, *Technologies of Freedom*, 24–25.

PART IV

Markets

We now turn to the last of the five value-added M's, *Market*. We will begin by looking at markets from the customer perspective, examining the broader market environment, its characteristics and trends, into which publishers' products and services are sold. We will then introduce the Media Universe, the three-dimensional Media Matrix, and profile each of the three major markets—consumer, business and professional, and educational. Part IV will close with a consideration of marketing issues from the publisher's standpoint by enumerating a number of marketing tasks critical for success in the changing market environment.

CHAPTER 9

Market Environments: Common Characteristics and Trends

This chapter looks at some of the key characteristics common to all the markets, including the increasing pervasiveness of the media in all areas of our lives—in the home, in the workplace, and at school; the changes in our information usage habits as a result of the changing media; and the simultaneous trends toward globalization and segmentation of markets.

THE MEDIATED ENVIRONMENT

As discussed in the Introduction, we live in an increasingly mediated world, an environment in which someone or something steps between us and the world to mediate reality in some fashion. The two types of mediated environments are the physical environment, the man-made environment of buildings and streets that blends with the natural world, and the psychological environment comprised of the media and their messages. The same way the architect-builder-developer team creates a building, a park, a shopping mall, or a highway for the physical environment, so does the author-publisher or producer-broadcaster team create a book, a film, or a television program for the media environment. One creates real properties, the other, intellectual properties.

A quick survey indicates the extent of the media environment. In the United States 40–50,000 new book titles are published each year, with over 500,000 titles in print. (The Library of Congress receives over 30,000 books and other materials for cataloging every day, 7,000 of which they keep.) More than 11,000 magazines are available, more than 1,700 daily metropolitan newspapers, 7,700 weeklies, and at least three national dailies—*The Wall Street Journal, USA Today,* and *The Christian Science Monitor.* Over 5,000 new videotapes are released annually, with over 70,000 total titles available. Approximately 350 new theatrical films are released annually—in essence, one a day, all year long. Including Fox Television, there are four national broadcast television networks, hundreds of independent stations, and more than 40 channels of basic and pay cable television (soon to be over 100 in some systems, with 500 channels available in prototype fiber optic systems), many of which are on 24 hours a day, not to mention direct satellite transmission, microwave services, and low power television. The AM and FM radio dial is jammed with more than 9,000 stations. Online computer information services already number over 500 and collectively carry more than 3,500 databases. In computer software, the home market, although never really considered to have taken off, consumes more than half a billion dollars of software every year, though this pales in comparison to the multi-billion dollar business and professional software market. In addition to the established tape and disc formats, new audio information services have emerged, including the rapidly growing 900 services available via phone. Supporting much of this activity, the constant flood of print, broadcast, and outdoor advertising messages that deluge us all is estimated to feed an average daily intake, per person, of an astounding 600 messages.[1] Hence, our next core concept:

Core Concept #24: The Mediated Environment

The mediated environment is symptomatic of our changed world. We exist today in a culture of overwhelming choice, of vast and multifarious inputs, a mature consumer society marked by a huge output of products requiring painfully detailed purchasing decisions. Often there is so much choice, so much information, that the individual chooses to turn off the stimuli and close off the environment, ironically prompting dysfunction in a society rich with information and choice. There appear to be few signs of abatement. The same baby boomers who rose up in revolution against the "material world" in the 1960s have rechanneled their energy into a consumer society extraordinaire, demanding products and services that meet diverse and specific needs and that match lifestyles now grown powerful with an enormous aggregate earning and spending capacity. The mediated environment is an inextricable feature of this consumer society landscape.

USES OF THE MEDIA

It is not surprising that media usage habits have evolved as the media environment has evolved. As McLuhan stated, "Man the food-gatherer reappears incongruously as information-gatherer. In this role, electronic man is no less a nomad than his Paleolithic ancestors."[2] But as consultant Christine Urban has observed from her studies, media users actually define a relatively conservative environment into which new media products are introduced. Urban says that "Consumers tend to behave in their own self-interest. They are accustomed to making routine, almost subconscious judgments about which media format would best meet their needs. Their choice of a particular format is guided by the relative cost of the format and by a long history of learned expectation about how well that format meets their information needs."[3]

As documented in Urban's survey of the available literature on the topic, consumer media users are generally seeking to gratify one of four major needs: (1) surveillance, (2) decision-making, (3) social connection, or (4) enjoyment.[4] According to Urban, these four basic groups encompass all possible needs, including the need for diversion, escape, even prestige, such as the display of a lavishly illustrated coffee table book or an up-scale magazine might provide. But Leo Bogart sees consumer media usage as even less directed, less purposive: "People seek inspiration, amusement, instruction and a sense of participation in the great events of the time. But above all else, the media experience is pastime, an activity that people engage in at certain hours of the day when they have nothing of overriding importance to do, and when they simply want to relax from chores or evade boredom."[5] MIT's Russell Neumann echoes Bogart's characterization and takes it a step further: "Media behavior is generally not purposeful. . . . People more often select a medium such as television or a magazine rather than the content within the medium."[6] These views suggest that, among consumers, active information-seeking is ancillary to the relatively passive consumption of the generalized media wash which surrounds us.[7]

These views are currently the subject of wide debate, a debate largely prompted by the introduction of newer, computer-based interactive media. But whatever the prevailing norm, the full range of media needs is still present in the total user population, and it is these needs that determine the ways in which we choose to obtain and use information. Even our physical position gives us a clue to the reasons for media use. While reading a novel, for instance, or watching baseball on television, an individual can lie back in a comfortable chair or sofa or in bed. But if the same person is doing his taxes, manipulating a spreadsheet on the computer, or figuring out a textbook mathematics problem, he is more likely to sit in an alert, upright attentive position at a desk.

To market products in this changing environment, publishers must be aware of the different media uses and customer needs. New media make possible different products and services, but in the end the market and user preferences are the final arbiter. As Urban cautions predictors, "Technology is a necessary, but not sufficient, component of the future media environment. . . . Technologically based projections tell us only what is *possible,* not what is *probable* [emphasis added] in a future competitive marketplace."[8]

In whatever market, new media technologies have brought and will continue to bring changes in user habits. As observed above, these habits are engrained on the user side just as industry norms and practices are institutionalized on the producer side. Successful new media will take the path of least resistance in order to win new users. Thus one major reason for the success of the VCR is its enhancement—through taping, time-shifting and increased variety of program selection—of television and movie viewing, two deeply engrained and popular habits. CD audio marked an improvement upon existing audio reproduction technology—records and tapes—by offering superior sound fidelity, zero deterioration of that fidelity over time, random access capability, and programmability.

On the other hand, videotex, until recently, has appeared to offer no clear benefits to the user. Television, radio, and newspapers currently provide adequate up-to-date news and information for most consumers. Previous videotex hardware-software packages did not address the information-entertainment needs nor the media habits of the intended audience, and failed. Or, they may simply have been too expensive. As the Prodigy service is attempting to prove, videotex may be most appropriate when piped in at a steady, predictable monthly price that is not based on connect time. Others are banking on the success of phone-based information services, which will display information on text-screen phones, such as AT&T's Smart Phone discussed above, rather than requiring a separate computer hook-up or a television peripheral device.

THE READER-VIEWER-LISTENER-USER

Usage habits also transfer across our individual roles—e.g., homemaker, office worker, student—in the different arenas in which we move. We are all omni-media consumers now. One would be hard pressed to find a reader only, a television watcher only, a radio listener only. Most consumers of information and entertainment read, view, listen, and use information products in all forms that satisfy their needs and wants. Hence the next core concept:

Core Concept #25: The Reader-Viewer-Listener-User

Consumers of the next generation will not have to be educated in information machine use, for they are growing up with such machines as everyday items in their environment. Twelve-month old babies can load and unload cassettes in a VCR, and many third graders simply assume they will write their book reports on a word processor. It seems plausible to expect that when the interests of the current generation of 8-year olds move beyond video games, they will already be groomed for interactive multimedia experiences on the television or computer, for play or for work. They will be used to controlling screen inputs and outputs and will therefore be more demanding of machine performance and interface characteristics than prior, book-bred generations.

At the same time, individuals of all ages are increasingly comfortable with electronic, interactive forms of information through consistent exposure to and use of ATM's, VCR's, home computers, video kiosks, automatic ticketing machines, credit card phones, cellular phones, and a proliferation of other devices. This will make the introduction of new electronic products and services all the more likely as it is less risky. The increasing exposure of employees to computer networks and online information in the office, for instance, will create an easier path for entry of similar information services into the home.

Information Age consumers not only have increased control but increased choice over what they read, view, and listen to, and this choice is an important element in the consumer marketplace. Once outside the coercive learning context of schools, the reader-viewer-listener-user comes freely to learn, to be stimulated, exposed, informed, aroused, angered, amused, delighted, and uplifted.

The changed information consumption habits of the reader-viewer-listener-user also affect the manner in which publishers present their material. *USA Today,* as noted above, owes a large part of its success to tailoring its material to a visually-oriented, television-viewing readership. As discussed in Chapter 8, the media cross-fertilize one another: books, newspapers, and magazines become more visual, audio cassettes become textual, and video-based material becomes non-sequential and random access when implemented in videodisc and interactive multimedia applications. Information Age users are subconsciously fluent in the various media metaphors, and the continuing dialogue between users and producers, between publishers and reader-viewer-listeners, will shape product and service offerings at least as much as the new media technologies themselves.

Inevitably a new set of user habits and skills will be engendered by the new information and media technologies. In human prehistory, people were orally literate in order to comprehend and communicate with one another. As recorded forms of communication were developed—clay tablets, papyrus scrolls, illuminated manuscripts, and later books printed by movable type—a new set of skills was required to operate in a written, versus an oral, communications environment. Later, more print forms were introduced—magazines, newspapers—and after them electronic point-to-point messaging media, such as the telegraph and telephone, each requiring different skills for comprehension and use. The 20th century brought the phonograph, radio, film, and television. The latest wave of communications technologies and services, such as online services and compact optical disc products, are based on computer and microprocessor technology.

This development from oral to written to printed to electronic forms of communication has led some observers to readdress the study of literacy. As noted in the Introduction, Benjamin Compaine has proposed the notion of the "New Literacy," referring to "the bundle of information skills that may be required to function in society, skills that may evolve from the capabilities made possible by the increasingly widespread use of inexpensive compunications (computer and communications) technology."[9] As Compaine characterizes the evolving environment, personal computers, the widespread use of automatic teller machines, the growth in electronic database publishing, and other developments are not isolated but are part of a broader cultural evolution akin to the major developments of the industrial revolution in the 19th century, including the steam-driven rotary press, the railroads, and improvements in optics for the manufacturing of eyeglasses. Those combined forces led to profound changes in the nature and breadth of written literacy in that period, creating the conditions for its spread from the elite to the populace at large. Now other forces are coming together to create new sets of skills. Students are learning how to use computers both at home and in school. This wider bundle of skills may be seen as central to the educational curriculum if they are perceived as necessary for proper social and worklife functioning in adulthood, skills which, says Compaine, may eventually have as profound an effect on thought processes as reading and writing do on ours.[10]

Compaine sees a three stage process not unlike the market life cycle phases of media technologies discussed in Chapter 8. His cycle moves from Literacy I, based on reading and writing, through a transitional Literacy II, which uses old format-derived content in the new electronic systems, to the New Literacy III in which we are "conceptualizing and processing information" in terms of the new media and information technologies. Although the changes will be gradual, if Compaine is right the implications could be profound for the way publishers select and prepare content in different media forms. Defenders of the printed word and its centrality in our culture will be alarmed by the unabashed relativism of literacy as an evolving concept. But should Compaine's notion be on the mark, it is further evidence of the Information Age paradigm shift, in which publishers must take a closer look at the user of information and see not just a reader, but a viewer, listener, and user as well, a receiver of information in all media and modes.

The retail market is also undergoing changes which represent the evolving view of the whole information consumer. While one trend is toward the format-focused superstore, be it in books, music, or video, another trend is toward mixing of media formats around a common theme. Stores such as WGBH/Learningsmith in the Boston area, which sell all types of home educational items, from books and music to software, audios, videos, toys, and other goods, typify this trend.

USER POWER AND RECOMBINANT PUBLISHING

The expanded skill set of the new customer is in large part a consequence of a shift in power to the market end of the spectrum, power that is both electronic and economic. The proliferation of user-premise machines means increasing sophistication in the generation, processing, and storage of information by customers. No longer does equipment and processing power reside solely at the originator end. At home, this includes televisions, VCR's, home computers, compact disc players, camcorders, and telephones, all of which are gaining in processing power. In schools, camcorders, VCR's, PC's and networks, laserdisc players and interactive multimedia, are all gaining in functionality. In the office, computers—from hand-held to notebook, laptop, and desktop devices, to local and wide area networks connected to file servers, CD-ROM players, phones, and fax machines—all represent increases in user-premise processing and storage capabilities. Mostly these are smart devices (i.e., they have programmed or programmable computer chips embedded in them) that allow users choice over and control of content. In many cases the content supplied is raw, unrefined data to which the user can add value with local processing power. It means a direct material to market link, or, from the user's perspective, a direct market to material link. Thus, our next core concept:

Core Concept #26: User Power

As Stewart Brand discovered during his year at MIT's Media Lab, "What's new at the Media Lab is the content-specific selectivity and repackaging at the receiving end that computer technology is offering. If printing and industrialization were revolutions that transformed civilization, a counterrevolution is underway."[11] This is a significant feature of the paradigm shift to publishing in the Information Age. Just as the information provider, or originating publisher, manages the value-added cycle of the 5M's, so the end-user can increasingly do the same because of enhanced local processing power. He can generate his own material and access outside sources. With digital multimedia he has the choice of mode and the ability to process in any mode.

Information technology also enables the user to subsume more of the publisher's traditional role in the selection and formatting of material, thus providing the user with greater choice and control. We can depict the relative shift in power by reversing the 5M's flow shown in Table 3-1 to the flow shown in Figure 9-1.

In this publishing environment, the user has the ability to interact directly with the information provider for his or her choice of material and how it shall be formatted for display—e.g., viewed on-screen or printed out. Information flows in many large organizations already operate in this fashion, where networked clients (users) access servers (information stores) for their specific needs, transporting the required data to their local computing devices for manipulation and display—screen or print—as they choose. Applications resident on the local devices allow them to process the information as they choose. The digital interactive television of the future will be, in effect, client-server television.

Former Times Mirror group vice president Jerome Rubin uses the Harvard

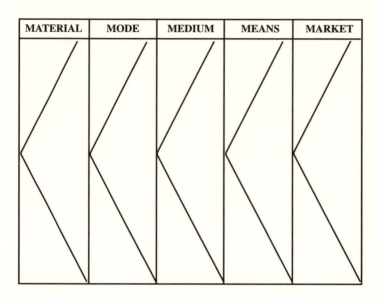

MATERIAL	MODE	MEDIUM	MEANS	MARKET

Figure 9-1
User Power: Reversing the 5M's Flow

Program in Information Resources Policy triad of substance-process-format to describe how Mead Data's online legal information service, LEXIS, which he launched in 1973, takes advantage of such user processing power: "When LEXIS was developed, legal publishers saw their role as providing substance to their readers in fixed and predetermined formats. By contrast, in building LEXIS, we put process in the hands of the user, so that he could control both substance and format at will." Rubin also states that "acknowledging the migration of process and format from the publisher to the user is essential as we approach the year 2000. . . . Selling multiple copies of the same substance in an identical format to large numbers of users will be an increasingly difficult way to turn a profit." Rubin observes that whereas Gutenberg's movable type enabled such mass distribution of identical copies upon its implementation in the 15th century, the 20th century's "electronic technologies allow the creation of infinite variations."[12]

The digital library (*see* Core Concept #6) can thus be viewed as converting the publisher's inventory from physical to electronic form, enabling users to select the content they want, when they want it, and in the format they choose. The digital library can feed the publisher's own packaging and derivative publishing mechanisms as well as online, on-demand, and custom publishing mechanisms. There are, of course, critical issues of content rights and content-provider royalties to be addressed, and Information Age publishers are taking steps to create the necessary information system infrastructure to support such requirements in a marketplace characterized by shorter development and to-market cycles, shorter product life cycles, and more intense competition.

In addition to connectivity, interactivity is also a function of user power. List publishers of pre-packaged electronic products also take advantage of user processing power, as do, to varying degrees, audio cassettes and discs, laser-discs, CD-I, and other multimedia formats. Some offerings combine disc-based products with online services, such as Lotus' CD-ROM *One Source,* which supports transparent access to Dow Jones News/Retrieval.

Despite the increase in user power, publishing organizations still have more access to capital, technology, and distribution channels, physical or electronic, and thus wield greater overall resources, than do individuals. Moreover, distinctions must still be made between performance and participative media. Lecture/performance content will continue to exist even as interactive/participative content evolves, just as both print and electronic formats will coexist in a pluralistic media environment.

GLOBALIZATION AND SEGMENTATION

Another trend in the market environment is the simultaneous movement toward globalization and segmentation of markets:

Core Concept #27: Globalization and Segmentation

The advances in media and information technologies are pushing the shape of markets in these seemingly contradictory directions. Broadcast technologies, especially with the advent of satellite communications, allow for the blanket transmission of signals to hundreds of millions, even billions, of people at once, making possible globally shared events and experiences. Motion picture studios and list and periodical publishers are also pursuing globalization strategies, both at the product and organizational levels. At the same time, segmentation or demassification of markets is pursued by list, periodical, and open channel publishers, including cable television and online services.[13]

Considering the historical development of consumer media, the rule has been to start with mass market coverage—newspapers, television, radio—and then, usually as a result of competitive pressure, to focus increasingly on marketing to targeted segments. Early in the development of a new medium, channels of publicity, advertising, and distribution are immature and therefore make it more difficult to reach intended audiences. But now most books published are read by only a few thousand at best, most cable channels are designed for narrowcasting, and radio is splintered among easy listening, all-news, talk-shows, classic rock, hard rock, jazz, and other types. Except for *People, Reader's Digest, TV Guide,* and a few other publications sold at the check-out counter, most magazines increasingly find their readers in small pockets, too: skiers, yachtsmen, numismatists, computer buffs, residents of the same city or state, members of the same age group, graduates of the same university.

As markets become segmented, publisher-user communities emerge focused on shared content areas. These communities knit publishers and audiences together by their common interests. As with all communities, they are interactions among their individuals, shaping and defining issues of common concern. These communities are of importance to publishers seeking to gain and hold market share. Typically, they are far easier to build and maintain for periodical and networked open channel publishers, whose customers are known and identified, than they are for list or broadcast publishers, whose customers are usually more difficult to identify or reach. However, those list publishers not serving mass markets can develop creative marketing strategies in their chosen market segments and achieve high returns. Moreover, the integration of information technology into the publishing process allows for customization of product to serve such communities' needs. On-demand printing from databases, for instance, allows customization of content at the individual level. McGraw-Hill chairman Joseph Dionne has stated that "we're trying to move the whole publishing industry in this direction," adding that customization in all print media in all markets is "a crucial part of McGraw-Hill's long-term strategy."[14]

SUMMARY AND CONCLUSION

In this chapter we have introduced four core concepts for the fifth value-added M, Market:

- *Core Concept #24: The Mediated Environment*
- *Core Concept #25: The Reader-Viewer-Listener-User*
- *Core Concept #26: User Power*
- *Core Concept #27: Globalization and Segmentation*

These four concepts identify features and trends that characterize the broader market environment into which the Information Age publisher's products and services are introduced, whether it is the consumer market, the business and professional market, or the educational market. The mediated environment is the psychological environment created by the proliferation of media technologies, outlets, and messages in our society. The multiplicity of media forms and messages not only creates a crowded media environment but brings changes in customers' information habits as well. The Information Age customer is no longer just a reader, but a viewer of images, a listener to sounds and words, and a user of information machines. The change in user habits is complemented by a change in the communications skills required for successful functioning in school, in the workplace, and in the society at large.

These new skills are also representative of the continuing shift in relative processing power from the information provider to the information user, where increasingly powerful on-premise equipment, much of which harnesses or embodies computing power, will continue to affect the manner in which publishers prepare, produce, and deliver their products and services. The new media and information technologies have also brought a simultaneous movement toward mass and global markets as well as smaller segmented markets, which will also have an effect on publishers' product and marketing strategies.

NOTES

1. Professor Frederick Williams, founder of the Annenberg School of Communication at the University of Southern California and now at the University of Texas, Austin, whose thinking helped shape my notion of the mediated environment, adds:

In America our television sets are on an average of six hours a day. Between the ages of six and eighteen, our children will watch about 16,000 hours of television and spend another 4,000 hours with radios, records, and movies. They will spend more time with media than with school or in talking with parents. We are increasingly living and working in an environment that is artifactual and electronic . . . rapidly fabricating a total psychological environment for ourselves. Television has become so ubiquitous as to be more environment than communications medium.

Frederick Williams, *The Communications Revolution* (New York: New American Library, 1983), x, 15, and 201. In 1984 the A.C. Nielsen Company reported the average daily television running time up to 7 hours, 2 minutes per household.

It is also interesting to note that, just as a strong movement has emerged to protect our physical environment, a similar though somewhat less organized movement has emerged to protect our psychological environment. Peggy Charren's Action for Children's Television (ACT), now disbanded, is a prime example of such a "media environment" advocacy group. Some critics state that the media environment is no less polluted than the natural environment. While former FCC commissioner Newton Minow once referred to network television as a wasteland, these critics would call it a toxic waste dump. New York University communications professor Neil Postman writes of the polluted river in our symbolic environment, and the pollutant is television: "We are now a culture whose information, ideas and epistemology are given form by television, not by the printed word. . . . Print is now merely a residual epistemology, and it will remain so, aided to some extent by the computer, and newspapers and magazines that are made to look like television screens. Like the fish who survive a toxic river and the boatman who sail on it, there still dwell among us those whose sense of things is largely influenced by older and clearer waters." Neil Postman, *Amusing Ourselves to Death* (New York: Viking Penguin, 1986), 28. *See also* Jerry Mander, *Four Arguments for the Elimination of Television* (New York: William Morrow, 1978).

2. Marshall McLuhan, *Understanding Media: The Extensions of Man* (New York: New American Library, 1964, Signet reprint edition), 248.

3. Christine Urban, "The Competitive Advantage of New Publishing Formats" in *Electronic Publishing Plus* (White Plains, N.Y.: Knowledge Industry Publications, 1985), 53.

4. Urban, "The Competitive Advantage of New Publishing Formats," 44. Urban's

chapter in *Understanding New Media* (Cambridge, Mass.: Balinger Press, 1984), Benjamin Compaine, editor, "Factors Influencing Media Consumption: A Survey of the Literature," is a summary and distillation of more than 350 major research reports on the topic through 1981.

Other media usage classification schemes exist. Communications researcher Elihu Katz classified 35 different information needs into five major groups, somewhat similar to Urban's scheme: (1) cognitive, relating to learning; (2) affective, relating to aesthetic or emotional experience; (3) integrative, relating to confidence and status; (4) social, relating to contact with family, friends, and the world; and (5) escapist, e.g., tension reducing. As cited in Christopher Burns and Patricia Martin, "The Economics of Information" (Washington, D.C.: Office of Technology Assessment, 1985), V-10.

5. As quoted in Burns and Martin, "The Economics of Information," V-10.

6. W. Russell Neumann, "The Media Habit" in *Electronic Publishing Plus,* 9.

7. It is important to distinguish, as these observers do, between media users in the consumer environment and those in other settings, such as the business or educational environments, where media usage is typically more directed and purposeful.

8. Christine Urban, "Factors Influencing Media Consumption" in *Understanding New Media,* 213.

9. Benjamin Compaine, "Information Technology and Cultural Change: Toward a New Literacy?" (Cambridge, Mass.: Harvard University Program on Information Resources Policy, 1984), 1.

10. Compaine, "Toward a New Literacy?" 3–4, 27. As an example, Compaine cites an interactive videodisc program, not unlike the MIT Media Lab's early Aspen Movie Map project, which maps in full video the entire city of Dusseldorf, Germany. The program "mixes detail and context. It has neither an obvious beginning nor end. And it is controlled in infinite variations by individual users. In time it may turn out to be as primitive in technique as was D.W. Griffith's early motion picture *Birth of a Nation* compared to George Lucas' high-tech *Star Wars*. But it suggests the potential break with the basic literacy skills that have shaped much intellectual behavior for nearly 1,000 years . . . [and] emphasizes the benefits that could accrue from combining holistic with sequential/logic skills."

11. Stewart Brand, *The Media Lab: Inventing the Future at MIT* (New York: Viking Penguin, 1987), 42.

12. Jerome Rubin, "Life After Print," *The Bookseller,* 17 August, 1990, 395–98. Personics Systems has developed an analogous system in the audio mode. The seven-year old system allows an in-store customer to create his or her own cassette tape from a variety of audio content sources. *See* Regis McKenna, "Marketing Is Everything," *Harvard Business Review,* January–February 1991, 73–74.

13. As used here, market segment refers to a group of customers with similar needs or wants who are treated in a similar fashion because they can be expected to respond in roughly the same way.

14. *See* Michael W. Miller, "Professors Customize Textbooks, Blurring Roles of Publisher, Seller, and Copy Shop," *The Wall Street Journal,* 16 August, 1990.

CHAPTER 10

The Media Universe: Profiling the Markets

This chapter adds the market dimension to the Media Matrix to create the Media Universe. We will profile the three major markets—consumer, business and professional, and educational—by briefly considering key characteristics before looking at the Media Universe in the global marketplace.

THE MEDIA UNIVERSE

The Media Universe is a three-dimensional depiction of the Media Matrix (*see* Figure 6–1). It adds a third dimension, market, to the modes and means which define it. The three major markets are represented as separate planes. The Media Universe thus depicts four of the five value-added M's—mode, medium, means, and market—and is the next core concept:[1]

> *Core Concept #28: The Media Universe: Modes, Means, and Markets*

CONSUMER MARKET

Media Formats, Preferences, and Trends

As shown in Figure 10-2, nearly all the media formats are present in the consumer market. The print products—books, magazines, and newspapers—

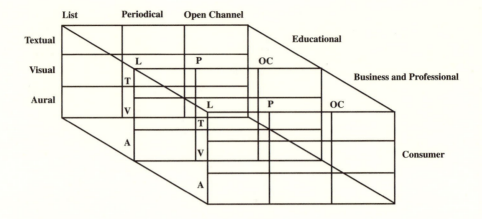

Figure 10-1
The Media Universe: Modes, Means, and Markets

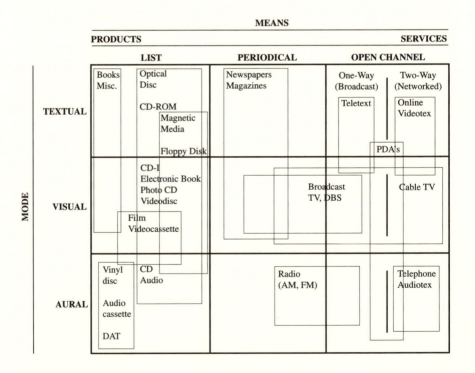

Figure 10-2
The Consumer Market

continue to demonstrate their versatility and appeal to nearly all segments of the market. As publisher and social forecaster Austin Kiplinger points out, even the most sophisticated electronic formats will serve to highlight the value of printed output: "The habit of reading the printed word is so engrained in educated people that it has survived every assault against it for more than 60 years: radio, the movies, television, and now 'videotex' versions of daily newspapers and magazines."[2]

While print products are still very much in demand, they are also faced with challenges, as the recessionary downturn of the late 1980s and early 1990s made painfully clear. As the largest single advertising vehicle of all the media, the decline in advertising hit newspapers the hardest. The persistent issues of content, design, and readership have been reexamined in light of the changed economic picture. To retain current readers and gain new ones, more papers, including regional weeklies, metropolitan dailies, and Sunday papers, continue to seek more ways to innovate in information presentation and advertising coverage. Magazines have also had to retrench.

But while print formats may continue to hold their own, the predominant consumer medium, if not the defining medium of the second half of the 20th century, is television, also a landscape undergoing dramatic change. The battle has been among the networks, the local independents, and cable. Most recently the prospect of multimodal optical fiber networks operated by the local telephone operating companies, along with newly-developed interactive broadcast technologies, has provided challenges to cable's limited two-way capabilities. The 1993 Southwestern Bell cable system acquisition referred to above also indicates the potential for cross-ownership of the two types of networks, opening up still other possibilities for service combinations.

Motion pictures, videocassettes and audio cassettes, and compact discs, all with moving images and sound, have established themselves as entertainment vehicles. Other newer consumer market media include software, videotex, and audiotex. Software tools have generally not fared as well in the consumer market as they have in the business market as the installed computer base is far smaller and the primary demand for computing has yet to materialize on a broad scale. The relatively low penetration of home computers has also inhibited the growth of videotex. With personal computer prices dropping into affordable ranges, and with the successful national roll-out of the flat-fee Prodigy service (and subsequent entry of America Online and CompuServe into the monthly flat-fee service arena), many are optimistic once again that consumer online information services will find their market. Phone-based home information services also offer promise, particularly in light of recent regulatory rulings allowing the local phone operating companies into the business.

Some analysts feel multimedia products will fuel the growth of computer-based home media, whether the players are hooked to computers or televisions. A variety of optical disc players and multimedia products are on the market, as discussed above, providing game applications (Nintendo, Sega) and more educational fare, such as *Microsoft Musical Instruments,* and a variety of encyclopedias, including those from Grolier, Compton's, and Microsoft. The last of these, *Encarta,* is the most recent entrant in the multimedia encyclopedia segment (released in spring 1993) with 21,000 articles, 7 hours of sound (6,500 audio files), 100 animations, 800 color maps, 7,000 photos, and an online dictionary and thesaurus.

Entertainment and Information-Driven

To make a rigid distinction between entertainment and information is not, of course, entirely accurate. The pursuit of information can be entertaining, and knowledge is often its own reward. Poppel and Goldstein speak of "infotainment," the convergence of entertainment and information, citing *Sesame Street* as an example. But it would appear that the demand for hard, decision-making information in the consumer market will never be the same as that in the business and professional market, as lessons from the first generation videotex ventures and home computer sales indicate. Despite the technological capability to deliver information through online systems, optical disc, and other means, consumers appear to be more interested in purchasing compact disc players and televisions for entertainment purposes.[3]

Still, there is strong demand for certain types of information in the consumer market: information for managing our lives, for planning careers, for finding a new home, for local shopping and education, or information about family issues, travel, health, home repair, as well as news, weather, and sports scores. There is also the need for enlightenment, knowledge, and art, fulfilled by fiction and non-fiction books and documentary programming on television. While sometimes the information in demand has mass appeal, often it is of a more specialized nature and of appeal to more narrowly segmented audiences.

Thus good access to information of real value may be the inhibiting factor in home information use. Intuitive, user-friendly retrieval technologies will become critical in high-volume, multimodal systems. As mentioned earlier, it is reasonable to expect that the Nintendo-playing generation will be predisposed to interactive television programs and applications, many of which will be information-oriented. The purchase and rental of pre-recorded video programming also marks a more purposive use of television than the relatively passive consumption of broadcast or cablecast material. It also fits the pay-as-you-go publishing model of choice before consumption, a departure from the way we have viewed television up to now. Moreover, as more and more consumers are exposed to online systems in the workplace, which typically combine the connectivity of remote information retrieval with the interactivity of a computer interface, we can expect a transfer of similar behavior and expectancies to the home.

The Mass Market and Segmentation

While the mass market and segmentation are at opposite ends of the spectrum, the consumer market encompasses both. List products such as books, videos, audio cassettes, and motion pictures, can all achieve mass market status. As noted in Chapter 9, the blanket technologies of satellite television and computer networks also allow for extensive reach by electronically distributed products, with minimal incremental costs.

The mass market creates a high stakes game for investors. While the potential for gain is enormous if a given property is a hit, its potential for loss if it's a flop is equally great. These risk-reward ratios are generally reduced in more niche-oriented approaches to the market, seen in books, magazines, cable television, and radio. Publishers and media firms can narrow their focus and create special interest products for considerably smaller sums, though each medium and its technology requirements will also determine the dollar outlay required. Typically, the development of sound and moving image programming will cost more than a print publication on the same subject, though no firm rules can be made as authoring tools and digitized content will lower costs, as will direct electronic distribution.

Discretionary Income and Advertising Dollars

All consumer media dollars are spent out of discretionary income. There are two schools of thought about the elasticity of consumer expenditure levels: the so-called constancy hypothesis and a newer school which foresees a growing level of expenditures devoted to media purchases.

The available figures document how steady consumer media expenditures have been over the years, including expenditures for both hardware and content. Since the 1920s, when the Bureau of Economic Analysis first started tracking personal consumption expenditures, the percentage of expenditures for the media has remained between 2.75% and 3.4% of total personal consumption. As the authors of the study *Consumer Media Expenditures, 1982–1987* point out:

There are only so many hours in the day and human beings can spend only so many of them absorbing communications messages. Since no communications invention has yet persuaded people to give up such non-media leisure time activities as sports, eating, conversation, or fraternizing with the opposite sex, it can be assumed that none in the future will do so either. The effect of new media will not be to stimulate a permanent increase in consumption of media, but only to rearrange the share of consumer expenditures going for existing media.[4]

If we agree with this analysis, the logical corollary is that producers of existing media hardware and software will have to adjust their shares and strategies to take account of an increasingly crowded marketplace competing for the same consumer dollars. Existing firms can either watch their established franchises erode, or they can seek to expand their piece of the finite pie.

Despite the historically flat media consumption rate, there is a growing group of prognosticators that feels we are on the cusp of something new that will break the pattern. Part of the redefinition of media usage habits, they say, includes new levels of expenditures. Home electronics is already the third largest purchase area for many consumers after their homes and cars, and with successive generations of equipment and new media forms causing obsolescence, replacement and upgrades, just as with cars, will be the rule. Typical future scenarios envision the installation of multimedia electronic centers in different areas of the household. The living room television and stereo will continue to evolve along the lines of the integrated audio-video systems now on the market to include full video and stereo sound with inputs for tape cassettes and optical discs, fiber optic and/or coaxial cable, and airwaves (satellite, broadcast), all programmable and remote controlled. An information-oriented desktop workstation would be found in the office or den, with the same video and audio outputs, supplemented by text and graphics and focused on interconnected data exchange and information manipulation for household budgeting, telecommuting, electronic messaging, and market services. The children's bedroom would house a learning station, with audio-video-text-data manipulation both online and on-site. A fourth smart-house control center would be in the kitchen, with text, video, and audio inputs and outputs for household management. A proliferating variety of hand-held devices completes the picture, with portable telephones either supplemented or displaced by PDA's and other read-write devices.

While such a vision may come to pass at some point soon, we must remember that in the consumer market such equipment and services must be paid from discretionary income. Any adverse economic condition could have a severe effect on this scenario. Moreover, fearful of technological obsolescence or lack of industry standards, consumers will typically not buy expensive electronic products until they are assured that the dollars expended will not be quickly rendered useless. As industry analyst Gary Arlen has stated, "the world at large doesn't care about machines—they just want results." Consultant Chris Burns concurs: "All the technology requires capital investment. The capital investment of $1,000–2,000 is trivial to a business, but it's very significant to a household." But Burns also points out the presence of another paying party in the consumer market: "What turns all the economics upside down in the consumer market is the advertiser. The whole rationale of advertising is to place your message in the path of somebody who is traveling along that way. That path is the media."[5]

In fact, the bulk of the cost of information preparation, processing, and delivery to consumers is not paid for by consumers, but by advertisers. This is clearly the case in magazines, where more than half of revenues come from advertisers, and newspapers, where more than two thirds comes from advertisers. In the almost exclusively consumer-oriented broadcast media, virtually all of television's and radio's revenues come from advertisers, the only exception being publicly supported stations.

However, even advertising revenues are not as dependable, especially in the print media, as they once were, regardless of economic conditions. Competition from electronic media and the high costs of physical distribution are driving prices up, which means consumers are paying a relatively greater share, as well as more overall dollars, for these media.[6] Other price supports may emerge. In Poppel and Goldstein's analysis, other potential third parties, such as banks and retailers, will play a role by funding and creating sophisticated, transaction-driven second and third generation videotex systems with full video, text, and sound.[7]

It must also be noted that while the giant broadcasting and periodical segments rely heavily on advertising support, other direct dollar consumer media continue to thrive, most notably books, video and audio tapes, and compact discs. These suppliers' ability to focus on narrower market segments and their independence from advertising support ensure flexibility, independence of content selection, and less vulnerability in economic downturns. The relatively low unit prices of these formats will also continue to provide excellent consumer value.

THE BUSINESS AND PROFESSIONAL MARKET

The business market includes all firms engaged in commercial and industrial activities, while the professional market includes legal, medical, scientific, financial (e.g., accounting), and technical occupations, defined by discrete bodies of knowledge and, in many instances, a community of government-certified practitioners.

Media Formats, Preferences, and Trends

Figure 10-3 depicts the media array in the business and professional market. Among list products, books continue to play an important role. The less decision-oriented the nature of the information the less likely we are to see a shift of its embodiment from print to electronic form. Material of a theoretical, reflective nature which attempts to explain a body of material or which requires prolonged study will most likely remain appropriate in book form. Many reference materials, too, will continue to reside in book form, though incursion will continue to be made by both online services and CD-ROM because of their high-volume storage and superior search and retrieval capabilities.

Computer software, whether in magnetic or optical media, will continue to see sustained growth. Software is at once an applications medium and an enabling tool for nearly all other applications. As the point of interface for

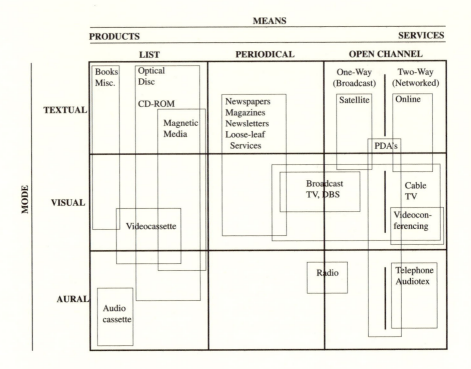

Figure 10-3
The Business and Professional Market

online systems, interactive video, CD-ROM, and other optical disc formats, it is the integrating tool in the convergence of textual, visual, and aural modes. As multimedia developer David Backer observed: "Publishers may maintain their competitive edge as much through the power and appeal of their software interfaces as through the quality of content materials. Emphasis on design and delivery of utilitarian software could significantly shift the focus in the publishing world."[8]

Software applications have also emerged as presentation tools, incorporating textual, numeric, and graphic material in interactive formats. Moreover the rise of multimedia personal computers will make software-based presentations even more prevalent, especially when hooked to large screens for group presentations.

Non-computer televisual media are also in increasing use in the business world. In the mid-late 1980s, videocassettes became an almost indispensable business tool. For years the business community had used 16-mm film and slides for presentations. But VCR's and televisions have invaded offices as well as homes and schools. The cost savings, speed of production, ease of duplication, standardized formats, and ease of use all favor video over film. The videocassette format will continue to be appropriate for motivating and training large audiences as well as individuals, especially when used in conjunction with print materials. Digital video delivered on multimedia optical discs, however, because of their interactivity, will erode the use of cassettes for certain applications, such as industrial training.

Due to the nearly ubiquitous, standardized players now found in homes, offices, cars, briefcases, and pockets, the audio cassette has also become a viable publishing medium in the business and professional market. The relatively low production costs for the conversion of print material or the creation of original audio material on cassette has attracted a number of players, both from the print world and elsewhere. While the audio medium does not represent a direct threat to the capabilities of print or electronic text products, it does provide a supplemental means of supplying focused business information, with sound allowing for vocal performances of inspirational and motivational quality. Unlike print and video, audio does not require the user's full attention and can therefore be played while the user is engaged in other activities, such as commuting to and from the workplace.

Print periodicals, particularly trade magazines and journals, will continue to play a vital role in both the business and professional markets. Their frequency and regularity of publication and permanent, referable output allow timely coverage of topics of interest to defined communities. General interest publications, such as *Fortune, Forbes, Business Week,* and *The Wall Street Journal,* will continue to serve a connective, cross-industry, cross-market role while competing heavily with each other. However, some impact has been felt by journal publishers from online computer networks, wherein scholars and professionals are able to communicate directly and more immediately with one another, bypassing the publishing intermediaries.

Broadcast television is probably the least appropriate medium in the highly segmented business and professional markets, but successful applications continue to emerge. What information is supplied via television broadcasts, including such programs as *The Nightly Business Report* and *Wall Street Week,* is not as useful for decision-making as it is for keeping viewers abreast of trends and changes. An example of an industry-focused broadcast business program is *The Computer Chronicles,* but it is a rarity. In cable, where narrowcasting is more the rule than the exception, the Financial News Network successfully maintained a daily television and radio programming schedule for the business and financial community beginning in the late 1970s. (Purchasers Dow Jones and Group W have continued the services since their acquisition of the firm in 1991.) Another possibility is the creation of regional business reports, weekly or daily up-dates on business news of interest to local viewers. Another possibility is more industry-focused programming. Other broadcast applications exist in radio, serving both as publicity tools and as information services, such as Dow Jones' nationally syndicated *Wall Street Journal Report.*

In sum, the electronic technologies employed in the business and professional market will be information-oriented—e.g., computers, online networks, optical discs—that allow users to input, store, and retrieve both internal and external data, versus the more entertainment-oriented broadcast media. However, the visual and aural modes will receive increasing emphasis in these markets, initially for purposes of presentation, education, training, and later for a broader range of uses. The rise of multimodal networks will also allow point-to-point communication in textual, visual, and aural forms. Groupware applications will be among the first to put multimedia to use in these markets.

Finally, although by our definition they are not true publishing formats, face-to-face events deserve mention in an examination of the business and professional media mix as they are important components in the total information marketplace. This includes such things as seminars, trade shows, and industry conferences, many of which are run by publishing firms in their respective areas of content expertise. Such face-to-face powwows have become increasingly important, bringing together industry participants to exchange views and understanding of industry conditions and prospects, promote new products, and make deals. Revenues from conferences are significant, often surpassing those of trade publications in the same field.[9]

Information Intensive, Focused Needs

Business means work, and any information that allows business people or professionals to do their work better will be of value. Such information can come in the form of training, as information for strategic purposes, or as information simply for keeping abreast of industry or general business news.

Training is big business, as businesses have discovered that better informed and trained employees will be more productive than those who are less informed and/or inadequately trained. A 1985 report from the Carnegie Foundation for the Advancement of Teaching estimated a population of eight million corporate learners. In 1987, corporate training specialists Leslie Steven May and Cynthia Ingols estimated that U.S. firms annually spend an aggregate $60 billion to educate these eight million corporate students, a figure that rivals the total expenditures of all the nation's public and private four-year colleges and universities combined. In high technology industries where the pace of change is rapid, manufacturing workers and executives are perpetual students of their own industries. As May and Ingols state, "Since technological innovations continue, the training/retraining cycle continues," leading to full-time schools within companies, with some firms, such as Arthur D. Little, even granting their own degrees.[10]

To survive in a competitive and changing business environment, organizations must also be outwardly focused, attuned to the market, the industry, and the forces of change. Information that meets these needs is used for strategic purposes, for competitive intelligence, and for market and technology awareness. Professor Ron Rice at Rutgers University says information technology allows businesses to "extend the boundaries of their organizations. In effect you say 'My organization's boundaries include an awareness of what other organizations are doing.' If you use an online database, for instance, to see how other companies in your industry are marketing their products, then you're using information technology to achieve competitive advantage."[11]

The firm's understanding of its operating environment plays a major role in shaping the organization's future direction. Publications that keep managers and workers abreast of their industry perform a crucial role in this regard, but more tightly focused data, both internally and externally generated, also provide the specific information companies require to plan their futures.

Availability of the right information, therefore, and access to it, are critical for business and professional users. Hence the early adoption, especially among professional users, of online services which allowed them to locate and extract the specific information they sought. With an information glut a premium is based on the specific information sought and intermediaries—both outside information brokers and internal groups such as MIS and research departments—provide a valued service by harnessing information technology to seek out, format, and present information that is pertinent to the operations of the organization. Coopers & Lybrand's John Clippinger speaks of the need for "information refinement" and foresees a significant opportunity for those information firms willing to assist their clients meet their specific information needs. Dun & Bradstreet refers to "the new rules in the information game. . . .Businesses are suffering more from information overload than from information scarcity. Thus the successful information companies of the 1990s may not be those that gather new data, but those that get existing facts to customers in the most useful form."[12] Thus in the business market the publisher's attention focuses on the customer and his information needs as a prelude to the development of product and service offerings. (*See also* Core Concept #21, Information Navigation and Access.)

In the professional and scholarly arenas, as more people pursue research and develop new ideas, those ideas must be reported. To avoid reinventing the wheel, scholars and professionals must remain plugged in to their respective practitioner communities. As a result, a proportionately greater amount of researchers' time is absorbed in secondary research, i.e., keeping abreast of colleagues' output in addition to their own new work, and in addition to studying, learning, and absorbing the work of the past. We may have already reached a point at which the mass of information is simply too great to absorb. Burns cites executives who tend to operate more on intuition than on hard data as they simply cannot keep up with all the changes in their field.[13] It raises the question of total systemic inefficiency if we do indeed "reinvent the wheel." It also reinforces the need for imprints and gatekeepers, authoritative sources for the latest and most significant information.

Deep Pockets

As the right information is vital to the success of their enterprises, business and professional organizations are more disposed toward spending money on information products and services than are consumers. While manufacturers and suppliers of information technology must endure cycles of expansion and retrenchment, the information providers are generally more resistant to these cycles as awareness and understanding of market and industry conditions are equally vital to businesses in up or down cycles. The willingness and ability of businesses to pay applies to content delivered in machine-readable formats as well as print publications, because if the information is timely or exclusive, customers will buy the machine as well. The financial exchanges are an excellent example of this dependence on machine-delivered information.

THE EDUCATIONAL MARKET

Media Formats, Preferences, and Trends

The media array depicted for the educational market (*see* Figure 10-4) shows distinct differences from the consumer and business and professional markets. List products predominate, with textbooks continuing to flourish and dominate the entire market. The centrality of the book to the classroom learning experience has been well established over a century of formal schooling. Books are a proven quantity, the repository of our culture and heritage and still the most trusted and authoritative of sources to teachers and students alike. Reading and writing are still primarily book-based activities that can be taught relatively cheaply with print materials, a fact of no little significance to school districts and administrators. Students can pore over books, unlike evanescent screen displays. Books are also a relatively cheap source of information because students do not need a machine to read their contents. Acting to control textbook costs is the increasing automation of the pre-press process. As publishers automate this process, from content capture, to page-layout, to typesetting, to printing, they are able to reduce production costs, increase content and design flexibility, and speed to-market times, for original texts, revised editions, and customized texts.

As the content of their texts is increasingly originated, captured, and stored in digital form, Information Age publishers explore derivative development of the material in both print and electronic media. Thus while education may continue to be centered on text-based materials and live interaction among teachers and students, the mix of media and materials in the process will continue to change, with more electronic components adding manipulability, sound, moving images, and other attributes to the printed page. These materials can include not only newer electronic media but, especially at the lower levels, other items such as posters, puzzles, games, and other elements of kits

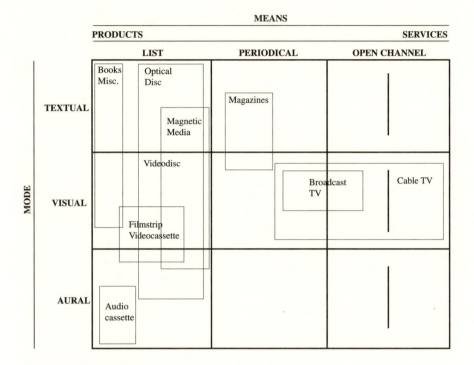

Figure 10-4
The Educational Market

that serve as classroom teaching aids. In the higher education market, for example, Course Technology, Inc., established in 1990, mixes print and electronic components to create integrated learning systems based on well-known existing software applications, such as *Lotus 1-2-3*.

Another avenue opened up by publishers' digital libraries is custom publishing. In the college market several initiatives have made possible the customized production of texts, including McGraw-Hill's Primis system and Paramount Publishing's joint-venture with Follet Corporation.

Computer software media are among the fastest growing of the electronic media in the educational market, due to computer manufacturers' heavy marketing push into the schools, with deep discounts off suggested retail prices, and the desire of parents and teachers to ensure that students are not left behind in the information technology revolution. Interactive multimedia programs are making their way into the classroom. Schools that are struggling to purchase textbooks and incorporate current computer programs are rightfully cautious of a bewildering variety of new, incompatible disc-based formats, but the technology's promise for educational purposes is clear to many. Straight text CD-ROM will also play a role, especially in higher education markets. As of this writing, at a comparatively early stage (phase 1–2 in the media life cycle; *see* Table 8-1), major multimedia projects for the academic and educational environments are often funded by a consortium of parties from the commercial and not-for-profit sectors. The Perseus Project at Harvard University's Classics Department, for example, a multimedia database of material on classical Greek civilization, is funded by a consortium including the Annenberg/CPB Project, Apple Computer, Xerox Corporation, Boston University, Bowdoin College, Harvard, and the Packard Humanities Institute.[14]

More traditional video-based media—i.e., non-interactive formats—are another educational market growth area. Nearly 30 years ago, with television still in its formative stages, Marshall McLuhan stated: "Whether there ever will be TV in every classroom is a small matter. The revolution has taken place at home. . . . The right approach is to ask 'What can TV do that the classroom cannot do for French, or for physics?' The answer is: 'TV can illustrate the interplay of process and growth of forms of all kinds as nothing else can.' "[15] By 1988, nearly 90% of school districts and over 90% of schools had purchased videocassettes.[16] The videocassette has been one of the most readily accepted of the new media technologies in the classroom, partly because it is now such a familiar item *outside* the classroom as well, making its adoption by teachers that much easier. No learning of complicated routines or equipment is required as with computers and software. Cassettes are small and portable like books and can be handed from teacher to teacher. Classroom cassettes are usually suited to specific subjects and needs. They can also be shown to groups, in contrast to computer software or interactive video which, unless the classroom is equipped with a costly large screen or an even more costly group of networked computers, must be used by students sequentially rather than simultaneously.

The videodisc, which combines broadcast-quality video presentation with computer interactivity, is also poised for broad acceptance in the classroom. As noted in Chapter 7, the videodisc's non-deteriorating image and sound quality, plus its ability to supplement sequential viewing with random access search functions, make it a strong competitor of the videocassette. The cassette's only technical superiority at the moment is its recordability. The late 1990 decision by the Texas Board of Education to approve Optical Data Corporation's *Windows on Science* videodisc-based elementary science program as a competitor for state textbook dollars, and the subsequent adoption of the program by more than 65% of the local Texas school districts, sent strong signals to the educational community as well as to publishers and developers of classroom materials. The company calls it an "electronic textbook," and Texas education officials say the company has "redefined the idea of textbook publishing and what goes into building a textbook company."[17]

Whatever the current regulatory and financial constraints, it appears likely that the superior learning benefits offered by a blend of modes and print and electronic formats will eventually make such integrated print-electronic learning systems a reality in most classrooms. As Paramount Publishing's Educational Group president Patrick Donaghy has stated, "The future [of educational publishing] will become a kind of joint venture. Media companies, [textbook] publishing companies, high-technology companies, and television companies will increasingly work together."[18]

Audio cassettes are also strong formats in the educational market. Phonograph records have been used for decades by schools and libraries to supplement text materials, and audio cassettes proved equally popular in schools upon the widespread purchase and use of cassette players in the 1970s. The technology is thus well-known and widely used, and the low cost of tapes make them the only audio-visual medium to rival the cost of printed material. At the lowest levels, book-cassette combinations are popular and successful components for pre-literate learners. At higher levels, dramatic readings of poetry—often in the voice of the original poet—and plays can bring language and literature alive with the sound of the human voice. Many current fiction and non-fiction books, released in audio cassette versions for the consumer market, are being used in the educational market as well. A newer phenomenon is recorded lectures available for resale and use beyond the originating university.

Periodicals will continue to play a supporting role in the educational market. Such stalwarts as *The Weekly Reader,* now over 60 years old and read by more than 11 million elementary school students across the country every week, will continue to thrive in the elementary market. Scholastic's range of magazines for the el-hi market will also maintain their respective niches. Other periodical publishers will continue to seek and find educational market applications, some as line extensions of their existing business and others as brand new opportunities.

Although there are not many newsletters in the school market, *Think, Inc.* is a general interest monthly newsletter published for grades 4–6 by a Colorado educator and textbook consultant, Tamra Keller, whose mission is to connect what students learn in the classroom to the world outside the classroom. At the high school, university, and post-graduate level, many magazine publishers such as Time Inc. and newspaper publishers such as The New York Times and Dow Jones, publishers of *The Wall Street Journal,* have built successful programs not only selling their publications into the educational markets but developing ancillary classroom materials based on the publications.

Open channel media are highly segmented in the educational market. On-line services are almost non-existent for el-hi segments, but more projects are underway and attracting attention each year. Budget constraints and alternative storage and delivery methods (principally print vehicles) have thus far prevented the widespread adoption of costly telecommunications services. In 1986, South Brunswick, New Jersey's Brunswick Acres School was one of the first in grades K–12 to experiment with Dow Jones News/Retrieval. In the New York City area, a consortium of WNET, the Corporation for Public

Broadcasting, and PBS runs an information service called Learning Link/
WNET for over 700 area schools.

Another use of online systems in the education market is for the creation
of custom texts via McGraw-Hill's Primis system, in operation since 1989. In
1991 the University of California at San Diego became the first college site
with the service on campus, allowing faculty members to search texts online
on the system's database and custom-design and create their texts on-site,
usually within 48 hours. Although the system is reportedly not yet profitable,
it represents an important new approach to textbook production that could
have far-reaching consequences for textbook publishers, at all levels. Although
enabled by a third-party on-site, in this case the campus bookstore, it clearly
demonstrates the shift from producer-selected, uniform texts to user-selected,
custom-produced texts that more closely meet the customers' needs (*see* Core
Concept #26, User Power).[19] Still, such systems are not without their detrac-
tors, who raise legitimate concerns about sequential learning as well as au-
thorship in an environment where chapters can be selected and recombined
at will, out of context of the original work. Concerns are also raised about
fragmentation of knowledge and the dilution of a core, shared curriculum with
such customized texts.

Until very recently, other open channel services, including broadcasting, had
only a very limited role in the formal classroom setting. The radical innovation
of Whittle Communications was to introduce an advertiser-supported news
program, Channel One, specifically produced for students. The controversial
service, which brings advertising into the classroom inside the Trojan horse
of free television and video equipment, demonstrates how a determined en-
trepreneur can find a new use for an existing technology in an established
market. The critics point out that children already watch countless hours of
television at home and that they should have neither television nor advertising
in the classroom. The state of New York and parts of California have banned
the service from public schools. Echoing McLuhan, management consultant
Peter Schwartz takes a more fatalistic view: "By far the dominant curriculum
in education today does not take place 8 a.m. to 3 p.m., it's 4 p.m. to midnight,
when the kids watch television at home. Electronic entertainment will be the
dominant educational medium that will shape global consciousness."[20]

Structured Environments, Defined Needs

From the publisher's standpoint there are many attractive features of the
educational market, not least of which is that the progression through the
grades makes for relatively predictable and stable markets. Moreover the purchasers of published materials are in most cases not the end-users—i.e., the
students—but intermediaries, such as administrators, faculty members, or
state or local adoption boards, making decisions to buy in quantity and for
specifically projected curriculum uses. While heavily competitive and highly

political, it is still a more rational purchasing environment than the consumer market, eliminating or greatly reducing impulse buys and other consumer market vagaries. While they may also reduce the prospects of creating a hit or a runaway bestseller, the stability and predictability of educational markets over time compensates for the relative lack of hits and potential up-side gain. Still, individual texts, like Paul Samuelson's *Economics* (McGraw-Hill) at the university level, can have extended lives, going through many revised editions and practically owning a marketplace niche for a number of years.

Thus we can characterize educational publishing as highly market-responsive, making it more akin to the clearly defined informational needs of the business and professional markets than the more diffuse consumer market, where segmenting, finding, and reaching target audiences is usually more difficult.

That the educational markets are attractive to publishers is evidenced by their consistent profitability. The industry is, however, highly concentrated, especially in el-hi publishing, where, as of 1986, the four largest companies accounted for one third of total revenues and nearly two thirds of all revenues flowed to the ten largest firms.[21] This means that garnering a consistent and sizable share of the established markets is tough for newer, smaller firms. At the same time it suggests that the path to entry may well lie with the newer electronic technologies, where growth rates and demand are high and market shares and buying practices are less well formed.

Defined curriculum needs also mean that developers of educational content materials must understand the nature of the subject matter and the level of sophistication—e.g., 8th grade reading level, mid-career professionals—with which it is presented. This is equally true of textbooks as it is for conversion of print material into an electronic format, or conversion of material from one mode to another. History or science, for example, readily lend themselves to audio-visual adaptation, whereas finance or accounting would appear to be more suitable for software development where repeated manipulation of no-tational forms is central to the learning process, as well as proper preparation for real-world computer skills.

The Third Wave of Electronics

To many educators, the new electronic publishing media are part of a third wave of electronic technologies now hitting the schools. In the 1960s publishers were sought out and bought up by electronics companies—Random House by RCA, Ginn by Xerox, D.C. Heath by Raytheon—in the expectation that a marriage of their hardware and the publishers' "software" was the wave of the future. In the late 1970s and 1980s, personal computers were introduced to the schools and adopted on a wide scale. Now school systems are being asked once again to purchase, at their expense, another wave of electronic technologies.

This third wave, however, is proving different from the first two, as a variety of the new technologies already have achieved significant levels of penetration. VCR's, for example, as noted earlier, were in 90% of the nation's 81,000 schools by 1988. Moreover, the attitude toward technology-based education has changed. In his 1987 report for the National School Boards Association, "Technology and Transformation of Schools," education consultant Dr. Lewis Perlman stated that the nation's education system must embrace the new information technologies or risk creating a future society of technologically deprived individuals at a competitive disadvantage in the world economy. In the report, Perlman points to the sweeping technological changes taking place in the environment *beyond* schools. But, echoing Peter Schwartz's observations on the mediated environment engulfing today's students, Perlman also believes that "merely injecting a few electronic tools—computers and videodiscs—into classrooms while leaving the basic design of education unchanged offers little hope for major improvement. . . . The school must become part of a total approach to learning that links it to the home and the entire environment in which learners live and work."[22]

Constrained Purchasing Power

Education has neither a mass market (it has the sheer numbers but they are sharply segmented), like the consumer market, nor the deep pockets, information-intensive purchasing power of the business and professional markets. Much of its purchasing power is subsidized, not by advertisers, but by budget-conscious state, local, and federal governments. Thus the schools are often the last to be able to acquire and incorporate the latest advances in information technology, technologies which often are more ideally suited to learning situations than any other.[23]

The lack of advertising as a funding source is another key purchasing constraint. As mentioned above, media pioneer Chris Whittle chose to turn this negative into a positive by introducing an advertiser-supported television venture into the high school classroom. The attractiveness of the idea from a business perspective was proven by the immediate entry of a competitive service from Turner Broadcasting's CNN.

New Learning Environments

If we look beyond the traditional institutional educational settings, a significant and clearly observable trend is the emergence of non-traditional learning environments. The case for lifelong education has not only been made but is being actively fulfilled. The United States has a well-educated population living in a society characterized by accelerating technological change, frequent workforce disruptions, and multiple career changes by individuals, with an attendant need for retraining. Traditional educational institutions struggle to keep up with a world that continues to change at a quickening pace, but often their resources are strained, and other organizations emerge to meet the challenge.

These new and different learning environments include the business and industrial workplace, where companies now routinely run full-time in-house educational programs for employees at all stages of their careers and in all areas of operation (*see* discussion in "Business and Professional Market"). They include the military, where the need for complex technical and other training has always been pronounced. They also include new forms of proprietary schools and private enterprises such as The Learning Annex now franchised across the country, which offers courses by professionals and practitioners on almost any subject. Established institutions of learning, from community colleges to public schools to four-year colleges and universities, have also expanded their student populations to include adult learners in their curriculum plans. Many colleges now offer degree programs for individuals at all stages of life, creating courses with nighttime, weekend, and other special schedules to accommodate the working population. New learning environments also exist in the home market, where broadcast television and other technologies service previously untapped student populations. Britain's Open University program is a prime example.

THE SIX GLOBAL SUPERMARKETS

The Media Universe can also be constructed for markets beyond the United States. We can divide the global market into six regional supermarkets, as shown in Figure 10-5. This is the next core concept:

Core Concept #29: The Six Global Supermarkets

The six supermarkets are: (1) North America, including the United States and Canada; (2) Latin America, including Mexico, Central America, and South America; (3) Europe—Western and Eastern Europe, which includes the Soviet Union; (4) Africa; (5) the Middle and Near East; and (6) Asia and the Pacific Rim, including Japan, China, Australia, and New Zealand.

The supermarkets serve as the locus of operations for a publishing or media firm in that region of the globe. Each represents a conglomeration of countries in a given region of the world, which can in turn be approached as separate markets with their own Media Universes. Most often, content products are customized to the needs of the individual countries within the supermarket as publishers are sensitive to cultural and linguistic barriers. Language, in fact, typically serves as one of the chief determinants in the granting of intellectual property rights. But even if world rights are granted for a given property in a given language, the publisher must be sensitive to local market needs. World English rights, for instance, do not automatically mean that a property will be

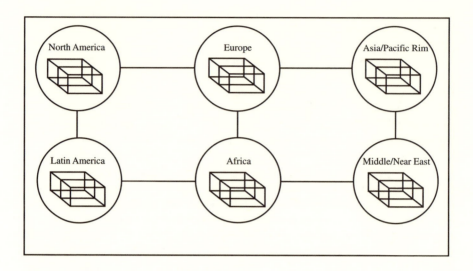

Figure 10-5
The Media Universe in the Six Global Supermarkets

equally salable in the United States, the United Kingdom, and Australian markets. Customization and content-tailoring may be required, as it often is for
translation editions. Still, while market customization may be the rule, some
properties are susceptible to global marketing. In the business markets, for
instance, both functional content (e.g., *Lotus 1-2-3*) and industry specific content (e.g., pharmaceuticals) can travel, though each product or service must
be viewed on a case-by-case basis.

The prospects for a global market for content products, especially for entertainment, are best in the consumer market. America has proven itself the
entertainment king, witness the selling off of the Hollywood studios to foreign
entrants eager for a piece of the action—Columbia to Sony, MCA to Matsushita, Fox to Murdoch, a piece of Time Warner Entertainment to C. Itoh—
as well as the success of Hollywood global megastars such as Arnold
Schwarzenegger.

Television programming, too, can travel, and the significant overseas revenues in both film and television can drive the conception and development of
properties that seek global returns on investment. Other consumer media have
also successfully sought and gained global franchises, including books, magazines, and motion pictures, though the economics and practices are different
for each.

The ongoing and dramatic changes in the international political arena will
also continue to create new market opportunities. Although it remains to be
seen whether the nations of the world can shape a new world order in the

wake of the collapse of eastern bloc communism, several large multinational firms have emerged to shape the global media market, such as the U.S.'s Time Warner, Australia's News Corporation, France's Hachette, and Germany's Bertelsmann.

SUMMARY AND CONCLUSION

In this chapter, we have introduced two more core concepts for Market, the fifth value-added M:

- *Core Concept #28: The Media Universe: Modes, Means, and Markets*
- *Core Concept #29: The Six Global Supermarkets*

The Media Universe adds the market dimension to the Media Matrix. Although they share certain characteristics, each of the three major markets is also defined by its own features. In the consumer market, where nearly the full range of extant media formats are purchased by either consumers or advertiser dollars, both entertainment and information are in demand and both mass markets and segments exist. While discretionary income constrains consumers' purchasing power, revenues from advertising significantly increase total media expenditures.

The business and professional market is characterized by information versus entertainment-oriented media in highly focused market segments. The spending power of organizations and constant demand for information makes the market less price-sensitive than the consumer market.

In the educational market, list products predominate, with an increasing number of electronic formats joining the text-based materials that still form the heart of most curriculums. Structured environments create more predictable and orderly purchasing patterns, though constrained purchasing power marks most buyers in the market. New, non-traditional learning environments are emerging, bringing new market opportunities for publishers' products and services.

The Media Universe can also be constructed for international markets, both for the six global supermarkets and for the individual countries within each of these markets. Opportunities for access to international markets is greater than ever before, though opportunities vary across the consumer, business and professional, and education markets in each country.

NOTES

1. In the same fashion that we could add other modes, such as haptic or olfactory, to the Media Matrix, we could also add other market planes, such as government, to the Media Universe. For the purpose of this study, we will consider the Media Universe as represented in Figure 10-1.

2. Austin Kiplinger, *The New American Boom* (Washington, D.C.: The Kiplinger Washington Editors, 1986), 190. Regarding his media format, *The New York Times* Vice Chairman Sydney Gruson stated: "When you hear the next prophecy about the fall of the newspaper business, ask yourself: What carries 30 million bits of storable information, weighs less than three pounds, provides hard copy, handles both text and graphics, allows random access, is available 24 hours a day, is completely portable, and costs less than 30 cents a connect-hour (because it is paid for mostly by someone other than the customer)? It is not the latest piece of fancy computer hardware. It is . . . the daily newspaper." As quoted in David A. Patten, *Newspapers and New Media* (White Plains, N.Y.: Knowledge Industry Publications, 1986), 7.

3. Chris Burns says: "From time to time information can play a pivotal role in the household's welfare—warnings of danger to health or safety, reports of opportunity beyond their immediate sphere, lucid instruction in something of direct importance. Once in a great while entertainment achieves the level of art, setting life on a new course. But these are the fruits of serendipity. Households do not systematically acquire information so much as they *scan* the horizon . . . [they] have only the most primitive methods for search and retrieval." Christopher Burns and Patricia Martin, "The Economics of Information" (Washington, D.C.: Office of Technology Assessment, 1985), V-12.

4. Editors of Knowledge Industry Publications, *Consumer Media Expenditures, 1982–1987* (White Plains, N.Y.: Knowledge Industry Publications, 1983), 5–7. As noted on page 5 of this report, Charles Scripps dubbed this steady rate of media consumption the "constancy hypothesis." *See also* Michael Tyler, "Productivity and the Economic Prospect" in *Electronic Publishing Plus* (White Plains, N.Y.: Knowledge Industry Publications, 1985), 354: "Microeconomic data show conclusively that there has been little long-term increase in the proportion of household income spent on information, communications, and entertainment ('ICE') goods and services." In *Information Technology,* Poppel and Goldstein report that for 1986 the average U.S. household spent about $1,600 on media, including equipment, services, and software for telephone, broadcasting, music, reading, and other entertainment-information related purchases. They also note that an additional $900 per capita was paid to the suppliers of these products and services in the form of advertising and telephone subsidies.

5. Burns, unpublished interview, 27 March, 1987.

6. *See* Jib Fowles, "The Upheavals in the Media," *The New York Times,* 6 January, 1991: "How will the media pay its bills in the future? Increasingly, consumers are going to be sharing their costs. The outline of this is already visible as cable viewers pay an increasing share of distribution and production costs. Readers will also pay higher prices for newspapers and magazines. Since the mid-1980s, single-copy magazine prices have increased by 72%. This trend will continue."

7. Harvey Poppel and Bernard Goldstein, *Information Technology: The Trillion-Dollar Opportunity* (New York: McGraw-Hill, 1987), 55. The authors state that

The major high-tech integrated market services revenue streams will not come from cannibalizing traditional information technology businesses, such as broadcasting and publishing. Rather, integrated market services will continue to carve most of its incremental revenues from such other industries as banking, retailing, education, and travel by helping to disintermediate less efficient stages of their marketing and delivery systems to consumers. Households already spend thousands of dollars annually within each of these other industries, and information technology suppliers will eventually take a share.

8. David S. Backer, "Prototype for the Electronic Book" in *Electronic Publishing Plus,* 138.

9. As Efrem Sigel states in his 1986 report on business information:

The modern trade show is a powerful arena for conducting business, combining show business, new modes of electronic presentation and questions and answers. The biggest trade shows attract more visitors, generate more revenues, and promote more interaction among attendees than any other medium. A major show like the Winter Consumer Electronics Show in Las Vegas, sponsored by the Electronic Industries Association, produces more revenue from exhibit fees than several of the trade magazines in the field sell in advertising in the course of a year.

Efrem Sigel and the Staff of Communications Trends, Inc., *The Business Information Markets: 1986–90* (White Plains, N.Y.: Knowledge Industries Publications, 1986), 97. Sigel reports that the trade show industry grew 400% in the ten years from 1975–1985.

10. May, in the Management Education Department at Digital Equipment, one of the world's largest computer makers with over 100,000 employees worldwide, outlined the educational effort of his company in 1987 (which, we should note, was prior to several rounds of layoffs in the firm):

The current size of this organization is comparable to a university of 25,000 full-time students. Every Monday morning, in over 100 worldwide locations, approximately 5400 students start classes that last from half a day to six weeks or more. In the fiscal year which ended on June 26, 1987 the educational services organization spent over $200 million to deliver 10,000,000 hours of education to 251,000 students. In addition to teaching more than 500 different courses delivered in 187 languages, the organization delivers a full range of communication services, including slides, scripts, videotapes, manuals, and technical books.

Leslie Steven May and Cynthia Ingols, "A Place to Work Is a Place to Learn: The Corporate Training Exercise," *Harvard Graduate School of Education Alumni Bulletin,* XXXII (Fall/Winter 1987): 15–16.

11. Ronald E. Rice, unpublished interview, 8 December, 1986. As MCI chairman William McGowan has stated: "Historically, management has looked at information technology—data processing and telecommunications—as just another major expense that has to be monitored and controlled by budget. But now many executives have realized that they can use information not only to manage their company but also as a profit-making tool. As soon as that corporate mind-shift takes place, everyone from CEOs to sales people in the field starts paying attention."

12. Claudia H. Deutsch, "MARKET-DRIVEN! Dun & Bradstreet's Bid to Stay Ahead," *The New York Times,* 12 February, 1989.

13. Burns and Martin, "The Economics of Information," V-6.

14. *See* Elli Mylonas and Sebastian Heath, "The Perseus Project," *Instruction Delivery Systems,* November/December, 1990, 12–13.

15. Marshall McLuhan, *Understanding Media: The Extensions of Man* (New York, N.Y.: New American Library, Signet reprint edition, 1964), 289.

16. "Number of VCR's in Schools Continues to Grow," *Home Video Publisher,* September 12, 1988. Based on figures from Quality Education Data of Denver.

17. *See* Udayan Gupta, "Optical Data Corporation Marries Technology with Education," *The Wall Street Journal,* 3 February, 1992.

18. As quoted in Therese Mageau, "Redefining the Textbook," *Electronic Learning,* February 1991, 18.

19. *See* Beverly T. Watkins, "San Diego Campus and McGraw-Hill Create Custom Texts," *Chronicle of Higher Education,* 6 November, 1991, A25.

20. As quoted in Stewart Brand, *The Media Lab: Inventing the Future at MIT* (New York: Viking Penguin, 1987), 242.

21. Bailey, et al., *The El-Hi Market, 1986–1991* (White Plains, N.Y.: Knowledge Industry Publications, 1986), 18 and 25.

22. *See* Fred M. Hechinger, "The Uses of Technology," *The New York Times,* 8 December, 1987.

23. As Professor Frederick Williams, founding dean of the Annenberg School of Communications at USC has stated: "Education, which is our most valuable strategy for preparing a new generation for change, is the last to adopt the technologies of change." Frederick Williams, *The Communications Revolution* (New York: New American Library, Signet reprint edition, 1983), 20.

CHAPTER 11

Marketing Tasks

Given the changes in the broader market environment discussed in Chapter 9 as well as the characteristics of the three major markets discussed in Chapter 10, publishers face new marketing challenges. This chapter considers five major marketing tasks facing Information Age publishers.

MARKET FOCUS

In a renowned 1960 piece in the *Harvard Business Review* entitled "Marketing Myopia," author and Harvard Business School marketing professor Ted Levitt drove home the point that businesses should shift their view of themselves from product to market orientation. The view has gained credence in the business world over the past three decades, thanks not only to Levitt, Peter Drucker, and other business theorists, but to thousands of successful market-oriented businesses. The Hollywood movie studios, for instance, initially saw television as a threat to the film business, and only after many painful years of attempting to resist the alleged incursion did they eventually join the business and exploit the new medium. By shifting their view from product (film) to market (viewer) orientation, they eliminated a threat and embraced an opportunity.

The publishing industry faces a similar definitional task in the Information Age. Publishers can continue to define themselves in terms of product—books, magazines, newspapers, print on paper products—or they can perceive their role as providers of ideas, information, and entertainment, regardless of the medium employed. In the emerging meta-industry known as the information industry, whose technological evolution has created opportunities for the embodiment of content in a myriad of print and electronic forms, the publisher's role is properly perceived as a provider of information and entertainment, a selector and packager of content, for specific markets:

Core Concept #30: Market Focus

The extent to which publishing firms are market- versus product-focused varies with the segment of the industry. A 1980 survey in *Publishers Weekly* found that most book publishers still viewed marketing as synonymous with selling, seeing it strictly as a post-product development activity.[1] It is arguable that book publishers, especially trade book publishers, have perhaps the least contact with their end customers of any segment of the media industry, and thus the fulfillment of customers' wants and needs is less explicitly pursued. But publishers in other segments, such as periodical publishers, advertising-supported media, and information service firms, must define their customer base and their needs in order to attract advertising revenue and to reach and service their customers. In marketing consultant Regis McKenna's phrase, they must "integrate the customer into the company," the reason that Market is one of the value-added M's of the publisher's mix: the customer is part of the product.

In the past decade, major publishing firms have made market focus the central tenet of their organizations, restructuring their operations into market-oriented groups. Paramount Communications regrouped its Simon & Schuster (now Paramount Publishing) subsidiary into consumer, educational, professional, and international groups, with over 100 operating units within these groups.[2] Perhaps the most thorough-going and highly publicized of the reorganizations has been McGraw-Hill's. In 1984 CEO Joseph Dionne announced a major reorganization, shuffling the company's divisions from product to market focus. McGraw-Hill's stated goal was to serve their customers' information needs in all forms by harnessing new information and communication technologies. Their entry into customized textbooks in the higher education market via the Primis system is an example of the market-focused strategy at work, harnessing technology to service expressed user needs. McGraw-Hill has invested considerable sums in the reorganization to date, and the effectiveness of the approach and its implementation will continue to be watched.[3]

Information and Media Technologies and Market Focus

The more publishers move toward information services the more value they add, as they have closer customer contact and can respond to user needs and preferences. The market focus and connectivity attributes of new technologies are pushing these services into personal and customized offerings, meeting the specific information needs of specific clients, just as lawyers offer legal services through in-person counseling and litigation, accountants offer financial and tax-related services, and doctors offer medical services.[4]

When the customer is linked to the publisher in a two-way interchange via networked information systems, another meaning of the fifth M, Market, as a value-added element, is revealed. As with subscribers to newspapers, magazines, and continuity book series, subscribers to online information and cable television services are "owned," an asset that can be identified, priced, and sold. They are part of the valuation of a media firm's total net worth. Reader's Digest, for instance, has a list of 50 million households throughout the United States and another 50 million around the world.[5]

With such "electronic publishing plus" systems, publishers must be increasingly concerned about what happens to their material *after* it reaches the reader-viewer-listener-user.[6] Changes in delivery technologies and new processing power at the user end mean that users can not only receive information but manipulate it and respond to the provider. Publishers often choose to play the role of information provider and let a third party handle the customer interface—e.g., a network operator or cable multiple system operator—but they can also add more value by integrating vertically to the customer. As the local phone operating companies and cable system operators know, customer contact is an invaluable and irreplaceable source of information, hence a source of market power. Some large content firms, such as Time Warner, are involved in owning and operating such systems.

As Stewart Brand has stated, publishers will increasingly "shift perspective from how information is sent to how it is sought." Brand proposes the term "broadcatch" to denote "content-specific selectivity and repackaging at the receiving end that computer technology is offering."[7] With the rise of end-user computing power, mass communications and interpersonal point-to-point technologies merge to provide instant conversations, breaking down the former one-way, one-to-many publishing definition. Moreover, the multiplication of channels of availability across all media provides increased market segmentation, a phenomenon found in almost all media. Except for certain shared events and those of broad social significance, segmentation leads to a decline of network power and mass audiences and the growth of niche publishing possibilities. Viewers return from shared public events to private lives.[8]

Still, as noted in Chapter 10, in consumer markets the possibility of mass markets—and there are actually many segments to the mass market—continue to make attractive prospects. The Olympics, for instance, provide programming that appeals to both genders, all ages, races, nationalities, and social strata. They run day after day for weeks at a time, holding viewer interest with new events and personalities every day. The entire spectacle then repeats itself in two years (the 1994 winter games in Lillehammer, Norway, will be the first games staged on the new two-year interval). To many advertisers this rare and unduplicated sustained viewing time is a tremendous buying opportunity. Viewing the opposite end of the market spectrum through the lens of cable television, NBC chose to supplement their regular network broadcast of the 1992 winter games in Albertville, France, with an experimental narrowcasting approach that provided three pay-per-view channels covering different events in depth. From a financial standpoint the venture was costly and reportedly unprofitable. But from the broader perspective of the user-defined, on-demand viewing paradigm within multimodal systems, the effort clearly points the way toward television's future.

Market-Focused Versus Market-Driven

The distinction between market-focused and market-driven is especially important to publishers. The distinction turns on the type of material provided by the publisher. Providers of information and the tools to manipulate it may pursue more market-driven approaches, while providers of knowledge, art, and entertainment may pursue more product-driven approaches. Scholarly publisher Irving Louis Horowitz speaks of

the new absorption by the publication world of a theory of information predicated on a doctrine of pure service to a market [which] in effect limits [publishers'] traditional role, abdicating the search for knowledge in favor of commercial criteria of success as measured by profitability or sheer longevity. . . . Instead of information being tested by its knowledge functions, knowledge is tested by its marketability, i.e., information functions, in part, the inevitable outcome of the computer revolution . . . [which] sets in motion a trust of data, i.e., information; and a declining use of knowledge, if not outright mistrust, of knowledge.

Horowitz terms this a dualistic warfare between the information industry and the knowledge industry, referring to a dual track "slow growth in scholarly publishing and fast growth in information."[9]

Knowledge publishers take a leadership role as they serve a purpose beyond that of meeting the explicit demands of the marketplace. In what we can term "leadership publishing," publishers lead the market, not follow, seeking out the newest and best statements of social or cultural value. The best trade book editors are market-aware in an in-built sense, participants in a conversation where both suppliers (publishers) and buyers (customers) talk *and* listen. Leadership publishers live with this uncomfortable dualism. On the one hand they can see the attractiveness of a purely market-driven approach, with the objective of maximizing revenues and profits. On the other hand they have a responsibility as mouthpieces of culture to publish statements of quality, innovation, and insight, to publish works of art. This often means putting money behind a product which may not have a proven market.

Customers often look to producers to innovate as they have the expertise and the means of production, the organization, and the mechanism for tapping innovation to fulfill the market's need for new ideas and expression. Think of fashion, food, cars, cosmetics—all are based on producer innovation, then customer reaction, choice, refinement, and new products. Thus to be market-focused does not necessarily mean simply to respond to stated customer needs. It means awareness of customers' values and interests and the creation of products which address those values and interests.

We must also make a distinction between wants and needs. Much of what passes for market-driven philosophy is in fact fulfilling an expressed market desire—i.e., a *want*—for a certain type of material. *Rocky IV* and *Scarlett* fall into this category. But while the creators of *Rocky IV* and *Scarlett* may have been fulfilling market wants, leadership publishers seek to fulfill market *needs*. Prior to its publication, the reading public did not know they "needed" Professor Allan Bloom's *The Closing of the American Mind,* for instance, nor did Simon & Schuster set about finding a writer to address the problems inherent in higher education in America today. But once the book was published and readers were attracted to it, then everyone "saw" the market for the first time, saw the expressed need that was, in retrospect, a latent need. Typically, once the customer base is proven, the market then forms around the concept, and other imitative suppliers rush in to fill the market-driven "need" which, by that point, is actually a want.

True innovation fills needs. Creative imitation fills wants. Leading into the market—true innovation—can make excellent business sense, as a firm can create a market where none previously existed. Being first in can also mean preemptive ownership of a niche. This is a large part of the excitement of leadership publishing, to publish the truly new and unexpected with little accurate foreknowledge of marketplace reception.

The commitment of resources to such unquantifiable ventures is at the core of leadership publishing. As risks and exposures are often high, such enterprises attract a certain type of individual willing to undertake such risks and live with the consequences of their investment decisions. The risk is reduced and the prospects of success heightened through constant market awareness and customer contact, the dialogue between producer and consumer that takes place not only through the buying and selling of products and services but through other channels as well.[10] This is where the efficiencies of a small company can pay off handsomely, focused in content, focused in market segment, for they are in tune with their customers. Similarly, the lesson for companies wishing to grow and diversify is to know customers' needs and values in the same fashion.

Inevitably the question of market research arises: how much can or should be done to reduce risk prior to development and launch of a given product? For general trade book publishers such research is especially difficult. The business is defined by thousands of new products every year, and the dollars and time expended would be impractical. Few of these products have known or identifiable markets, and there is typically no advertising or other third-party revenue to offset costs. End-users are expected to cover the entire outlay, hence the observation that for book publishers, market research is the first printing.

As Powell, Coser, and Kadushin observe, in book publishing "there are basically three approaches [to market research]: formal market research, informal (in-house, sales records, etc.), and intuition."[11] Each level is successively less rigorous, less quantitative, and more risky. Industry consultant Christopher Burns has stated that even in the more information-oriented firms, market research is not necessarily the key to success: "I think [publishers] should do market research. But the very successful publishers in all media have been the ones where there were one or two people at the top who intuitively understood the market."[12]

MANAGING THE PRODUCT LIFE CYCLE

Another reason to stay close to the customer is that the life cycles of many information products and services are severely shortened in the Information Age marketplace. Managing each product or service through its life cycle thus becomes another key marketing task:

Core Concept #31: Managing the Product Life Cycle

As with media technologies (*see* Chapter 8), the life cycle of an individual information product or service can be tracked through the stages of birth, growth, maturity, and decline or renewal. The investment of time, attention, dollars, and other resources at different stages of the product's life cycle have always been important, but planning and other management tasks are even more critical for Information Age publishers as the typical life cycle is severely shortened, and managerial decision times along with them. There are many causes for the shortened cycles, among them the crush of products in the mediated environment vying for buyer's attention. This means retailers must clear space for new products, forcing them to make quick decisions on non-performers. The increased penetration of information technology in the wholesale and retail distribution channels have also provided instant and accurate product performance data to support such decisions. In response to this pressure, publishers are increasingly forced to allocate heavier resources at the time of product introduction to ensure quicker customer awareness and response. Word-of-mouth marketing, a book publisher's oldest and most effective marketing tool, is often not enough in such hastened times.

The daily flood of information also means a higher level of information saturation. Yesterday's news fades quickly to make way for today's. Value is ascribed to information based on its currency, making it difficult for list publishers to sustain interest in any given topic or trend. Windows of opportunity are shut as public attitudes and interests shift with dramatic and unforgiving swiftness.

Publishers can counter such effects in different ways. One strategy is to collapse to-market times by foreshortening the product development period. This can be risky, however, perhaps even damaging the product which requires a lengthier gestation period for proper research and development. Another strategy is market research, to pinpoint buyers' interests and tastes. Another is to publish content less tied to the rapid cycles of periodical information, seeking properties of more durable interest. Another is to harness the power of distributed processing in online systems such as McGraw-Hill's Primis, creating an on-demand publishing mechanism, which one could also call "pay-per-view text," to supplement the initial, physical distribution of multiple identical texts. However, by definition, publishers must present material of interest, in whatever form, and judging the market's interests, tastes, and needs will always remain as much a part of the publisher's art as the publisher's science. The key lies in the appropriate deployment of resources for each property at any given point in its life cycle (we will address this further in our discussion of the intellectual property management program in Chapter 14).

BUILDING AND EXTENDING BRANDS AND IMPRINTS

A third key marketing task for Information Age publishers in a crowded media environment is to create and leverage brand and corporate identities:

Core Concept #32: Building and Extending Brands and Imprints

Publishers and media firms are gatekeepers, interpreters, known names and reliable sources, especially important in a world plagued with information overload. We cling to the familiar—*Reader's Digest, National Geographic, The New York Times,* Walt Disney. These imprimaturs are guides and friends, as familiar and trusted elements of our man-made environment as Coke and Kleenex. Because of the goodwill and credibility built around these names, publishers can extend them into other media in their respective areas of content expertise.

The power of legitimation through imprints and labels is undeniable. The handbill passer on the corner cannot compete with the daily paper, though his message may be equally vital or even better expressed. The publishing apparatus has grown up specifically because media users seek validation of statements, an ascribed social function which sifts, sorts, and delivers statements of value. A gatekeeper's stamp of approval organizes the market for information and ideas and serves a vital, asked-for function in the total realm of messages.

Thus for publishers it is often more important to own a customer base and a recognized imprint than a technology base. *National Geographic* successfully extended their imprint from magazines to television and video; *The New York*

Times from newsprint to online; Microsoft from software to print (Microsoft Press); Turner Broadcasting from broadcasting and cable to book publishing.

In the newer machine-readable media, where non-browsable audio, video, and software products cannot easily be perceived by potential buyers, imprints are also of importance. Like magazines, publishers of such products often must sell themselves in advance of selling the actual material. Perceived value is part of the total product sell that differentiates each publisher from the next. The prospective buyer must be assured of the product's value, for in the absence of other information, he can only base a purchase decision on the provider's reputation.

Imprint and brand extension can exist at both the corporate and product level. Even if copyrights in underlying works expire, derivative products, product line extensions, or other new products developed under the same corporate umbrella or registered trademarks can continue to yield value. Perhaps the premiere example of this phenomenon is the management of the Disney name, library of films, cartoons, and characters. Introduced by creator-animator Walt Disney in the 1920s—Mickey Mouse was Steamboat Willie in the original 1928 cartoon—the Disney name and cast of characters was reintroduced for the postwar baby boomers in the 1950s and 1960s. Television, via the weekly *Mickey Mouse Club* show, was an effective blanket medium for mass awareness as well as an ideal vehicle for displaying the Disney library of existing and new material. Disney films, cartoons, and characters have now been revived for an entirely new generation of viewers, baby boomers' children, whose parents revisit their own childhood memories while introducing their children to the material. New characters and material, such as the films *The Little Mermaid, Beauty and the Beast,* and *Aladdin,* have been introduced, spawning entirely new multimedia domains for exploitation. Disney content has been repackaged to appear not just in movie theaters and broadcast television but on a dedicated pay cable channel, on videocassette, in audio cassettes, and in myriad non-information merchandise forms, as media technologies have continued to evolve. Moreover, Disney creatures do not just live as intangible creatures in the minds of their fans. They are alive at Disneyland and Disney World, the world's largest theme parks, at another park in Japan, and at EuroDisney outside Paris. Thus the Disney name and magic, in the hands of able custodians, has been successfully extended across both space and time, creating a multi-billion dollar response to the question, "What's in a name?"

Extending imprints into the merchandising of non-information products is virtually limitless. Hybrid information products exist, such as Talking Big Bird with a cassette inside. A single feature film such as *Batman,* itself based on a comic book character, spawned an orchestrated mini-industry of dolls, guns, toys, uniforms, and other paraphernalia upon its release. *USA Today* extended its name into a line of clothing, "designed in accordance with the newspaper's upbeat, colorful, graphic style."[13] But depending on the underlying property driving the merchandising, product life cycles can either be long and luxuriant or brutally short. Peter Rabbit is perennial, while the *Batman* blitz soon gave way to *Dick Tracy* and the next Hollywood comic strip character super-promotion. (However, the successful release of *Batman Returns* created an echo effect which rejuvenated the life of the property.)

Another manner in which firms can extend brands and imprints is through visual means, especially via logos, company trademarks, colophons, typefaces, symbols, trade dress (the overall look and positioning of design elements on a given product's packaging), and other pictorial and graphic elements. The importance of such imagery cannot be overstated. The goodwill issuing from visual elements can have a direct and far-reaching impact on company morale and performance, for they are intimately connected with the organization's identity, both in the marketplace and within the organization. One need only consider the emotional response evoked by an image of Mickey Mouse—or even a set of mouse ears—to recognize the effect. Subliminal forces are at work. The distinctive yellow border of the *National Geographic* magazine cover has come to suggest stability and a known and expected level of quality, hence comfort and reassurance that the product is reliable and meets certain standards of editorial, design, and production quality. Publishers and media firms are custodians of such symbols and imagery, and their maintenance is of great value to their caretakers.[14]

INNOVATIVE MARKETING

In our discussion of the other four value-added M's, we have noted the erosion of some of the publisher's role and power. This is true to a certain extent in marketing, as well, where network connectivity can provide direct customer contact for individual content creators. But publishing and media firms still have the market access and the power to publicize and reach customers. If they do it well enough, marketing can provide a differential advantage versus other publishers in the competition for content experts, authors, and other information providers:

Core Concept #33: Innovative Marketing

In a crowded media environment, Information Age publishers seek value everywhere: in a series name; in authors' names, reputations, and promotability; in content; in imprints; in package design; in media format attributes. They seek it beyond the 5M's, too, in the goodwill of the company name, in the serendipity of events, in the timing of release (hot, topical, seasonal, anniversary), in titles, in cross-media awareness and resonance. Advertising executives speak of "mindshare," doing whatever is possible to pre-sell products, searching for the key selling factor, something that will stick in the mind of the prospective buyer. The two infrastructure M's of Management and Money can also provide value and differential advantage. The right marketing executive can mean success, not failure, for a new product line, and access to funding and pricing and credit policies can offer advantages to customers and over competitors.

As noted above, the crowded media environment often means increased marketing spending to obtain customer awareness of the product. Film studios routinely spend millions of dollars at the time of a feature film's theatrical release to ensure broad public exposure. The awareness persists through the time of the film's release on cassette and in cable and other after markets. Film companies exploit not only print media—primarily newspapers because of their broad local reach and graphic display capabilities—but television as well to give viewers a "sneak preview" or glimpse of the actual product, the equivalent of a test drive. Book campaigns typically focus on print media with reviews and advertising in newspaper and magazines—again, allowing potential buyers to "test drive"—as well as publicity via radio and television talk show spots for touring authors. Staying within the same mode can be critical. Book publishers can employ online services as a reviewing and publicity medium to provide sneak previews of their upcoming products. Other innovative marketing communications for book publishers include television advertising (network, cable, local) and outdoor advertising (bus, subway, billboard, or other outdoor media).

Publishers can also innovate through marketing techniques. Automation allows direct marketers to create databased information profiles of actual or prospective customers. Magazine and catalog subscription lists are among the most desirable of direct marketing tools, for they provide an accessible group of potential buyers about whom interest areas, location, purchase tendencies, income and spending levels, and a variety of other criteria are known. Direct marketing techniques are more easily implemented by some publishers than others. Magazine publishers, for instance, with their subscription lists, can target markets more easily than book publishers, for whom virtually every book is a new product with a new market. Thus for book publishers, strategies which provide direct customer contact—e.g., direct mail, direct response advertising, bounce back inserts for mailing lists, newsletters for series buyers—will help identify customers for future direct marketing efforts.

Information Age publishers are also aware that different media formats require different marketing approaches. New and unfamiliar media require new marketing techniques as product awareness is not enough. As noted above in Chapter 8, new-to-the-world products typically suggest a more complicated purchase sequence, thus more effort and imagination required in the selling. Marketers must innovate to get intangible, machine-readable information products into users' heads before they can get them into users' hands. Prospective customers can buy and eat a new breakfast cereal as the entry ticket is cheap. They can test-drive a car, feel a table, sit in a chair, try on a shirt. As noted above, publishers of video and software must provide similar opportunities for customers to sample the product. Applications software, for instance, is a high involvement product, not a simple impulse buy. Software publishers are selling an environment that in many cases is entered and lived in every day by the customer. It is more akin to selling a house in a neighborhood than a read-it-once paperback book or a 2-hour movie experience. Customers are aware that switching costs are high after they are locked in to a given application. They need information on products and how they work and not only need to see them demonstrated but need to use them before purchasing. A free tutorial and demonstration disk, for instance, with print support materials and a toll-free number, would greatly aid a purchase decision.

Moreover in newer electronic media it may not be clear that primary demand has been established for a given device. Thus publishers may have a two-tiered sell: generic demand for the medium and a sell for the specific content product. The best products break through both and are intuitive purchases by the customer. The purchase adds up instantly in the buyer's mind. Software sells the hardware.

CROSS-MEDIA/CROSS-MEANS SYNERGIES

Another marketing task in a crowded media environment is the exploitation of product and service synergies across media and across means:

Core Concept #34: Cross-Media/Cross-Means Synergies

In Chapter 7 we introduced the idea of cross-media interaction (*see* Core Concept #17) in the discussion of multimodal publishing. Product development and marketing work in tandem to exploit these synergies. Among aural media, for instance, the synergistic fit between radio and records, tapes, and discs, is well established. The broadcast medium provides the broad exposure and awareness that leads buyers to purchase the published product. Similarly, producers of television and video programming use broadcasting and cablecasting to gain program exposure which leads to videocassette and disc purchases. This can be true in the consumer and educational markets—Ken Burns' *The Civil War*—as well as the business market—Nathan and Tyler's *In Search of Excellence.* The online book review and excerpting referred to above is another example of cross-means synergy, "broadcasting" text excerpts to whet the customer's appetite for the purchase.

While cross-means synergies exist within a given mode, cross-media synergies also exist. Certain synergies are established and known among existing formats. The same book publishers seeking review coverage in textual media will also pursue opportunities in open channel visual media (*The Today Show, Bookmark*) and aural media (radio talk shows) for market awareness. Movies can sell books, too, as can software, albeit for different reasons. With new formats emerging, new synergies will be sought and found by innovative marketers in publishing and media firms.

SUMMARY AND CONCLUSION

In this chapter we have introduced five more core concepts for Market, the fifth value-added M, each of which defines an important task for Information Age publishers:

- *Core Concept #30: Market Focus*
- *Core Concept #31: Managing the Product Life Cycle*
- *Core Concept #32: Building and Extending Brands and Imprints*
- *Core Concept #33: Innovative Marketing*
- *Core Concept #34: Cross-Media/Cross-Means Synergies*

Publishing and media firms will continue to adopt market-focused strategies for a number of reasons. New information and media technologies provide connectivity with customers and offer new opportunities for market segmentation and contact. The multiplicity of new media formats and channels of distribution also mean changing user information habits, hence the need for publishers' awareness of those habits in order to appropriately serve customers' information needs. While many firms in the information industry are market-driven, market-focused leadership publishers will continue to fulfill their broader cultural role in the provision of new knowledge, artistic expression, and other types of material. The increased speed of product life cycles puts additional pressure on marketing managers to make fast decisions and commit resources on tighter schedules. Information Age publishers also build new imprints and extend established brand, product, and corporate names into new media as part of their marketing strategies. Other innovative marketing techniques are employed to differentiate products and services in a crowded media environment, with different approaches required for different media formats. In marketing their products and services, Information Age publishers also seek to exploit synergies across the means of distribution as well as across media formats.

NOTES

1. *See* Michael Wendroff, "Should We Do the Book?," *Publishers Weekly,* 15 August 1980, 30: "According to the survey results, publishers define marketing simply as selling. This narrow definition was supplied by 72% of all respondents and 82% of all respondents for the large house sub-group, although it was abandoned decades ago by companies in other fields which have now become proficient marketers using a defi-

nition that stresses the discerning and satisfying of customer needs and makes *selling* [my emphasis] the product the final step in a long, well-thought out process."

2. *See* Edwin McDowell, "Is Simon & Schuster Mellowing?" *The New York Times,* 28 October, 1990, and company annual reports.

3. From the company's 1984 Annual Report:

McGraw-Hill's historic shift in 1984 from product to market orientation comes as major developments in the information industry itself—the rapid changes in computer and communications technology and in the new ways in which customers obtain information—dictate bold moves to help ensure the corporation's reaching its goals of market power and increased profits. . . . With market-centered operations, each of McGraw-Hill's strategic units becomes a multimedia information provider, capable of serving customers by whatever medium best suits their needs—by print in magazines, newsletters, books, and loose-leaf files or electronically through software and interactive and broadcast communications facilities.

For a dissenting opinion on the McGraw-Hill reorganization, *see* Suzanne L. Oliver, "Management By Concept," *Forbes,* 26 November, 1990, 37.

4. In H.P. Gassman's depiction of the information industry, the Knowledge Industry is one of three major sectors, comprised of mass communications (advertising, broadcasting, newspapers, publishing), education and market research, and professional service occupations (lawyers, accountants, etc.). As cited in *Intellectual Property Rights in an Age of Electronics and Information,* prepared by the U.S. Office of Technology Assessment, PB87-10031 (Washington, D.C.: U.S. Department of Commerce, National Technical Information Service, April 1986), 10.

5. *See* Dierdre Carmody, "Reader's Digest Looks Beyond Itself," *The New York Times,* 28 January, 1991, D1.

6. In his preface to the book *Electronic Publishing Plus,* Martin Greenberger states: "The term 'publishing' is too narrow in context to convey the full meaning of what is taking place. Therefore, throughout this book the name we use is *electronic publishing plus* (with thanks to Richard Hooper). It includes not only the operations familiar to traditional publishing and broadcasting, but also the software, transactions and communications functions sprouting up throughout the new industry. We suspect the 'plus' may be the tail that wags the dog in future developments." *Electronic Publishing Plus* (White Plains, N.Y.: Knowledge Industry Publications, 1985), xiii–xiv.

7. Stewart Brand, *The Media Lab: Inventing the Future at MIT* (New York: Viking Penguin, 1987), 42–43.

8. As Irving Horowitz has stated it: "The act of making public has been closely identified with the process of marketing. One must surmise that in the new information technology environment marketing activities will both increase and become more focused and segmented." Horowitz, *Communicating Ideas: The Crisis of Publishing in a Post-Industrial Society* (New York: Oxford University Press, 1986), 19.

9. Horowitz, *Communicating Ideas,* 89–90 and 96. As publishing analyst Walter Powell has observed, "Cultural industries can be classified as either distributor- or producer-oriented. Publishing is unusual precisely because it nurtures both kinds of enterprises simultaneously (sometimes in a single house)." Walter Powell, "The Good Books Business," *The New Republic,* 15 and 22 September, 1988, 35.

10. Industry analyst Efrem Sigel has stated:

How, short of the most wasteful process of trial and error, do publishers divine what their readers desire? . . . The long answer is that in an information-rich society like the United States, or in other industrialized countries, readers communicate their wants in all sorts of ways—by professional concerns, by the movies and television programs they watch, by the plays and concerts they attend, by the records they buy, by the sports teams they root for, by the athletic and leisure activities they engage in. If publishing is to succeed it must be a mirror of society's activities, hobbies, business and professional pursuits, intellectual endeavors and political concerns. Not that there can be one such mirror, or more precisely, not that such a mirror can be without many facets. But the more diversity exists in the activities and interests of a society, the more diversity must exist in its publications—in all forms, print (newspapers, magazines, books) as well as audiovisual or electronic.

Efrem Sigel, "The Future of the Book," in *Books, Libraries, and Electronics* (White Plains, N.Y.: Knowledge Industry Publications, 1982), 20–21.

11. Walter Powell, Lewis Coser, and Charles Kadushin, *Books: The Culture and Commerce of Publishing* (New York: Basic Books, 1982), 142. Publishers do employ other pre-publication risk reduction measures, such as manuscript evaluation by expert readers for non-fiction and professional works.

12. Christopher Burns, unpublished interview, 27 March, 1987.

13. *See* "USA Today Ready to Wear," *The New York Times,* 11 December, 1990.

14. For an extended treatment of this topic, *see* Wally Olin's *Corporate Identity: Making Business Strategy Visible Through Design* (Cambridge, Mass.: Harvard Business School Press, 1990).

PART V

Management and Money

Having addressed the five value-added components of the information construct in Parts II, III, and IV, we now address the final two M's, the two essential infrastructural elements of the publishing enterprise, *Management* and *Money*. We will consider the requisite traits for publishing management in the Information Age before considering the question of maximizing return on investment, which we will consider from both the corporate and product level perspectives.

CHAPTER 12

Strategic Vision and Integrative Management

Management, the first of the two infrastructure M's, conceives of and determines how the organization will engage in its affairs. This chapter highlights six key management principles for Information Age publishers.

LEADERSHIP, VISION, AND ORGANIZATIONAL PURPOSE

In the past few years, there has been much attention paid in both the general and business press to the subject of leadership. Throughout his presidency, George Bush was hounded by "the vision thing," his seeming inability to articulate a bigger picture and a plan for the country's future. Meanwhile the United States' declining industrial performance, especially vis-à-vis the Japanese, has led many to question our system of management, asking "where are our leaders leading us?" USC management professor Warren Bennis has speculated on the lack of clearly articulated direction in American business:

In the current climate, vision is a fragile thing and needs to be nourished and developed in executives as well as employees and co-workers. . . . It isn't easy, of course, or without risks, which is why too many executives prefer to deal with simple, day-to-day problems and settle for small wins, rather than trying to deal with the overarching problems. But, as I see it, one of the greatest threats to American business, perhaps the ultimate threat, is its narrowing of horizons, its tendency to restrict its vision to devote its principal energies to just hanging in there, denying the sense of wide-ranging possibility, of entire worlds to conquer, that used to animate American business and made it one of the wonders of the world.[1]

Bennis' notion of "wide-ranging possibility" is particularly true in those industries undergoing change, because change brings opportunity. As addressed throughout this study, the information industry is undergoing fundamental changes, changes which management must not only respond to but participate in. In other words, leaders must lead, not follow, in an environment in which new and unknown territory is more the rule than the exception. A vision of the environment in which the firm operates is the critical first step:

Core Concept #35: Strategic Vision

Former MIT President Jerome Wiesner has stated that "Leadership is a mysterious talent, an amalgam of vision, energy, understanding of institutional goals and purposes, knowledge of the substance of the basic work involved, and a genuine concern for human beings."[2] Strategic vision, then, to be of value, must articulate not only leadership's view of the environment but the organization's role within it, i.e., the organization's mission.

A clearly articulated mission statement focuses and motivates individuals throughout the organization. To be meaningful and effective, however, it must translate into a strategy, or like a rudderless ship, the business may stay afloat but go nowhere, drifting with the tides. The strategy, in turn, is translated into action plans and procedures at the operating level. Then the firm as a whole, and divisions, departments, and individuals, can proceed step-by-step toward objectives and goals within that mission:

Vision—of the environment

Mission—of the organization within the environment

Strategy—to fulfill the mission

Plan—to implement the strategy

A strong mission statement, then, within the context of leadership's vision of the firm's environment, makes organizational purpose explicit. It lets the world—the firm's customers, suppliers, employees, and any who come in contact with the business—know what the business is about and where it is headed. A clear mission statement also guides the firm's strategic business decisions, issues of merger with or acquisition of other businesses, divestitures or spin-outs of current businesses, and appropriateness of joint venture and alliance partners. A firm's strategy to fulfill its mission takes into account the circumstances of the firm, both its industry environment and its resources.

As part of the meta-industry known as the information industry, Information Age publishers operate with an expanded worldview. They are aware not only of their own firm's strengths and weaknesses, but of blurring industry boundaries and new and unknown competitors. They are aware that young entrepreneurial firms, for example, devoted to a new media technology, will not have a vested interest in established methods and formats and can often move more quickly and decisively than the larger, established firms with vested interests—witness Microsoft's purchase of a share of UK-based reference publisher Dorling Kindersley. They are aware that some hardware firms, their counterpart organizations in the information industry that create the machines on which and the conduits through which content flows, also see themselves in the content business, and will also pay to play the game—witness Sony's acquisition of CBS Records and Columbia Pictures and Matsushita's purchase of MCA.

Even with a framework of understanding, change will always outstrip management's ability to accurately predict the shape of things to come. This constant change reinforces the need for a technology-neutral view of the business. Media executives must ask: what do we provide for our customers? Is it books, films, records, software? Or is it ideas, information, entertainment? Viewed in this fashion, technology is a tool in the service of the publisher's mission: to serve customers by entertaining, inspiring, informing, educating. Information Age publishers cultivate this broad vision throughout their organizations and articulate organizational purpose within this vision. Further, they define a strategy for the future that is based upon this vision and this purpose, a strategy that is itself dynamic in response to a changing environment.

PLANNING

If mission articulates organizational purpose, then the strategic plan states how the firm will accomplish that mission. As with any plan, it is a tool which serves as a bridge from intuition to action and provides a focus for daily efforts.

In large, multidivisional firms, there are three planning levels: the strategic plan at the company level; the business plan at the business unit level; and product and marketing plans at the product level. The three levels are integrated, with product and marketing plans providing implementation plans for the business unit plans, which in turn correlate with the organization's strategic plan. In addition to being integrated vertically, the plans are also linked horizontally across business units to provide for maximum corporate productivity and return by harnessing organization-wide resources in fulfillment of organizational purpose. Hence, the next core concept:

Core Concept #36: Integrated Planning

The strategic plan merges the outward and the inward. Starting with an analysis of the firm's operating environment, including the economic, technological, social, political, regulatory, and other environments in which the firm operates, managers create a set of assumptions about external factors that form the context for operating decisions. The operational aspect of the plan, flowing upward from the business unit level, details what businesses the firm will engage in, how it will pursue its business, and what its operating and financial objectives are.

It is incumbent upon managers to decide where the business is heading before they can decide how to get there. Where do they want the business to be in five years, ten years, fifteen years, and what steps must they take today to get there? John Sculley refers to such long-term planning as "back-to-the-future" planning: "It is particularly appropriate for firms in high technology fields such as the information industry, where time is compressed [and] the sustainable advantages don't last as long. . . . Planning," says Sculley, "becomes a flexible, sometimes intuitive process of navigation rather than a tight set of procedures based on trends and projections."[3]

The business unit plan is set within the context of the company's strategic plan and focuses more specifically on the demands of the near term, creating operational plans for product development and marketing. In addition to individual business unit plans, in an integrated planning process, as noted above, divisions and groups think cross-divisionally, as well, specifically incorporating into their plans how the divisions will work with other units in the firm. Harvard's Michael Porter speaks of the need for such planning to maximize the firm's resources and competitive advantage, emphasizing that such strategy is a corporate as well as a business unit responsibility.[4] As it is different from that of divisional managers, the perspective of the organization's senior management is critical. For if the horizontal strategies are to be effectively implemented, they must be given strong support from above, with incentives for and emphasis upon the consolidated bottom line in addition to individual business unit performance.

At the product level, the plan is the tool which reconciles the creative impulse with organizational demands. It satisfies the left-brained demands of the organization for analysis of the information which will dictate the size and scope of the envisioned project and how it will be managed, attempting to quantify it through such aspects as return on investment, market size, and projected costs. These are necessary steps to go through in validating the feasibility and attractiveness of the concept to others who will ultimately be involved, in one fashion or another, in its funding, development, and implementation.

In many creative organizations, planning is anathema. Oft-cited reasons for not creating a plan include not only the stultification of the creative impulse but reluctance to get locked into—or measured against—stated goals or rigid operational procedures or the desire to move quickly and not spend time at the drawing board. Sometimes it is a genuine lack of procedural knowledge or training that inhibits managers from developing a plan. Other managers claim that after years of experience they operate well enough on instinct and an intuitive understanding of industry and market conditions.

But all of these reasons are outweighed by the benefits of a good plan, especially for large, multi-divisional organizations and those venturing into new territory, where managerial instinct, while always valuable, is usually not enough. Moreover, the competitive environment in which most media firms operate requires planning, not only because of changing conditions but because a firm that does not plan will be at a competitive disadvantage. Marshalling and managing the range of resources required for operations simply requires foresight, structure, and specified processes or the business cannot operate effectively enough to achieve its aims.

While a complete absence of planning would certainly be detrimental to effective firm operations, an over-emphasis on planning is also dangerous. Conditions change too quickly in the environment, and technological development and market behaviors are not always predictable. A good plan and a good planning system are thus flexible and take account of these variables. Moreover, good firms recognize that severe organizational constraints will indeed stifle the creativity essential to the enterprise's products and services and will take measures to create conditions whereby creative impulses are not burdened or constrained. Indeed, the best managers know that planning is a process; that it is dynamic, not static; that it is an outlook, an approach, a mentality, suffused throughout the organization. Good planning is dynamic in response to changes in the environment. As conditions change, plans change.

INTEGRATIVE MANAGEMENT

While leadership molds the vision and states the mission, management creates the strategy and the plan for its implementation.

Both the firm's leadership and its senior operating management must track the trends in a changing publishing environment and make appropriate responses. In the evolving information industry, this means coordinating an increasing variety of resources across a range of markets, media, technologies, and functional disciplines. Paramount Publishing's Richard Snyder typifies those publishing executives who have not only witnessed but played a role in the vast changes in the publishing industry. Having cut his teeth on trade book sales, Snyder is now president of Paramount Communications' publishing operations, a billion and a half dollar publishing and information group which has operations in all major media in all major markets. If his market focus and understanding were limited to the trade book field and his functional focus and understanding limited to sales, he would not be where he is today.[5] The need for management that can operate effectively across industry, technology, and market boundaries, integrating the resources of the organization for effective operation, is the next core concept:

Core Concept #37: Integrative Management

Among senior management's critical tasks is to put in place the organizational infrastructure that will allow the firm to fulfill its mission. This means investments in personnel, management, systems and procedures, training, and technology. Continuing professional education, for example, is an investment in the firm's most critical resource—its people—in an industry undergoing constant technological change.[6]

Also at the top of integrative management's agenda is the integration of the organization's parts. Although a firm must organize its operations vertically to fulfill the development, production, and marketing of its products and services, the component pieces of the organization must also work together in order to achieve the greatest possible benefit from the firm's combined resources. As Harvard Business School's Kenneth Andrews has stated: "The ability to handle the coordinating function in a way that brings about a new synthesis among competing interests, a synthesis in harmony with the special competence of the organization, is the administrator's most subtle and creative contribution to the successful functioning of an organization"[7] (*see* Core Concept #44, The Horizontal Organization).

Publishing is a world in change, and the changes require organizations that are structured to handle complexity and require management that can manage it. Different media technologies attract different types of people: computer hackers and software programmers, video and audio producers, the literary set. Management must integrate wordsmiths and number crunchers and create conditions where they can talk to—and understand—each other.

Thus integrative managers are bridge builders, connectors between merging cultures. They are ambassadors, diplomats who know the various worlds and can communicate effectively within and among them. In order to do so they must have a good understanding of these worlds and be able to effectively persuade and communicate across camps during this turbulent transitional period.

Integrative management is also the link between the firm's executive leadership and its product-level operations. It integrates the organization by forming the one-two punch with product champions (*see* Core Concept #38), serving as the champion placed high enough in the organization to ensure that the right projects and initiatives receive proper funding, senior management commitment, and support from other parts of the organization.

Where do such managers come from and who is training or developing the integrative management of tomorrow? We can expect that some blend of in-house, on-the-job training and formal education will be components. Experience and training across functional disciplines, for example, finance, marketing, product development, as well as industry segments—book, video, software—will be required, as will experience in different market settings, domestic and international. The issue of succession of senior management is also critical to a firm's long-term success, and the intentional rotation of potential senior executives through different management experiences in different segments of the organization is essential.

Evidencing the need for integrative management in publishing organizations was the creation in the last couple of years of new positions in technology and new media at several major print-based firms, including Random House, Putnam Berkley, HarperCollins, Paramount Publishing, and Penguin USA.

PRODUCT CHAMPIONS

The very best products—in any industry—have an individual with a vision, and that vision is transmitted through his or her enthusiasm to others. The vision may be refined over time, but the individual still carries the torch. Later, as the project is defined, business strategies are developed. But in essence each new product is a leap of faith. Someone has to champion it within the organization in order for it to succeed. That person is the product champion. In publishing it is the property developer, the creative product manager, who orchestrates the development and marketing of a given intellectual property:

Core Concept #38: Product Champions

The product champion works with the executive sponsor, with knowledge experts and creative teams, with designers, producers, and developers, and with marketers, both inside and outside the organization, for development, marketing, and licensing of a given property in its various media forms. It is senior management's task to identify, hire, and nurture these product champions, providing them the necessary top echelon support for product development. Gilbert Maurer, president of Hearst Magazines, has said "You have to create a structure in which idiosyncratic people can flourish. It is hard to institutionalize creativity."[8] John Sculley called Apple's product champions "impresarios" and explained their unique requirements as creative product managers: "Management and creativity might even be considered antithetical states. While management demands consensus, control, certainty, and the status quo, creativity thrives on the opposite: instinct, uncertainty, freedom, and iconoclasm. . . . To nurture the creative impulse of any organization there needs to be some reconciliation of the two states."[9]

In order to attract and retain skilled product champions, senior management seeks ways to provide incentives for them, some of which may be financial, such as participation in product returns, and others of which may relate to work conditions or other forms of reward. They will often seek performance-based rewards to motivate them.

RESOURCE MATCHING

Management also integrates the 5M's of the publishing process, matching the appropriate resources for a given product or service both inside and outside the organization:

Core Concept #39: Resource Matching

Every firm, by dint of its history and current make-up, will be strong in some areas and weak in others. Firms must seek those elements they don't have. The necessary first step, then, is to heed Aristotle's advice to "know thyself." By knowing their own strengths and weaknesses, and what resources they need to accomplish their objectives, firms will be better able to seek those resources that complement their own and aid in achieving their goals.

Firms can define their core expertise in terms of the five value-added M's, either singly or in combination with each other. Some firms are focused on a certain type of material, such as entertainment, regional information, business or medical information, or information for a specific age group (e.g., children). Most media firms are skilled in at least one mode. Television broadcasters, for instance, are adept at the manipulation of moving images and sound, newspaper publishers at text and still images. Medium—books, CD-ROM, software—is another element defining the firm's core expertise, and therefore by exclusion what resources it requires to venture into a new area. Means, too, define the firm—a periodical publisher, an online service, a broadcaster. The market perspective, too, is critical: "We are a consumer publisher but require an entree into the education and business markets."

Many of the resources required are managed outside the company. This is as true with new publishing media, where specialized technical skills are required for product development and/or distribution, as with existing media, where industry patterns of resource matching are well established. Publishers will continue to seek alliances and cooperative efforts with knowledge experts, modal processors, technology experts, manufacturers, distributors, and others, for these parties have skills and resources which complement their own. Such alliances will increase as many large, diversified firms will choose not to house all expertise and functions internally, both to lower overhead and provide greater flexibility across the 5M's.

For Information Age publishers, resource decisions are increasingly made not just within media but across media, as well, as content developed for one format can be converted and sold in another. Market access, for instance, is an issue for those firms seeking distribution of their products and services beyond their primary channels and territories of distribution. Thus in addition to make or buy decisions requiring inputs (material, medium) into the final product, Information Age publishers are also increasingly facing make or sell decisions—do we license the material to a third party developer or publisher, or do we develop and market it ourselves? These decisions can only be properly made with an understanding of the firm's own resources and within the context of the firm's organizational strategy.

Two recent examples of resource matching to take advantage of new media opportunities are the Microsoft-Dorling Kindersley alliance and the Scholastic-WGBH partnership. Since 1991 Microsoft has been working with U.K.-

based reference publisher Dorling Kindersley to develop interactive multimedia programs based on Dorling's content. The first product release from the collaboration was the late 1992 release of *Microsoft Musical Instruments* for the consumer market, based on a Dorling Kindersley title from their Eyewitness book series. The Scholastic-WGBH arrangement marries the former's content and educational marketplace presence with the latter's video content and multimedia skills. The initial *Interactive Nova* science products (which, incidentally, were developed with the help of a third partner, Apple Computer) were supplemented by a social studies program as well as a multimedia version of the *Bank Street Writer* word processing program. Part of the appeal for Scholastic of partnering with WGBH is the reduction in video content costs. WGBH is also partnering with Optical Data Corporation, the producers of the laserdisc-based *Windows on Science* program adopted in Texas, for additional videodisc and interactive multimedia titles for schools.[10]

TECHNOLOGY MANAGEMENT

For all firms in all industries, the management of information technology throughout the organization is critical for success:

Core Concept #40: Technology Management

For Harvard's Michael Porter, technology management, or "technology development" as he calls it, is part of both product processes (the 5M's) and support activities (the 2M's): "Technology development may support any of the numerous technologies embodied in value activities, including such areas as telecommunications technologies for the order entry system, or office automation for the accounting department. . . . Technology development that is related to the product and its features supports the entire [value] chain, while other technology development is associated with particular primary or support activities."[11]

For Information Age publishers, product technology is to be managed like any other resource. Companies must harness it and wield it profitably. At the core of this is the digital library (*see* Core Concept #6), the digital embodiment of the publisher's material for maximum product development opportunities in a variety of print and electronic formats. While senior management need not be technically trained, at a minimum they must be technologically aware and have the necessary technical expertise on staff. For product development, this can prove to be a delicate balancing act: providing a nurturant creative environment blended with technical proficiency that still remains cognizant of and responsive to marketplace needs.

Product technology also stirs up the pot, presenting boundary-crossing management challenges. Who at the magazine talks to the video producers about product development? Who at the book publisher talks to the audio producers or software developers? Only technology-aware management can successfully manage these critical intersections.[12]

As stated throughout this study, value can be sought and gained in all aspects of the organization's operations, and information technology in the infrastructure is no exception. Effectively implemented information technology is essential for cost control. Publishers' profit margins are typically eroded by heavy overhead, and smart firms seek all possible ways to keep overhead low without damaging the capabilities of the organization. In more and more areas, publishers can automate to cut overhead and boost productivity. Book publishers, for example, can reap multiple benefits from installing electronic contract processing and royalty reporting systems for authorized multi-point access throughout the house, so that authorized users, from editorial to royalty accounting to subsidiary rights, can call up on screen, in their offices, in multiple fields, up-to-date royalty, property rights, and other contract-based information. Groupware applications providing imaging and workflow management also offer great potential.

The best firms are able to turn information technology—indeed, the application of any technology—into a competitive advantage, not just a cost-saving, productivity-enhancing tool. Investment in the proper technology and applications can boost revenues, improve workflow, and allow firms to out-maneuver the competition through better views of their own business and of industry opportunities. If, for example, a content firm creates a comprehensive rights database that yields multilateral views of its information assets as embodied in its intellectual property contracts, it will enable full deployment of those assets for maximum return, in acquisition decisions, licensing negotiations, the assessment of derivative publishing opportunities, and other areas. Firms can also use information technology in the infrastructure to knit the organization together cross-divisionally, both for revenue-enhancing opportunities and operating efficiencies.

In the past two to three years, a number of major print-based firms have recognized the centrality of technology management to the firms' futures and have put in place a senior technology officer or, in at least one case, an entire division, to address technology issues. These firms include, among others, Paramount Publishing, which created the Paramount Technology Group for the entire corporation.

SUMMARY AND CONCLUSION

In this chapter we have introduced six core concepts for Management, the sixth M:

- *Core Concept #35: Strategic Vision*
- *Core Concept #36: Integrated Planning*

- *Core Concept #37: Integrative Management*
- *Core Concept #38: Product Champions*
- *Core Concept #39: Resource Matching*
- *Core Concept #40: Technology Management*

Successful firms are led by those who articulate a clear mission for the organization, set within the context of leadership's vision of the environment in which the firm operates. Out of that mission grows the firm's strategy, a statement of how the firm will achieve its objectives. A dynamic planning process throughout the firm serves as a tool to enable the firm to enact its strategy. Integrated planning incorporates not only vertical, division-driven objectives and resource deployment but horizontal, cross-divisional objectives as well to optimize the firm's capabilities in pursuit of its strategic objectives. Integrative management knits together the multi-media, multi-market publishing firm, operating across technology and market boundaries. Product champions are the creative property managers who conceive, acquire, and oversee the development of the products and services which comprise the firm's offerings. Such property management requires the matching and deployment of resources both within and without the firm, including content, technical, and marketing resources, among others. Information Age publishers also manage information technology in the firm's product processes and its infrastructure, both for cost-saving productivity purposes and for strategic advantage in a competitive industry environment.

NOTES

1. Warren Bennis, "Leading to Make a Difference," *National Business Employment Weekly*, 4 June 1989, 33–34.

2. Jerome Wiesner in "Foreword" to Koji Kobayashi's *Computers and Communications* (Cambridge, Mass.: MIT Press, 1986), ix–x.

3. John Sculley, "Planning for the Future," *Odyssey* (New York: Harper & Row, 1987), 292–7.

4. *See* Michael Porter, *Competitive Advantage* (New York: The Free Press, 1985), Chapter 10, "Horizontal Strategy," and Chapter 11, "Achieving Interrelationships."

5. *See* Edwin McDowell, "Is Simon & Schuster Mellowing?" *The New York Times*, 8 October, 1990, and "Profits—Dick Snyder's Ugly Word," *The New York Times*, 30 June, 1991.

6. *See*, for example, "Kodak Pays the Price for Change," by Claudia H. Deutsch, *The New York Times*, 6 March, 1988. Continuing education for employees is among a list of management programs and ideas designed to revitalize and redirect the organization in response to a changing, more intensely competitive business environment. The list also includes: product development teams; internally competing technologies; market-driven competition; faster product life cycles and product development cycles; more products out the door for greater chances of success; joint ventures; less staff,

more strategic business units; outside contract bidding; and a new venture division, with seed money to back employee new product ideas and embrace new technologies.

7. *See Business Policy: Text and Cases* (Homewood, Ill.: Richard D. Irwin, 1983), 550.

8. As quoted in Geraldine Fabrikant, "Hearst's 8-Year Buying Spree," *The New York Times,* 26 April, 1987.

9. John Sculley with John A. Byrne, *Odyssey,* 183–89. Sculley's guidelines for the creative "incubator" require: (1) make it safe; (2) give directions, not goals; (3) encourage contrarian thinking; (4) build a textured environment; (5) build emotion into the system; and (6) encourage accountability over responsibility.

10. *See* "Scholastic Goes Public: Stock a Hit With Investors," *Educational Marketer,* 23 (2 March, 1992): 1ff.

11. Porter, *Competitive Advantage,* 42–45. In Porter's scheme, technology development is part of the overall support activities of the organization, which also include procurement, human resources management, and the "firm infrastructure," which includes general management, planning, finance, accounting, legal, government affairs, and quality management. In *Information Technology: The Trillion-Dollar Opportunity* (New York: McGraw-Hill, 1987), Poppel and Goldstein cite technology management, along with marketing and people-culture management, as one of the three critical strategic management arenas for all information technology firms (pages 168ff).

12. Peter Drucker observes the merging of all types of technologies, how they come from different bases but now need to be understood together. He urges "awareness of and concern with science and technology outside of one's own lab, outside of one's own field, outside of one's own industry . . . [because] technological streams no longer run parallel. They increasingly cross each other, with frequent spillovers from one to the other." Drucker favors free-standing research labs outside the corporation, such as the MIT Media Lab, that draw on many of these streams for research and development. He also suggests that the sponsoring client corporations would have a "technology manager . . . who can develop business objectives based on the potential of technology and technology strategies based on business and market objectives." Peter F. Drucker, "Best R&D Is Business-Driven," *The Wall Street Journal,* 10 February, 1988.

CHAPTER 13

Maximizing Return: Organizational Strategy and Structure

This chapter looks at maximizing return on investment from a corporate perspective, considering organizational strategy for Information Age publishers and the structural issues linked with strategy. We will consider issues of diversification and company strategic stance before reviewing strategic and structural options, including a discussion of the need for horizontal as well as vertical structure.

ORGANIZATIONAL STRATEGY

As defined by business theorist Alfred Chandler, organizational strategy is "the determination of the basic long-term goals and objectives of the enterprise and the adoption of courses of action and the allocation of resources necessary for carrying out these goals."[1] As discussed in Chapter 12, corporate-level strategy is an outgrowth of the firm's mission, the stated purpose of the organization. In actuality, say Raymond Miles and Charles Snow, strategy is often less a plan itself than "a *pattern* or *stream* of minor decisions about an organization's possible future domains . . . decisions [that] take on meaning only as they are implemented through the organization's structure and process. In other words, an organization's strategy can best be inferred from its behavior." Further, say the authors, organizational strategy is rarely conceived or implemented in isolation, for while strategy may determine structure, the existing structure of the organization acts as a constraint on strategy. Thus firms conceive and implement strategy out of a given set of existing organizational realities. How radically they are willing to reengineer these constraints for the sake of strategy is a critical ongoing question for the firm's senior management.[2]

ASSESSING VALUE ACROSS THE 7M'S

For publishers, strategic considerations begin with the 7M's: where do we have value already, and where can we seek additional value? Publishers are the investors in the products, those who take a risk on the entire enterprise and provide sufficient capital to empower and sustain the operation. Thus, management and money are the two givens. Where firms vary is in their engagement in the five value-added M's throughout the media universe. Consultant Christopher Burns has observed that "profits flow for the most part to the investors, not to those who found the data or organized the presentation or crafted an efficient expression." Burns and co-author Patricia Martin tabulated 1984 revenue figures for all information content firms—books, magazines, newspapers, print and online information services, document retrieval, direct mail, radio, television, cable, motion pictures, records and tapes, performing arts, and software—totaling $143.7 billion. Although there were variations across media segments, their findings showed that for the industry as a whole 55% of revenues went to cover sales and distribution, 15% to media conversion and production, and 17% to the material itself, with the remainder going to profits. The authors observe that "The information industry appears to be primarily involved in converting knowledge into an appropriate information form and delivering it to a market where it is highly valued. Relatively less is spent developing the knowledge itself."[3]

One school of thought posits ownership of all value-added stages on the part of content firms. Booz Allen Hamilton's Jennifer Bater cited the importance for content firms to "expand participation in all three content value-added segments [development, synthesis, distribution]."[4] Management consultant Peter Schwartz feels that the big entertainment firms will try to integrate vertically as the oil companies have done, "owning the whole process from oil discovery to gas tank, from writer to theater seat or TV set or headphone." The movement of the large consumer electronics firms into entertainment would seem to bear this out, albeit from the opposite direction. Schwartz also foresees that "computer intelligent 'ticket-takers' might emerge that could extract income from information flows with great subtlety and reliability."[5]

What is required of publishers for the most profitable deployment of limited resources? A book publisher specializing in travel information, for instance, may be considering whether he should also make the content available in electronic form, either online, in stand-alone software packages, or in audio or video formats. Should he do it himself? Should he license the content to a technology house for development and retain marketing rights? If he sells it via an online system, how much will he charge the vendor? Who will format and structure the material electronically, the vendor or the originating publisher, and how much control should he maintain over the content, its structuring, and its formatting? Will electronic versions of the information cannibalize his current print offerings, or complement and synergize with them? How does he value the conversion from one medium to the other, and what price does he set on these? How much control should he keep at each stage, from development in other media to packaging, marketing and distribution? If he chooses to go into these other media, what is the optimal sequence and marketing strategy for the entire content-media roll-out to maximize the life of the information and obtain the fullest possible return on the material? These are questions Information Age publishers must address if they are to succeed in a multi-format, multi-market environment. The questions are asked anew with each product.

While firms may start by looking at new media opportunities, they must also look at their own resources: what they've got, where they're strong, what they're good at, what they know how to do, what markets they're in, what competitive advantages they have, and what they bring to the table. The 7M's framework is useful in performing this analysis.

A 7M'S VALUE ASSESSMENT: TRADE BOOK PUBLISHING

A value assessment of trade book publishing reveals it as a business beset by an unusual number of constraints on all sides: Material—while material is typically their chief differential advantage over other publishers, most trade publishers are almost entirely dependent on outside sources for content—not only its development, but its *conception*, as well. In competitive product bidding situations, the publisher is often at the mercy of the seller, the agent or author, who can drive the price to what the market will bear, in some cases with little relevance to projected sales or publisher profits. Mode—a printed book is principally confined to text and still images. Medium—while the publisher adds value to the content by designing, packaging, and distributing a book, he does none of these appreciably differently from other publishers. In fact, he typically does not do it himself, but relies on third parties to produce and distribute the material.

In addition, his product, which requires effort to consume, is sold into an increasingly televisual, electronicized culture, where people have less and less time for the sustained effort required to read a book-length work. Moreover, nearly ⅓ of the population is illiterate and can't use the product. Means—he distributes his products on consignment—all of them can come back if the buyer/retailer so desires—yet he must constantly fill the pipeline with new products to remain viable in all eyes—authors, retailers, etc.—and amortize the overhead he has invested in the firm's operation. He typically gives away 50% of revenues to those in the distribution chain, seeing but half of each dollar from the end customer. Market—each book—and he may publish upwards of 200 a year—is a new product, and he must market each totally anew, but with limited marketing resources. He doesn't know who his market is, having little or no contact with his end customers, and he has little or no idea what they think of the product after they purchase and use it. Money—if end-users won't buy, he has absolutely no income from advertising to offset the loss. His raw materials costs—paper, ink—not to mention the cost of inventory, are constantly rising. *Management*—he has few, if any, direct, head-to-head competitors for his products to focus and sharpen strategic efforts. The publisher's senior management has typically risen through the ranks of one functional discipline or another—editorial, marketing—with no general management training, and is often ill-equipped to meet the complex demands of multi-market, multi-media enterprise management on the scale required in a rapidly changing, highly technologized industry environment.

Each of these constraints can be seen as a challenge. Continuing with the 7M's framework, responses to these challenges could include the following: *Material*— while mindful of the industry's role and strengths—a cultural leader whose existence is dependent upon the intuition and craft of its product managers, the editors, and their ability to seek out and develop statements of value—publishers can also engage in active content development in addition to passive acceptance of externally developed ideas which they must wait for, sift through, and, often on their heels, bid competitively for. They can lock-up talent and create a more predictable supply of material through long-term contracts. They can seek alternative sources of material— e.g., works for hire, public domain—by commissioning and developing material and owning copyrights, as do newspapers and software developers. They can seek "presold" products—big name authors, series, TV tie-ins, institutional affiliations— which capitalize on existing awareness in buyers' minds and boost marketing efforts. They can sustain and revitalize backlist properties that are proven sellers and require minimal reinvestment. They can develop and acquire new types of properties that will yield multiple revenue streams in multiple media formats and markets. *Mode/ Medium*—they can add different modes—motion, sound, touch, and even smell—to supplement existing print formats. They can squeeze maximum value from information assets by exploiting derivative rights, either via internal development or licensing. They can reduce costs by automating as many aspects of product development as possible, inputting and structuring content for embodiment in multiple print and electronic formats from the point of inception. *Means*—they can seek alternative distribution channels within their existing markets, through direct marketing, continuity series, and other non-retail channels, either on a license basis or in-house. They can feed online custom-publishing systems from their digital content libraries. *Market*—they can balance the volatility of consumer market publishing with less volatile market segments, such as educational and business and professional publishing. They can seek new markets for existing and future products via cross-market selling to educational, international, and special markets. They can focus on segments with favorable purchase and/or usage habits, such as children's books, reference books, libraries, and special sales. *Management*—they can own more of the value-added by integrating vertically, owning all aspects of the publishing process from creation to distribution, or by purchasing a percentage stake in these areas— e.g., a software developer, a book packager, an online service, or a retail chain. They can joint-venture with technology and/or market partners for new product development and market access, or they can acquire firms in these areas. They can seek out and hire management expertise in areas where they are weak or in businesses they seek to enter. *Money*—they can develop additional sources of revenue from active licensing programs in new areas—e.g., electronic rights—and seek alternative financing arrangements for products via pre-financing or laying off rights up front to reduce their exposure. They can seek advertising or other third-party support.

THE MEDIA UNIVERSE AND DIVERSIFICATION

The large print publishing firms have historically diversified, either defensively or offensively. In the earlier part of the century book publishing, which viewed itself more as a craft than an industry, was confronted by changes in the operating environment. The move from trade to educational and subscription publishing after the turn of the century was the first major diversification for book publishers, broadening the range of products they offered and types of customers they served. As Lewis Coser reports: "The shift from a simply organized house that published for one market to a more complex firm that published for several markets and encountered a variety of environmental demands can be viewed as a key stage in the transformation of publishing from a cottage business or occupation to a corporate enterprise. . . . People at the top of publishing houses found themselves less concerned with day-to-day activities and more involved in developing long-range plans, coordinating and reconciling the activities of various departments."[6] With the addition of new publishing formats and international markets, this transformation continues.

If firms are to take advantage of these new opportunities, they must think strategically. More specifically, says management consultant Peter Drucker, "Entrepreneurial innovation will have to become the very heart and core of management," due primarily to advances in technologies. Drucker sees innovation as purposeful, systematic, and manageable. It is capital intensive, he says, especially in development and market introduction stages. Thus large corporations must be capable of rapid and continuing innovation: "What existing organizations will have to learn is to reach out for change as an opportunity and to resist continuity."[7]

The Media Universe introduced in Chapter 10 can be used to define the

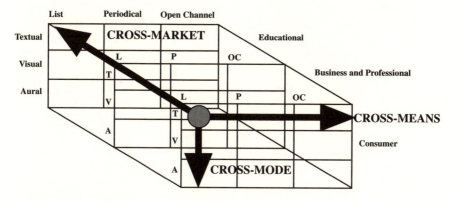

Figure 13-1
The Media Universe and Diversification

product-market scope of the company's operations (*see* Figure 13-1). The universe shown here depicts a text-based consumer market publisher. For this firm, cross-market diversification would be into the educational or business and professional markets. Cross-means diversification would be from list to periodical and/or open channel publishing. Cross-modal diversification would be into visual or aural modes. The firm could also diversify across two different M's simultaneously—e.g., from book publishing into television, which is both cross-means and cross-modal—which moves the organization two steps from its core expertise.

Firms must define which cells of the Media Universe they are currently in and which cells they want to be in. Where are the growth opportunities? What resources are required? Where do the firm's strengths lie? A publisher can choose to reside in one market plane and even in one cell of the entire matrix, defining himself, for example, as a "list text publisher in the consumer market." This defines his predominant communications mode, his target market (prior to segmentation) and his typical publishing cycle. Should he choose to diversify in terms of market only, he would stay in the same matrix section but move across planes. Should he choose to stay in the same mode—e.g., visual—but deliver both stand-alone physical products and electronically delivered services, he would move across the matrix into open channel delivery mechanisms. Should he choose to develop and publish material in a different mode—e.g., move from text to predominantly visual or aural media—then he would move vertically up or down the matrix. The choice of the medium for the material and market is, of course, at the publisher's discretion and is at the core of the Information Age publisher's strategic challenge.

It should also be noted that a strictly attribute-based approach to media choice is not adequate. The dynamic equilibrium is not just a natural equilibrium of media attributes, but is affected by third parties, especially advertisers. Manufacturers, network operators, and monopolistic forces also exert influence.

In general, it is wise for the diversifying firm to have some connection via one or more of the 5M's, what is known as related diversification, or what publishing industry analyst J. Kendrick Noble calls a "plus connection." For instance, with audio and video being marketed through bookstores, book publishers have a channel of distribution in common with video and audio publishers. Successful diversification, Tom Peters and Bob Waterman found in their 1982 study of successful companies, *In Search of Excellence*, is based on a strategy of controlled diversity. They cite Richard Rumelt's 1974 Harvard Business School study, based on a sample of a broad range of Fortune 500 firms over a 20-year period, which found that "those businesses with 'dominant-constrained' and 'related-constrained' diversification strategies were 'unquestionably the best overall performers.'" Dominant-constrained is defined as very closely related to one skill—e.g., coating and bonding at 3M—and related-constrained is defined as close relationships between businesses, but perhaps in different technologies, such as a trucking firm that enters the railway business: transportation remains the focus. "These companies have strategies of entering only those businesses that build on, draw strength from, and enlarge some central strength or competence," say the authors. "While such firms frequently develop new products and enter new businesses, they are loath to invest in areas that are unfamiliar to management."[8] Hence, the next core concept:

Core Concept #41: Related Diversification

For book publishers, diversification into videocassette publishing, for example, is a related-constrained diversification. Both involve the seeking out, development, packaging, marketing, and distribution of list information and entertainment products. It is a cross-modal (textual to visual) diversification wherein the media technologies are different, as are certain of the required skills for success in the business. But the mission to publish still applies, the market and content focus remain the same, and thus the diversification fits with the content business.

Conversely, the farther afield from its current base of operations a firm goes, the more unrelated the diversification becomes. To engage in distribution changes within one's market, *and* in cross-modal conversion, *and* in cross-market selling simultaneously, would be a test of the firm's resources and would heighten the risk in the new venture. The largest of publishing concerns, however, what I call full-service publishers (*see* Core Concept #43, below) are increasingly coming to occupy all cells of the universe.

In a market-based diversification approach, the accepted format-focused industry definitions—e.g., book publishing—are suspended in favor of a broader, market-focused view of the business. As cautioned earlier in this study, however, too broad a view of one's business will dilute the firm's core competitive advantage. On the other hand, too narrow a definition will lead to missed opportunities, stagnation, and decline for the firm as competitors successfully invade the firm's markets and steal customers. The optimal approach is a balanced one. The firm remains committed to its successful core operations while remaining aware of and pursuing profitable diversification opportunities.

We are currently witnessing trends in the industry toward both diversified and focused firms. In the takeover environment of the 1980s characterized by cash-rich buyers looking for fat or undervalued companies or those with a high break-up value, some firms found it made sense to slim down and focus. Two major information industry players made such decisions in the merger-mad 1980s. CBS, under the direction of Lawrence Tisch, sold not only its book and magazine publishing operations but its historic and highly prized record group to Sony to return to its broadcasting roots. On the hardware side, Xerox decided it was a facilities company and divested itself of its significant content operations. They sold R.R. Bowker to Cahners, University Microfilms to International Thomson, Ginn and Company to Gulf and Western (now Paramount Communications), Xerox Education Publications to Field Corporation, and Xerox Learning to Times Mirror, in order to focus their efforts on office automation.

As the larger firms consolidate and the industry concentrates, opportunities will also open up for niche players, as is true in most maturing, concentrated industries. A variety of media and market-focused firms will emerge to address gaps in the marketplace not served by the larger firms. Barriers to entry will exist—e.g., cost of material, distribution channel access—but innovative firms will discover sustainable niches, particularly in the emerging technologies.

PORTFOLIO APPROACH

How do diversifying firms manage the risk? In investment theory the portfolio approach holds that one diversifies risk by holding a range of investments. Some are holdings in more mature, stable businesses, while others are shares in younger, higher growth businesses, volatile businesses with greater risk and uncertainty, but also a greater prospect of return. Still other investments are held in between the lowest and highest risk, offering some more immediate return on investment.

Information Age publishers can employ a similar portfolio approach to a broadening array of media formats. They can maintain the successful core media formats while experimenting with others that represent the promise of future return. We can depict this portfolio of media formats across the market life cycle, as shown in Figure 13-2.[9] The media portfolio concept is an extension of Core Concept #23, the Dynamic Equilibrium. It is a management tool to assess the firm's participation in a changing media marketplace.

Many firms will choose to grow incrementally. If 75% of a firm's revenues are from newspapers they will not suddenly pull out of print and jump into online delivery, which holds a considerably smaller share of the information marketplace. However, they will take a close look at online service because it may prove a popular medium for information access, and 5 or 10 or 15 years down the line, the relative media shares may shift.

The privately held Hearst Corporation is an example of a diversified media firm that holds a portfolio of properties in various media. The company is organized in media groups: newspapers, magazines, book publishing, broadcasting (television and radio), cable television, and other non-media activities, such as real estate. When asked why the firm had diversified over the years from its base in print media—originally newspapers, then magazines and books—into broadcasting and cable, Hearst President and CEO Frank Bennack, Jr. said: "We were too heavily skewed to publishing. As the move to electronics continued, we felt we needed a heavier participation there. Our

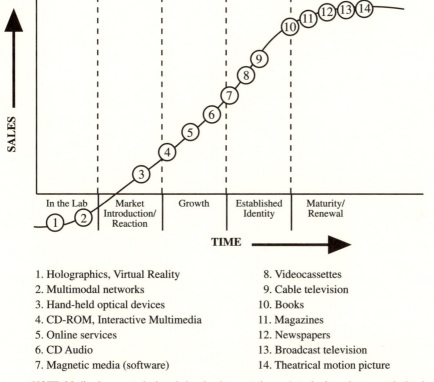

| 1 | 2–3 | 4 | 5 | 6 |

SALES

In the Lab | Market Introduction/ Reaction | Growth | Established Identity | Maturity/ Renewal

TIME

1. Holographics, Virtual Reality
2. Multimodal networks
3. Hand-held optical devices
4. CD-ROM, Interactive Multimedia
5. Online services
6. CD Audio
7. Magnetic media (software)

8. Videocassettes
9. Cable television
10. Books
11. Magazines
12. Newspapers
13. Broadcast television
14. Theatrical motion picture

NOTE: Media placements depict relative development phases. Actual sales volumes not depicted.

Figure 13-2
The Portfolio Approach: Today and Tomorrow Media

decision revolved around the perception that internal growth was not adequate to a changing media marketplace."[10]

If viewed historically for each firm, the portfolio concept may also serve as some indication of the firm's potential involvement in other future media. Figure 13-3 depicts a hypothetical publisher's media portfolio as it might change over the last decade of the 20th century. Successful diversifying firms know that they must be patient in order to learn about the new formats and that they must be prepared to lose as well as gain. New media will develop at their own pace and user habits along with them in a gradual give and take process. Over time the marketability and profitability of products in the in- dividual new media formats will become more clear. As certain new media

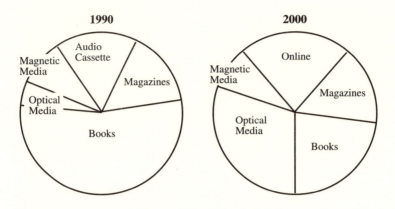

Figure 13-3
Publisher's Changing Media Portfolio

begin to make money in certain markets, a firm can shift its resources to take advantage of the opportunities.

While the media portfolio theory can be applied at the corporate level, it can also be applied at the divisional and product level. Within a division of the publishing firm a product initiative may be launched that is clearly speculative but important for a variety of reasons: meeting a perceived or determined customer need, gaining a toehold in a new market, gaining an understanding of a new technology, or demonstrating technical awareness and proficiency to customers, competitors, the investment analyst community, or other parties.

DEFINING STRATEGIC STANCE

As with all business ventures, each diversification initiative must be set in the context of its organization and its culture as well as its industry and market. Every company has its own approach to the pursuit of new business opportunities. A company which has an established manner of recognizing and promoting the efforts of its entrepreneurs with a full commitment to their success is more likely to succeed than one which approaches new opportunities in a lukewarm manner or defensive posture. For every large company grinding the bureaucratic levers to create the new enterprise a dozen small independent firms will be committing their heart and soul to achieving the same goal. Sometimes the best approach is the marriage of the independent's enthusiasm and technical prowess with the larger organization's financial, marketing, and management resources.

As the industry is in a crucial transitional phase, many firms are performing an identity check, asking themselves "who are we and where are we going?"

Business strategists Raymond Miles and Charles Snow identified four basic types of organizations in regard to their interaction with their environment, a typology detailed in Table 13-1, Strategic Typology of Organizations:[11]

Core Concept #42: Strategic Stance and Entrepreneurship

Defender

Defenders see themselves as defending the status quo in the industry and the marketplace, holding the ground, not wishing (or caring) to be perceived as innovators in technology, markets, or otherwise. In some media or market areas this is a wise strategy as the incursion of new media may not be that strong or a threat to existing business. But in other areas where the environment is moving away from the status quo, where ground is being gained by other players—e.g., the broadcast television networks' yielding market share to cable and VCR's—then the defender is at a competitive disadvantage.

Another defender strategy is to focus, to be an expert in a market segment and/or media format. This can also be a differential advantage. A book publisher focused solely on books will do his craft and do it well. Many publishing firms are known for their specialty—e.g., a military publisher, focused on content; a software publisher, focused on technology; an educational publisher, focused on market. Any intersection of material, medium, and market, as well as mode and means, further defines the publisher's core competence.

Such defender strategies are not without dangers, however. Defenders must be aware of environmental trends. The environment around the firm may change, and along with it the process or product mix, customers and their habits, or the techniques and technologies for processing, distributing, and marketing information. Even if defenders choose not to diversify, their businesses do not operate in isolation but as part of an organic industry environment. As documented throughout this study, the changes in process technology and media vehicles throughout the information industry will make it increasingly difficult for format-focused defenders to survive. Content-based, media-diverse defender strategies—e.g., National Geographic—are clearly less vulnerable and more sustainable.

Another defender danger is opportunity cost. While a firm may see no perceptible advantage to being first in, eager entrepreneurs will be the first to seize new market opportunities, as for them necessity is the mother of invention. Those who stay in one medium only will not participate in these new-found opportunities.

Analyzer

Analyzers are often fast followers, watching the industry leaders closely. Most analyzers cannot afford to be the industry leader in R&D, manufactur-

ORGANIZATIONAL CHARACTERISTIC	DEFENDER	ANALYZER	PROSPECTOR	REACTOR
STRATEGIC DISPOSITION	Hold ground	Fast follower	First in	Uncertain, blow with wind
VIEW OF CHANGE	Not germane	Situation-specific	Opportunity	Threat
ENTREPRENEURSHIP	Limited	Follow the leader	Risk and reward	Hit and miss
MARKET SHARES	High, tightly focused	Varied; some high	Expansion, market creation	Varies with segment
ENVIRONMENTAL AWARENESS	From a distance	Watch closely	Knowledge of cutting edge	Aware but unresponsive
PERSONNEL	Expert in niche	Steady as she goes	Attract the best, dreamers that do	Best people go elsewhere
FINANCIAL ORIENTATION	Invest for efficiency	Choose safe bets	Invest for future	Tentative, inconsistent
ORGANIZATIONAL HEALTH	Good, in limited areas	Slow, steady growth	Growth, continuous renewal	Stagnation, decline
LEADERSHIP	Drive for efficiency, narrow market dominance	Conservative followers	Visionary, inspirational	Mixed messages; internal focus

Table 13-1
Strategic Typology of Organizations

ing, or marketing. But when a competitor innovates successfully, the analyzer will soon follow. Their preferred learning style is watching the efforts of others, rather than pioneering.

How do analyzers maintain their market and technology intelligence? In addition to watching competitors' moves, they track industry publications and the general press for signs of relevant innovations and developments, attend industry conferences and shows, use outside consultants, appoint a staff or divisional level director of technology, and encourage company-wide awareness of the issues. Industry licensing trends will also indicate areas of significant activity. Some analyzers will enter into project-basis alliances with outside partners in order to learn. Perhaps most importantly, they listen to their customers.

Prospector

While the defender focuses inward and the analyzer watches the environment closely, the prospector explores, pioneers, looks for opportunity, and takes the risks and consequences while hoping for reward.

Prospecting can be costly and a drain on resources, but if successful it can also lead to prosperity. Prospectors spend to know and spend to gain. They see "gold in them thar hills" and feel they must embrace new opportunities in market, media, or any of the other value-added M's. Prototypical content prospectors in the media business include, among others, Michael Eisner's Walt Disney Company, Time Warner, and Paramount Publishing. In media hardware, Sony Corporation is a prototypical prospector.

In addition to providing a knowledge of cutting edge technologies, prospecting also creates more frequent occasions for introspection, in which the company must assess its direction and degree of commitment before it determines which way it will go. This in itself is a healthy exercise as it keeps the organization alive and aware. In the best instances, where the direction of the company is clarified or reaffirmed and the new venture proves successful, it can lead to organizational rebirth and renewal.

Most prospectors have both product champions committed to finding a way to get the job done and executive sponsors willing to make the necessary sustained commitment to make it work. Prospectors know they may make mistakes, but they recognize their value as learning experiences and feel they are worth the effort and expense. They believe that some bias toward action, toward first-hand experience, is necessary for true understanding. Knight-Ridder spent substantial sums of money on Viewtron, perhaps a costly learning experience. Nonetheless, they learned. The cost of doing business was to explore the technology not only in the laboratory but in the marketplace. The experience places them at a comparative advantage over other newspaper firms now exploring entry into the next wave of online services.

Good prospectors understand the costs of true innovation. As management consultant Peter Drucker has stated, "The essence of economic activity is the commitment of present resources to future expectations, and that means to uncertainty and risk."[12] The predictive model, whereby known factors aid in reducing risk, is of limited value in true innovation. Those companies that lead into the marketplace recognize and accept that the elimination of uncertainty is an impossibility. The only way to truly know whether a medium or a given application will succeed is to get it into the hands of a population of users, which means putting it on the market and finding out what it will do. The firm then listens and either redesigns in response to marketplace reaction or drops out.

As Drucker has stated, "Successful innovators are conservative. They are not 'risk-focused'; they are 'opportunity-focused.' " Further, says Drucker, successful entrepreneurs "try to create new and different values and satisfactions, to convert a 'material' into a 'resource,' or to combine existing resources in a new and more productive configuration.... Systematic innovation therefore consists in the purposeful and organized search for changes and in the systematic analysis of the opportunities such changes might offer for economic or social innovation."[13] Prospectors adopt this attitude and these tactics for true innovation.

Reactor

Miles and Snow's fourth strategic type, reactors, are the wallflowers, those firms that are too shy to step forward and wait to be chosen before joining the dance. Their risk, of course, is never joining the party at all, being left to languish on the sidelines. If the firm ventures nothing, it will gain nothing, and if it doesn't grow, it will stagnate. The firm's total market and technology domain will shrink. Suppliers and buyers will recognize that the firm is not awake to industry trends. The best people inside the organization, frustrated by the lack of movement and energy, will go elsewhere. Eventually, such companies, failing to see the trends in the market, will face decline, senility, and death, either via takeover or bankruptcy and reorganization.

For publishers in the Information Age, it is clear that a reactor strategy will not lead to long-term organizational health. The pace of technological change in all areas of publishing processes, formats, and infrastructure will overtake the uncertain firm. Reactor firms' undervalued and underutilized assets will be sought out by buyers seeking a greater return on those assets. Thus if they have assets of value, they are most likely to be purchased, merged, or absorbed in some fashion into an organization that is actively pursuing opportunities in the changing environment.

The four-part typology described above can be viewed as the producer or supply side equivalent of the innovators, early adopters, late adopters, and laggards on the buyer side. It should also be noted that a business may not necessarily have a uniform strategic stance throughout the organization, perhaps choosing to defend one area and prospect in another. It may also combine these stances in a given area, as a defensive prospector, for instance, that ventures into a new medium to defend its current investment. Whatever the stance, the firm's human resources must match the strategy. Prospecting companies require entrepreneurs and growth managers while defenders require steady state maintenance managers, usually two different types of people.

STRATEGIC OPTIONS

There is a range of both short- and long-term strategic options open to publishers choosing to take advantage of new business opportunities presented by the changing industry environment. The short-term options look at the generation of revenue and income off existing properties, while the long-term strategies look at full entry into a new medium or market. A short-term strategy can evolve into a long-term strategy should the market prove attractive or the endeavor successful.

Whichever option is chosen in a given area, it is important, especially for publicly held companies, to demonstrate responsible pursuit of new media and other growth opportunities to improve shareholder value. Not only must fixed costs be covered, but maximum return must be realized on information assets through planned property development. If a firm owns the rights to a given property, it is incumbent upon it to responsibly pursue one of these strategies. If they do nothing, then they are underutilizing their assets, thereby failing to achieve full return on their investment.

To determine the appropriate organizational strategy for a specific publishing opportunity, the firm must review the above-considered issues of value assessment, diversification, portfolio position, and strategic stance. The company will then be in a position to evaluate the opportunity properly, as a long-term, strategic opportunity, a short-term, tactical maneuver, or a no-go.

SHORT-TERM STRATEGIC OPTIONS

As stated above, short-term options typically look to generate incremental revenue off existing assets. Starting with the least degree of commitment, investment, and control, the most common short-term strategic options for publishing firms include the following.

Passive Licensing

The firm has no capability in developing properties beyond a defined medium and/or market. Other development opportunities are achieved strictly through reaction to outside interest. The de facto policy is to license all rights and retain none for internal development as the organization's capabilities are narrow. Similarly, acquisition strategies do not emphasize obtaining broad rights as no plan for their development or licensing is envisioned.

While some incremental revenue may be gained and there is little risk or investment involved, the firm receives only a portion of the revenues that would be gained through in-house development and marketing. Moreover, the organization typically relinquishes control over the development of the licensed property as well as the coordinated development and sale of the property in its various media incarnations through the media cycle.

Active Licensing

In active licensing programs, the firm shares in revenue but still relinquishes a measure of control over product development and distribution. As with passive licensing, there is lower risk, lower revenue, and less learning by the organization. However, with an active licensing program, the firm can play a greater role in coordinating the media life cycle by sequencing the development of the property in its various media forms. Active licensing also allows the firm to create development plans for selected key titles, those with a major brand name, trademark, or content franchise, or those with the greatest potential for revenue.

Active licensing recognizes the firm's need to evaluate and select the right licensees. It starts with thorough research on both backlist and frontlist properties to develop a list of existing license and rights situations on key properties under license or owned by the firm. Development opportunities in the various media are scrutinized for incremental revenue possibilities. Product ideas are generated based on existing content, then screened in consideration of the various formats, markets, and other licensing opportunities: would the content published in that format add value for customers? Would there be demand for it in that form? What directly competitive products are already in the market or under development? If an electronic format, what is the player population? How has the medium performed to date and what are the trends? What synergies or cannibalization might there be with the same content in existing or other media forms?

After combing the property rights base for these possibilities and generating a range of products for potential license, the properties are prioritized and license opportunities identified and pursued. At this point other questions about the firm would be addressed regarding other resources the firm has to leverage beyond its information assets, such as product development skills, marketing capabilities, or distribution channels in the various media formats. After a development plan has been prepared, the firm can prepare a prospectus for each potential development option, e.g., multimedia CD-ROM, and, based on an evaluation of solicited responses to the prospectus, select the appropriate licensee for that implementation. On major properties, auctioning exclusive rights for a specific implementation, such as is done for paperback book rights, may be a desirable approach.

An active licensing program can also affect the acquisition strategy of the division or firm. To control the rights for one medium—e.g., book—is the least risky. The publisher produces, manufactures, and distributes in that medium only, and all other media rights are retained by the original copyright holder, and licensed elsewhere, if at all. He has no control over development or marketing of other media versions of the same content, nor does he share in the return. But with an active licensing program, the firm can obtain broader rights in a property and sub-license them to third party developers and publishers in other media and markets. Here a royalty share of the income is received—which in turn is shared with the copyright holder or proprietor of the material—and some control gained over development and release. More control is usually maintained over development in the same mode. Cross-modal licensings, such as in book to film, generally dilute content control, though these are negotiable items, particularly in newer media formats.

Development and Marketing Arrangements

Product development and marketing arrangements go one step beyond active licensing programs by involving the originating publisher more fully in some aspects of a product or product line's development and/or marketing. The firm uses developers or other resources in limited term arrangements to pursue the development of products which either the publisher or outside vendors manufacture and bring to market. While still not a full-fledged publishing program, the publisher can in this manner leverage his information assets and control product development, manufacturing, marketing, or distribution, as required. The increased involvement also means increased risk and investment, but with the prospect of increased return and greater control over management of the given property.

The originating publisher can choose which areas of product development, marketing, and distribution it would like to be involved in, using third parties in areas where it needs assistance, from development to distribution. The objective is to protect the property's and the publisher's interests in terms of revenue, product quality, and trademark and brand names.

Joint Ventures and Strategic Alliances

The joint venture or strategic alliance is an intermediate-term option that typically goes beyond the limited scope of a development or marketing arrangement for a single property. While development and marketing arrangements are generally proscribed regarding term and other aspects, allowing the publisher to enter into and exit from such arrangements as and when he sees fit, a strategic alliance is a heavier commitment of time, energy, organizational focus, and other firm resources. A specific partner or partners is chosen in pursuit of a specific objective, but the magnitude of the opportunity is usually greater than that of a development or marketing arrangement, as are the prospects of its transformation into a longer-term strategic initiative. The implicit statement behind an alliance is that "we need each other for now, but we're not exactly sure whether we'll need each other in the future." Such a statement implies that the venture could be a failure, in which case the alliance dissolves. Even if it is a success, the parties must reevaluate their desire to continue ensemble, or at least under the existing arrangement.[14]

As of this writing, no area of the information industry is the focus of more strategic alliances than digital or interactive television. As discussed earlier, major players from all segments of the industry, including IBM, Apple, AT&T, Microsoft, Time Warner, TCI, General Instrument, and Intel—in essence, a "who's who" of the information industry—are entering into alliances with each other to stake claims in the new territory. As indicated above, such a flurry of alliances indicates not only the expected magnitude of the rewards to be gained but carries the implicit message that these resource matchings are essentially expeditious arrangements during a transitional phase. When the new medium of digital television emerges, there will be both winners and losers, and no longer alliances but new firms, whether combinations of pre-existing entities or newborn organizations, will populate the industry landscape.

LONG-TERM STRATEGIC OPTIONS

Those organizations more intent on longer-term participation in a new area have several options available, including internal start-ups, external start-ups, and merger or acquisition. Unlike the short-term approach of generating incremental revenue off existing assets, the long-term strategy says: "While some synergy will be available across domains, these businesses must be attractive enough on their own, as stand-alone businesses apart from our existing enterprises, for us to get into them. They must head us in the right direction. Since we want to be in these businesses, let's devise a suitable entry strategy that uses our strengths to their fullest, and also tells us where we are weak and therefore what other resources we need to be successful."

I should also point out that licensing, although also the lowest risk short-term strategy, is usually part of the established firm's long-term strategy as well. No media firm can cover all the possible forms and exploitations of its range of properties, no matter how many segments of the business it is engaged in. At a minimum, a passive licensing program will continue to respond to opportunities brought to the company by outside parties. A long-term active licensing program also makes good strategic sense should the firm, whether due to limited resources or other reasons, choose to define its format focus more narrowly than broadly. Even broadly focused firms will continue to commit resources to licensing, witness Paramount Communications' creation of a central licensing group in 1993 to service all Paramount business units' licensing needs.

Internal Start-Up

Internal start-ups are entrepreneurial units within the larger organization designed for the pursuit of new technologies or markets. While the firm maintains its bread and butter cash flows, the start-up unit allows the firm to commit resources to explore a new opportunity. Start-up units provide a toehold if a technology or market develops, as well as providing first-hand knowledge of the new area. They also allow the firm to pursue new opportunities in an open, entrepreneurial, creative fashion by creating a separate entity— what Tom Peters would call a "skunk works"—within the larger organization.[15]

To create the best conditions for its success, the start-up should ideally be a stand-alone operation, either within a division or the firm as a whole. For instance, a new media unit could be a start-up within a market-oriented group, while a new market group could be developed within a format-oriented division.

If either established as or developed into a stand-alone operation, a new media unit, for example, should not be expected to rely strictly on the parent firm's properties as product source, although it is certainly a logical starting point. If so, the unit's growth will be restricted and it will be placed at a severe competitive disadvantage. Multiple product sources should be cultivated. While serving a legitimate business purpose, it should not remain a value-added development option that is simply a service function to the parent firm's products. HBO is not dependent only on Time Warner books and magazines or Warner Brothers films for product supply. Disney's book publishing venture encompasses more than the print versions of other Disney properties. However, the full media development capabilities of the total firm should not be ignored, and the parent firm's offerings will remain components, sometimes as dedicated product lines, of the new unit's offerings.

External Start-Up

The firm may also choose to acquire a percentage stake in an existing concern already in a targeted business. Typically the acquiring firm brings specific resources such as capital, product direction, or marketing and distribution to the new unit's capability.

The extent of the investment and involvement on the part of the acquiring firm can vary widely. Some firms keep their distance, viewing their stake strictly as a financial investment, regardless of its connection to their current business, seeking only return on the investment with the long-term possibility of its growth into a full-fledged business. Others may choose to observe the product-to-market cycle, gaining knowledge as well as financial return. If successful, the minority stake may be raised to a majority stake, or the unit purchased outright and operated as a full subsidiary or folded into the main company.

An example of such a minority stake is the early 1991 purchase by Microsoft, the world's largest microcomputer software developer and publisher, of a 26% share of Dorling Kindersley, a London-based book packager and publisher. As part of the arrangement, Microsoft was granted multimedia development and distribution rights to certain Dorling Kindersley products, highly visual reference books for readers of all ages. The move was significant as it marked the first time a software publisher bought into a book publisher, evidencing the trend in the convergence of software tools and content formatted and sold on the same platform.

Like some internal start-ups, an attraction of such external business units is the recognition that creative groups thrive in an entrepreneurial environment outside the confines of the parent corporation. Apple Computer has chosen to "spin out" creative groups, such as Claris Software, from the parent organization, to ensure the optimum creative environment and operating freedom essential for innovative product development. In essence, book publishers use a similar approach to content development as the bulk of their material is prepared by outside individuals and groups, both knowledge experts and modal processors. On the other hand, periodical publishers, especially newspapers, develop relatively more content in-house, due chiefly to editorial control, deadline demands, and the need for close editorial-production coordination.

Whether internal or external, most start-ups begin with a firm product definition in a specific niche. Having a clear identity and sending clear signals to the marketplace are critical for success. Then, after initial products are launched and a presence established in the marketplace, the unit can think about follow-on products. The immediate bias is for action, to develop the products and get in the game. Investing firms should typically expect long development periods, poor initial cash flow, and relatively high risk, especially on new-to-the-world products.

Mergers and Acquisitions

Beyond an investment in an outside entity that harbors a given media expertise or market entree lacking in the investing firm, a firm can choose full-scale entry into a new business or market (or an enlargement of its existing operations) through merger with or acquisition of another firm. It is often easier to buy market presence or acquire media expertise than to build it from scratch. In the book business, for instance, with retail distribution dominated by a few powerful wholesalers and chain-store retailers, merely obtaining access to shelf-space can be difficult. An established backlist means instant books, instant distribution, and instant cash flow, some or all of which may be sustainable almost indefinitely. Firms can also acquire market entrees with the possibility of future development potential in any and all media through the extension of the acquired imprints and product lines.

As discussed above, related-constrained and dominant-constrained diversifications on average prove most successful. Reviewing a study of mergers and acquisitions by McKinsey and Company, *The Economist* reported that healthy businesses kept their core business active and well-managed, which allowed them to retain cash flow for other, newer ventures. Successful acquisitions were relatively small and close to the acquiring company's existing operations in one area or another, and careful and active integration of the new business into the existing one after the acquisition proved critical for success.[16]

Another type of combination seen in the 1980s was the large firm combining with or acquiring another large firm. Time, Inc. and Warner Communications combined in 1989 to create the world's largest media organization, yet it was still a combination of two content firms whose product lines complemented each other. Perhaps of greater note is the purchase by hardware firms of software firms, i.e., content providers, as noted earlier, such as consumer electronics giant Sony's purchase of Columbia Pictures and CBS Records, and rival Matsushita's purchase of MCA, which has operations in film, television, records, and book publishing.

The message in these business combinations is that the map has truly expanded beyond the media arena and across the information industry as a whole. Content firms may now be blind-sided by a different type of player, in a different league, with a different agenda and investment capabilities on a different order of magnitude. They will also increasingly be scrutinized for underutilized assets in any of the 5M's and sought for acquisition if acquiring firms feel they can reap greater return on those assets under their direction.

THE FULL-SERVICE PUBLISHER

The business combinations discussed above represent one of the grand strategies that emerged in the last decade: creating the mega-firm to participate in all major media formats in one or more of the major markets. Typically these enterprises are not confined by national boundary but seek global marketplaces for their products. They engage in activities across the media spectrum. They select and process the material, choose the appropriate mode, medium and means, and target, position, and deliver their products and services to all appropriate markets. We call such firms full-service publishers, our next core concept:

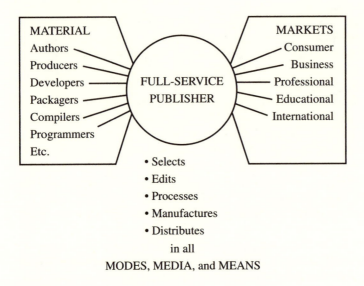

MATERIAL
Authors
Producers
Developers
Packagers
Compilers
Programmers
Etc.

FULL-SERVICE
PUBLISHER

MARKETS
Consumer
Business
Professional
Educational
International

• Selects
• Edits
• Processes
• Manufactures
• Distributes
in all
MODES, MEDIA, and MEANS

Figure 13-4
The Full-Service Publisher

Core Concept #43: The Full-Service Publisher

A true full-service organization has the capability of developing products in all formats for all distribution means in all markets, including internationally. But full-service publishers can also exist on a narrower scale, those firms that focus on a specific market or market segment's information needs and meet those needs in any and all appropriate media. Dun and Bradstreet, for instance, is a full-service publisher in the financial information arena.

Full-service publishers recognize that the greatest property control and greatest return to the rights holder come through total development of the property under the publisher's supervision. This means overseeing the development and marketing of the content in all its appropriate forms within market-focused segments, where they understand the information wants and needs of the customers and deploy the appropriate media for the content and its uses. Since this strategy requires enormous resources and has complex management demands, many publishers will choose instead to focus on a technology and/or market niche—e.g., a regional book publisher or a business video publisher. While these are valid strategies, publishers must decide which type of business they will be and how they will grow. Those mid-size companies choosing not to pursue a full-service publisher strategy will be ripe either for combination with other mid-sized firms or acquisition by the media conglomerates.

There are compelling competitive reasons publishers will continue to move in this direction. In list publishing, authors and content experts will increasingly seek publishers (and agents) that can manage the development of their properties in all media, extracting full value from their efforts and sustaining the life of their products. Those publishers with the demonstrated full-service capability and vision will attract valuable content providers seeking greater return from in-house development than from licensing to outside parties. Perhaps the ultimate full-service contract to date was the 1991 deal between Sony and Michael Jackson, providing the performer with a multi-million dollar guarantee for products in recording, video, film, and other formats over several years. The full-service development and marketing capabilities of Sony made the contract possible. Similar deals are Madonna's and Martha Stewart's with Time Warner.

Whichever markets are chosen, the demands of full-service publishing are great. They involve greater expenditures of time, money, and manpower. They involve heavy overhead expenditures to sustain the enterprise, heavy marketing expenses to promote products into multiple media, and a bias toward those properties which are appropriate for development in multiple media and markets. They entail greater risk, greater knowledge of the media and the markets, and an overall greater need for resources. They also entail the most difficult management challenges. But if the firm can do the best job of adding the value at each stage and in each medium, it stands to reap the maximum return for the risk and expenditure.

STRUCTURE

Given its strategy, the organization must then decide on the optimal structure for its pursuit. As noted earlier in this chapter, strategy is rarely conceived or implemented in isolation, but is instead formulated within the context of existing organizational constraints, which are both positive—e.g., high market share, media expertise—and negative—e.g., existing formats and distribution mechanisms.

The structure of the operation must allow the firm to maintain the environmental awareness critical to continued success. Each of the strategies enumerated above will lead to certain organizational structures best designed to pursue them. Within a company or division, the most common type of departmental focus is functional, in which the firm's operations are focused on the discrete components of the product development and marketing process—e.g., editorial, production, manufacturing, promotion, and sales—with an administrative group supporting any or all of the aspects of these processes as required. While this organization makes sense within a division or firm focused on a single medium or market, larger, diversified firms face more complex structural issues. Specifically, they must strike some balance between the demands of developing content in multiple media and selling content to one or more markets.

MEDIA-FOCUSED

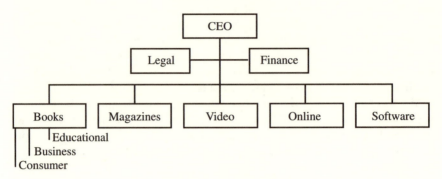

MARKET-FOCUSED

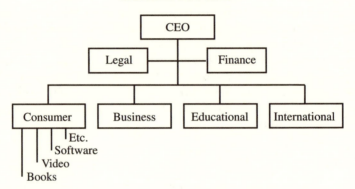

Figure 13-5
Media-Focused Versus Market-Focused Organizations

There are essentially two structural approaches for such diversified firms, as depicted in Figure 13-5. The first type is the media-focused firm, organized around technologies—e.g., a book division, a magazine division, a video group, a software division—that serve all markets. The other approach organizes around markets and wields all appropriate technologies, print and electronic, for the content and customers in the market or segment served. Depending on the organization's size, needs, marketplaces, and product mix, there are many variations on these basic structural themes, including hybrid structures which mix both media and market-focused units. A market-focused firm, for instance, may wish to explore a new media technology through the creation of a separate division dedicated to its research, development, and deployment.

An example of the media-focused organization is Time Warner, which is organized around book publishing, magazine publishing, video, and cable television, all in the consumer market. Reader's Digest is another consumer firm organized around media, with a magazine division, a book division, and a music division housing records, tapes, and videocassettes. The advantages of media-focused firms lie in their grouping of product development skills and their ability to build tight cultures around the demands of a given media technology. The demands of software development, for instance, are clearly different from those of weekly magazine publication. The potential drawbacks of media focus, however, are that the firm may lose its customer focus. It may also fail to see or exploit technology synergies or trends. It may further duplicate marketing to the same customers, spending more to do so and losing content and service synergies.

The implicit statement behind the structure of market-focused organizations is that the focus is on the content and the customers. Such firms are in a position to be sensitive to their market's information needs—a counterbalance to the product-driven approach to content—and are structured to deploy all appropriate media in service of their customers' information needs and wants. Disadvantages include a dilution of media development expertise, missed opportunities in cross-market selling, and a lack of centralized production and manufacturing.

Such market-focused groups are increasingly popular among large diversified firms, however, as they allow the firm to consolidate several market-related businesses under one umbrella despite differences in content or media focus. Paramount Publishing's Consumer Group, for instance, includes not only trade adult (e.g., Simon & Schuster, Prentice-Hall Press, Summit Books) and mass market publishing (Pocket Books, Washington Square Press) but a variety of other imprints and operations, such as travel books (American Express, Frommer), reference (Betty Crocker, Webster's New World dictionaries), and audio cassette publishing (AudioWorks). The Paramount Publishing Education Group develops and markets materials for all ages, from pre-school to continuing adult education, including books, videocassettes and discs, audio cassettes and compact discs, and CD-ROM. The Professional Information Group is even more diversified across media formats, meeting "about one half of our customer needs . . . via print products and the remaining half by a wide spectrum of other media and services, including computer software, online data delivery, videotapes, audio cassettes, live services, and fee-for-service transactions," says Peter Nalle, group president.[17]

THE HORIZONTAL ORGANIZATION

Conglomerate firms with superior performance are not just holding companies of separate businesses but are fully-integrated organizations, knit together across as well as up and down by what Michael Porter calls horizontal interrelationships. The sum of such interrelationships across the firm's vertically-structured business units is the horizontal organization, the next core concept:[18]

Core Concept #44: The Horizontal Organization

As Porter has stated, "The unique corporate assets of a diversified firm are the existing and potential interrelationships that reside in the value chains of its business units. These interrelationships represent the major contribution of a diversified firm to its business units, and to the industries it might enter. The central role of the diversified firm is to nurture and expand these interrelationships."

Structuring the interrelationships is critical, for as Porter says, "organizational structure balances the benefits of separation and integration." Porter exhorts firms to "create horizontal organization mechanisms to assure implementation. Firms cannot successfully exploit interrelationships without a horizontal organizational structure that encourages coordination and transfers skills across business unit lines. Such tasks as defining the right business units, clustering them into the proper groups and sectors, and establishing incentives for business unit managers to work together are vital to success."[19]

While "grouping is perhaps the single most powerful device for focusing attention on and reinforcing interrelationships,"[20] other mechanisms include centralization of key firm-wide activities (e.g., purchasing), cross-divisional operating committees, task forces, cross-divisional senior management groups, structured interdivisional business arrangements, management information systems, and human resources policies, as well as more informal approaches, though these last are usually least effective as they carry no explicit organizational weight.

The wielding of several technologies in several markets demands that diversified publishing and media firms face these challenges. The market-focused company will develop products and services that can sell into more than one market and thus should be made available for marketing through those channels. They will also need to draw upon technical expertise in other divisions as media development tasks will often be performed in parallel, not in sequence. The media-focused firms, on the other hand, will need to interact for the sake of cross-media property development. In all cases there are varying degrees of in-house development versus jobbing out.

How the various tentacles of the firm interact must be led from the top, where senior management must encourage the component parts of the organization to promote synergistic ideas, then aid in developing procedures and mechanisms to promote and routinize interdivisional and intracorporate relationships. As Porter stresses:

Top management must reinforce interrelationships by sending clear signals about their importance, and promoting a culture where the corporation has an identity that transcends and reinforces that of business units. Achieving interrelationships usually requires the creation of some shared values within a firm. Managers must perceive that collaboration with other business units is important and will be rewarded, and that senior management will act fairly in measuring the performance of the individual units involved.[21]

As new markets and new media develop, organizational solutions that take advantage of the new opportunities are not always readily apparent, and trial and error is often the case. Companies should be prepared to live with reorganization in a post-merger or acquisition environment. The ideal organization is that which can respond quickly and capably to attractive publishing opportunities, which means the ability to draw upon its full resources to assess opportunities as they arise and coordinate those resources to capitalize on the opportunities.

SUMMARY AND CONCLUSION

In this chapter we have introduced four additional core concepts for Money, the seventh M:

- *Core Concept #41: Related Diversification*
- *Core Concept #42: Strategic Stance and Entrepreneurship*
- *Core Concept #43: The Full-Service Publisher*
- *Core Concept #44: The Horizontal Organization*

Publishers seeking to pursue new business opportunities will raise their chances for success through diversification related in some fashion to their current business. Their organizational strategy will be based on an assessment of their own resources and where value can be added. Firms will define their strategic stance before assessing the short- and long-term strategic options available to them, from passive licensing through full entry into a new business via start-up, merger, or acquisition. The firm's strategy determines the firm's structure as a market or media-focused organization. However the firm is structured, it should be integrated horizontally (e.g., cross-divisionally) as well as vertically to wield the organization's full resources in pursuit of business opportunities.

NOTES

1. From *Strategy and Structure* (1962) by Alfred D. Chandler, Jr., 1962, as quoted in Raymond E. Miles and Charles C. Snow, *Organizational Strategy, Structure, and Process* (New York: McGraw-Hill, 1978), 7.

2. Raymond E. Miles and Charles C. Snow, *Organizational Strategy, Structure, and Process* (New York: McGraw-Hill, 1978), 5–8. The authors point out that these ideas are based on "three pivotal ideas" underlying the theories in their book: "(1) organizations act to create their environments; (2) management's strategic choices shape the organization's structure and processes; and (3) structure and process constrain strategy."

3. From Chapter IV, "The Distribution of Rewards," in "The Economics of Information" (Washington, D.C.: U.S. Congress Office of Technology Assessment, 1985), IV-14.

4. In "Consumer Content," Booz Allen Hamilton, *Information Industry Insights*, Issue #9, 12.

5. As quoted in Stewart Brand, *The Media Lab: Inventing the Future at MIT* (New York: Viking Penguin, 1987), 238–39. Some online information services already track customer usage by specific area of the service.

6. Lewis Coser, et al., *Books—The Culture and Commerce of Publishing* (New York: Basic Books, 1982), 176.

7. Peter Drucker, *Technology, Management, and Society* (New York: Harper and Row, Colophon reprint edition, 1970), 36. For an introduction to strategic analysis of business opportunities, *see* Philip Kotler, *Marketing Management,* Chapter 4, "The Strategic Management and Marketing Process" (Englewood Cliffs, N.J.: Prentice-Hall, 1980), 63–91. Kotler defines diversification as developing new products for new markets. Three other growth opportunities—existing products in existing markets (market penetration), new products in existing markets (product development), and existing products in new markets (market development)—are not seen as diversification per se in Kotler's scheme. I use the term "diversification" here to include all growth opportunities beyond the firm's existing business.

8. Tom Peters and Bob Waterman, *In Search of Excellence* (New York: Harper and Row, 1983), 294. Rumelt's work was subsequently expanded and published as *Strategy, Structure, and Economic Performance* (Boston, Mass.: Harvard Business School Press, 1986).

9. *See also* the four cell Boston Consulting Group growth-share matrix (Cash Cows, Dogs, Question Marks, and Stars) and the General Electric nine cell Business Screen, as discussed in Kotler, *Marketing Management,* 75–80.

10. As quoted in Geraldine Fabrikant, "Hearst's 8-Year Buying Spree," *The New York Times,* 26 April, 1987.

11. Raymond E. Miles and Charles C. Snow, *Organizational Strategy, Structure, and Process,* 28–29. Miles and Snow also review other organizational typologies, and David Patten, in his book *Newspapers and New Media* (White Plains, N.Y.: Knowledge Industry Publications, 1986), writes of four investment strategies that roughly mirror Miles and Snow's typology: (1) the conceptual approach (defender), (2) hold your place (defensive prospector), (3) R&D (analyzer/prospector), and (4) market experiment (prospector).

12. Peter Drucker, *Innovation and Entrepreneurship* (New York: Basic Books, 1985), 25.

13. Drucker, *Innovation and Entrepreneurship,* 34–35, 138, and 140. Drucker cites three characteristics for successful innovation: (1) innovation is work and requires a solid understanding of the environment; (2) to succeed, innovators must build on their

strengths; (3) innovation is an effect on economy and society, changing behavior in customers and people in general.

14. Strategic alliances are addressed in Poppel and Goldstein, *Information Technology: The Trillion-Dollar Opportunity* (New York: McGraw-Hill, 1987), pages 93–94, where the authors provide guidelines for successful external alliances; Michael Porter on coalitions in *Competitive Advantage* (New York: The Free Press, 1985); and Kathryn Rudie Harrigan, *Strategies for Joint Ventures* (Lexington, Mass.: Lexington Books/D.C. Heath, 1985), among other sources.

15. For an extended treatment of start-up business units within a sponsoring corporation, see Gifford Pinchot III's *Intrapreneuring* (New York: Harper & Row, 1985).

16. As reported in Stephen C. Coley and Sigurd E. Reinton, "The Hunt for Value," *The World in 1988, The Economist Publications*, 141–42. The same study also found that one-third of the top performing British companies and over one-half of the U.S. top performers look to internal, organic growth as a prime means of developing a portfolio of business opportunities over time, some of which succeed and others of which are cast off if unsuccessful.

17. Paramount Communications, *Annual Report, 1990,* 23.

18. Michael Porter, *Competitive Advantage* (New York: The Free Press, 1985), 364ff. Chapter 10, "Horizontal Strategy" and Chapter 11, "Achieving Interrelationships," serve as the basis of the discussion in this section. While Porter refers to horizontal organization as the "procedures that facilitate interrelationships," I use the term to refer to the sum total of interrelationships which define an organization's cross-business unit structures and mechanisms.

19. Porter, *Competitive Advantage,* 380 and 375. Porter cites the environment at Koji Kobayashi's NEC as "a clear culture . . . which reinforces finding and exploiting interrelationships" (*Competitive Advantage,* 413). Mechanisms used at NEC include business group orientation, over forty standing corporate-wide committees, a strong corporate theme and mission, personnel rotation, and an explicit cross-business planning system. In the United States, General Electric is an example of a firm striving to develop interrelationships. The company's 1990 annual report discusses at length the $58 billion company's efforts to create "the boundaryless company" across its thirteen businesses. Customers, suppliers, and internal functions intentionally blur in GE's effort to create "integrated diversity . . . the elimination of boundaries between businesses and the transferring of ideas from one place in the company to another. . . . Integrated diversity means the drawing together of our 13 different businesses by sharing ideas, by finding multiple applications for technological advancements, and by moving people across businesses to provide fresh perspectives and to develop broad-based experience. Integrated diversity gives us a company that is considerably greater than the sum of its parts." General Electric Company, "To Our Share Owners," *1990 Annual Report,* 1–4.

20. Porter, *Competitive Advantage,* 396.

21. Ibid., 410.

CHAPTER 14

Maximizing Return: The Intellectual Property Management Program

In the previous chapter we saw how different strategies and structures are available to companies wishing to pursue diversification and new business opportunities. In this chapter we are concerned with product level strategies, which are based on the resources and structure of the organization and set within the context of the organization's strategy, i.e., how the firm evaluates and chooses which development opportunities to pursue, both for existing information assets and for future properties. We will discuss how firms maximize return on their information assets before introducing the seven step Intellectual Property Management Program.

MAXIMIZING RETURN ON INFORMATION ASSETS

A firm's information assets are the rights to the properties it owns or has licensed for development. Information Age publishers seek maximum return on that bundle of property rights by managing each property to extract its maximum value over the longest period of time. In the valuation of a publishing or media firm, its information assets are among the most significant as they represent the firm's most exploitable resource.

To maximize return, firms scrutinize their existing information base for incremental revenue lying dormant in properties, imprints, trademarks, and other assets already owned or under license. New technologies, as well as new markets, bring new development and revenue possibilities for such assets. This means choosing specific information assets and developing strategies for them. This is true of any content firm, in publishing or other media segments. As one analyst stated regarding Paramount Communications' success: "Paramount may be most distinguished by its willingness and ability to milk the most in revenues from its established properties . . . 'They're able to keep their long-term assets current.' "[1] Henry Becton, president of Boston-based public broadcasting station WGBH, refers to this strategy as "multi-versioning," creating multiple products from the same programming base for both educational and consumer markets: "The net effect is that we bring in other revenues, which help pay for the production to begin with."[2] In 1988, Turner Broadcasting formed a licensing unit, Turner Home Entertainment, to exploit merchandising and other rights to the parent firm's Warner Brothers and MGM film and television libraries and Hanna-Barbera cartoon collection. Executive vice president Steve Chamberlain refers to their strategy as "rejuvenating the characters." Classic films the company has revitalized and re-released on video, usually in major anniversary years, include *The Wizard of Oz, Gone with the Wind, Citizen Kane, Casablanca,* and *King Kong.* The company also plans a Wizard of Oz theme park in Kansas.[3]

While not always the case, maximum return strategies typically involve gaining the widest exposure for a concept in all appropriate embodiments. Information Age publishers can learn from their media partners—advertisers—who use all appropriate media to gain maximum message exposure, awareness, and mindshare. Advertising agencies develop cross-media campaigns in print (magazines and newspapers), broadcast (TV and radio), direct mail, outdoor, and other media, all coordinated for maximum exposure and message retention via selected media vehicles. With the same range of media options open to them, Information Age publishers intent on maximizing return will increasingly develop, plan, and manage the same kind of cross-media, cross-modal campaigns. These will be extensions of the film and television tie-ins we see now, where a theatrical release or broadcast run stimulates sales of books, videocassettes and discs, audio cassettes and discs, and a range of other merchandise in their wakes.

There are, of course, significant differences between advertising and content-based publishing. Advertising messages are shorter and their campaigns typically more sustained. Also, while the simultaneity of messages in multiple media is effective in advertising, a publishing program may require different approaches, such as a sequenced roll-out instead of an omni-media blitz. In publishing it is also true that some product forms are not considered complementary but mutually exclusive, such as paperback and hardcover editions of the same title. Perhaps the single biggest difference is that publishing's customers typically buy the products and services, whereas advertising messages are free.

Full-service publishers (*see* Core Concept #43) take a step toward accomplishing cross-media property management strategies when they acquire as broad a bundle of rights as they can at the time of initial property acquisition. Certain properties and certain authors and content experts will be responsive to such "one-stop shopping." The publisher acquires total development and marketing control for a sequenced or simultaneous release, either in-house or via managed and coordinated sub-licensing, and in addition to gaining property control, maximizes return. Even if the acquiring firm cannot fund the broader acquisition of rights on its own, it can seek other sources of backing by, for example, pre-financing rights sales or using outside investors, as is the case with WGBH's "multi-versioning" strategy cited above.

THE INTELLECTUAL PROPERTY MANAGEMENT PROGRAM

The Intellectual Property Management Program (IPMP) takes a content-based, property management approach—the property being the underlying intellectual property from which the products and services are developed—to the development of a cross-media campaign that cycles content through all appropriate media forms to sustain the property's life and obtain maximum return on investment:

Core Concept #45: The Intellectual Property Management Program

The key for publishers is to study the content and determine how best to deploy it in the appropriate media in a staged program from conception through birth, development, maturity, and reincarnation. The most successful properties will be maintained throughout the life of their copyright, after which they go into the public domain, though derivative and adaptive versions

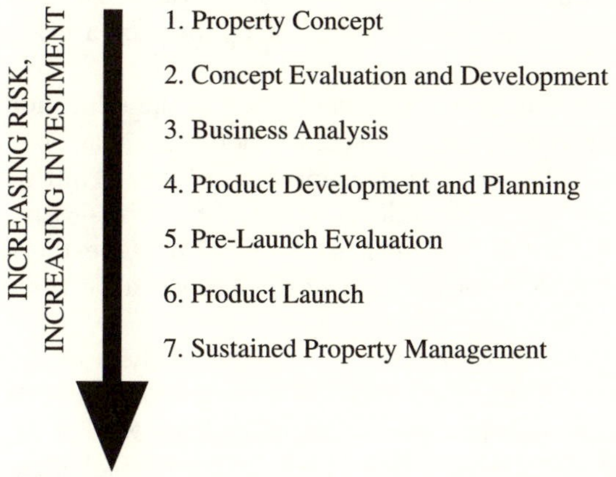

1. Property Concept

2. Concept Evaluation and Development

3. Business Analysis

4. Product Development and Planning

5. Pre-Launch Evaluation

6. Product Launch

7. Sustained Property Management

INCREASING RISK, INCREASING INVESTMENT

Figure 14-1
The Intellectual Property Management Program

of the original property may continue under copyright protection. Registered trademarks can provide additional forms of protection for imprint names, logos, and colophons, and therefore, by extension, content franchises. The protectable asset, though, is the intellectual property, that is, the expression (property) of the idea (intellectual) as recognized by copyright law.

The IPMP consists of seven basic steps, as shown in Figure 14-1. As a firm proceeds through the seven step sequence for a given property, both risk and investment increase.

Step 1: Property Concept

Property concepts can be either internally or externally generated. Those coming from the outside are received and evaluated by the firm in the same sequence as those ideas internally generated. But whether from the inside or outside, there are two basic sources of new concepts: inspiration and purposeful innovation.

Inspired concepts are those that emerge from creative wellsprings, sparked by intuition or a flash of insight. Oftentimes such ideas are born to fit the form and are thus technology-inspired. Television producers and directors will come up with ideas that fit their medium. Other developers and publishers will have ideas for laserdisc programs, magazine articles, books, or multimedia products. Often intuition combines all 5M's, or even all 7M's, in a wholistic flash, without analysis of component parts.

The opposite approach, purposeful innovation, is championed by Peter Drucker in his book *Innovation and Entrepreneurship.* Purposeful innovation uses a structured, orderly approach to new product concepts. In publishing it would employ such tools as the five value-added M's matrix (Table 3-1) and the 5M's wheel (Figure 4-2) to assess the full range of options for a given property concept.

Using another tool, the Media Universe, a firm could look at the education market as currently configured and see a gap in the aural mode, one-way open channel cell—radio. Is there a viable product concept there? Chris Whittle's Channel One service exploited a gap in the education market matrix—visual mode, one-way open channel—i.e., television. Prior to Channel One there was little or no in-school broadcast television, and none that was advertiser-supported.

Another approach to purposeful innovation is through an analysis of the firm's existing information assets, as discussed above. The firm first studies its content closely to understand its possible uses and applications. Next it assesses the licensing history and rights status of the property to see which areas are free for development. With development and/or licensing rights established, the publisher can generate product possibilities, considering medium formats separately as well as in conjunction with one another. The publisher will also consider the various means of distribution as well as different markets and market segments.

Another purposeful innovation approach is brainstorming, where a group—for instance, an author, editor, and marketer—use both structured innovation based on the 5M's and free-form approaches to generate a range of ideas. Such brainstorming sessions can also be held with focus groups comprised of customers from target market segments.

Step 2: Concept Evaluation and Development

Once the property concepts are on the table they are assessed for potential development. Those ideas deemed worth pursuing are run through an initial concept screen using the five value-added M's:

Material: What type of content is it? Does the firm know the content area? Will it be developed in-house or outside? Are the proposed developers capable of doing the project? If no developers are proposed, can the appropriate parties be engaged for its development?

Mode: Is the material already embodied in one symbolic mode? What other modes—textual, visual, aural—either singly or in combinations, are most appropriate for the material?

Medium: Is there a "happy medium" for the content and its expression? How will the content be developed to take full advantage of the medium's strength and provide maximum benefit to end-users? How might its embodiment in one medium interact with others? Will the products envisioned cannibalize or synergize with the firm's existing and future products? What media will provide maximum reach? At what stage in the life cycle are the respective media envisioned for use? What is the installed player base for machine-readable formats? For instance, in many cases a book is a book, period. But increasingly an audio version, a video version, an optical disc version, or merchandising opportunities will point to added revenue.

Means: Should the property be developed as a list, periodical, or open channel product or service or some combination of the three? What specific distribution channels will be chosen? Will the firm undertake distribution itself or seek third party resellers?

Market: For which markets are the envisioned products intended? Will the property sell to one or more markets or segments? Does the property have mass or global appeal? How could it be positioned, both purely and vis-à-vis competitive products? Can the customers be identified? How will they be reached?

As part of its evaluation, the concept is reworked and developed in different product and market scenarios. Prior to its analysis for viability as a commercial prospect, the concept must be developed into an identifiable set of products susceptible to business analysis. For these questions the firm may develop a media release plan, as shown in Figure 14-2, as well as depicting the media array in the Media Universe, as shown in Figure 14-3.[4]

These two figures depict the array of products projected for a property to be developed initially as a book, audio cassette, and audio disc, in conjunction with the airing of a broadcast television series, subsequently released as a softcover book and on videocassette and disc, and later rerun on cable television. At least one book format is always in print, and the visual and aural publishing media of cassette and disc remain in distribution after broadcast and cablecast runs. While the release plan shows both sequenced and simultaneous releases, the Media Universe adds the market dimension. As depicted here, this property is designed to sell to both consumer and educational markets.

The movement from the initial concept to evaluation and development is a movement from intuition to analysis. Concept evaluation then trades right-

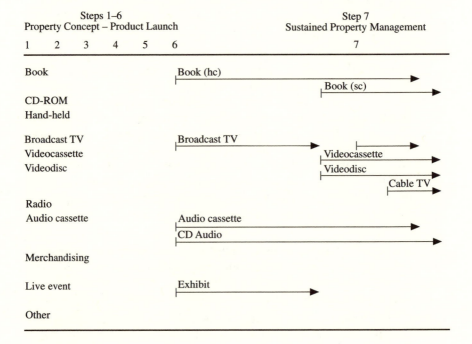

Figure 14-2
Media Release Plan

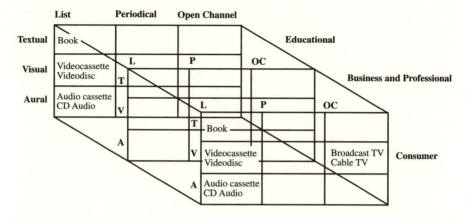

Figure 14-3
The Media Plan in the Media Universe

brain thinking for left, running the concept through the screens. Aside from pure product-oriented criteria, other aspects are preliminarily assessed: are there existing competitive products? What resources does the firm bring to the table? What resources does it lack and where can they be obtained?

Where applicable, market research can be of use in concept evaluation by giving some idea of product salability. It can cut up-front development costs, especially on bigger projects, through focus groups, expert testing, and other methods, and sometimes table a project before it's too late.

Step 3: Business Analysis

If a property concept has successfully moved through evaluation and initial development in Step 2, it will next be scrutinized for profit and loss in various scenarios, e.g., licensing versus in-house development. This is where the 2M's, Management and Money, come into play, in the creation of development scenarios that assess the economic attractiveness of the opportunity. Moreover, management will also ask (and answer) questions concerning the firm's capabilities and appropriateness for the project: Who is the property's executive champion? Is there a product champion? What does the firm bring to the table and what other resources does it require to successfully publish the property? Which scenarios maximize return? Are they reasonable and reliable? The analysis is undertaken of the entire property and its full development possibilities, quantifying and assessing profit and loss on specific products and services.

Step 4: Product Development and Planning

If the business analysis yields satisfactory results and other authorizations are passed, the decision is made to proceed with the property. If necessary, rights are acquired from the outside, in which case the contractually agreed terms form the foundation for the property and the firm's development options.

In addition to the actual development of the initial product or products, the publisher will also initiate planning for the product launch, including all aspects of marketing, such as advertising, publicity, promotion, distribution—in essence, how the property will be introduced to the world. This planning is concurrent with product development, but as the initial product nears completion, the plans will adjust accordingly. A multiple product roll-out, for example, might become a staged, sequenced development rather than a simultaneous release.

Step 5: Pre-launch Evaluation

More common in some segments of the industry (e.g., software, theatrical film) than others, product evaluation prior to the launch or release is designed to ascertain weaknesses in the product and correct any remaining defects. This is usually the final stage at which a product can be killed prior to commercialization. Software is routinely shipped to beta test sites, and pre-release prints of multimillion dollar films are screened in front of test audiences. Regional roll-outs of products are also common, and with magazines, test issues are often used. For other formats, such as trade books, the additional investment in evaluation at this stage often does not make economic sense, although early signs of the book's strength or weakness based on the response from advance readings may influence the size of the initial print run and marketing plans.

Step 6: Product Launch

By this stage, all is ready for market introduction. Marketing, packaging, positioning, pricing, the communications plan, distribution channels and support—all become reality as the initial product or products are introduced to the marketplace. For multi-product launches, a coordinated approach integrates the various product components in a single campaign. Each such campaign will be tailored to the intended market and based upon the specific property content.

Step 7: Sustained Property Management

As depicted in Figure 14-2, the initial product launch is the culmination of the first six steps of the IPMP. It lays the foundation for ongoing property management, which in successful properties is continually reinvented and far outlasts the preparation for the initial launch. Thus while the initial property planning is critical to the future success of the property, the majority of property management takes place in the post-launch phase, where the objective is sustaining the life of the property in its multiple incarnations. Once the new product is born it begins its life in the market and will cycle through the stages of development—i.e., market introduction, reaction, growth, maturity, and decline and revitalization, similar to the media life cycle discussed in Chapter 8.[5]

Sustained property management is not concerned solely with maximizing return, for a property that is poorly managed or whose reputation is damaged in some fashion can quickly lose marketplace value. It is also concerned with quality control, including how the various manifestations of the property are developed; brand and trademark protection; cannibalization and/or synergy with existing and future derivatives and adaptations of the property; and over-exposure or market glut, which could turn potential buyers and users against the property. All of these are set within the context of the objective of sustaining the life of the property.

The key to successful sustained property management is continued organizational commitment to the property. Rarely are a property's full possibilities envisioned prior to the initial product's launch. Opportunities arise for new development possibilities both from within and without the firm, and products succeed and fail in unexpected ways. Property managers must adjust accordingly, for it is a dynamic process for each property. They must continually track the property's vital signs and reevaluate, reinvent, and seek points of revitalization over the life of the property, especially as markets and media change. Thus scanning the marketplace for feedback and the environment for technological and marketplace change, as well as new competitive threats, are part of the publisher's ongoing responsibilities in property management.

Such revitalization and extension is the lifeblood of sustained property management. Many children's books, for instance, have taken on new life in audio and/or video form with the introduction and proliferation of cassette players. Optical disc formats provide new and different opportunities for the same properties. A broadcast television program may sustain its life through spin-off print components as well as video and audio components, or it may go cross-market, such as the sale in the educational market of both print and non-print components of Ken Burns' *The Civil War* and Robert MacNeil's *The Story of English.*

Understanding how the media interact—and such interaction, as noted throughout this study, is continually evolving (*see* Core Concept #23, The Dynamic Equilibrium)—is critical to successful property management in the Information Age. As noted earlier, one such firm engaged in full property management is the Walt Disney Company, which manages its *real* properties—the theme parks and associated accommodations and facilities of Disneyland, Walt Disney World, EuroDisney, and Disney Japan—as extensions of its *intellectual* properties, which themselves have been created, revitalized, and reintroduced to markets and generations anew around the world over a span of decades.[6]

Each property requires a property manager to sustain it over time. As discussed in Chapter 12, the property manager is typically at the point of origin of the property within the organization, the original product developer, the product champion who is the focal point for all plans and decisions related to the property's management throughout its life. By engaging in-house and outside resources, the property manager seeks to orchestrate an integrated publishing program across media and markets. He both initiates ideas for new development and responds to and evaluates outside proposals for development of new products and services that are extensions of the underlying property. Each development possibility suggests different strategic partners. License arrangements, development deals, distribution deals, and other types of alliances typically proliferate for the more successful properties.

As Information Age publishers pursue integrated property management strategies, they will establish procedures for new media product development that will become as habitual as the familiar media development cycles already in place. Such development procedures typically revolve around the same three major parties: the author/content expert, the producer-developer in the given medium, and the publisher as property manager, financer, and marketer.

Just as Hollywood seeks and develops film properties with an eye toward after-markets, such as videocassette and international sales, so Information Age publishers seek properties with multiple revenue streams, i.e., properties that can be developed in more than one format and for more than one market. They will also seek properties that, like good real estate, sustain or gain value over time, either because core product sales continue or because the property is rich in derivative product possibilities, or both.

While publishers often seek such evergreen properties, faster product life cycles often mean that today's content is obsolete more quickly than ever before, washed out of the public consciousness. Windows of publishing opportunity open and close quickly. Thus custom-publishing and quick concept-to-market turn-around become increasingly important for publishers to manage. Periodical publishers are already in this game, but it increasingly affects many segments of book publishing, as well, especially those in the consumer market. In the educational market, the move toward custom texts at the post-secondary level also means quicker to-market times and more rapid obsolescence of material. In the business markets some segments, such as the financial markets, require information that is not even seconds old, while the pace of knowledge growth in the professional markets demands constant updating. Due to the quickened pace, it is essential for publishing firms to develop the infrastructure to support such initiatives, including not only acquisition, editorial updating, production, and marketing capabilities, but a mechanism for proper rights clearance, which means constructing and maintaining a database of contract information with an accurate, up-to-the-minute inventory of property rights bought and sold.

SUMMARY AND CONCLUSION

The final core concept for publishing in the Information Age is for the seventh M, Money:

- *Core Concept #45: The Intellectual Property Management Program*

Publishing firms wishing to maximize return on individual properties can follow the seven step Intellectual Property Management Program, which takes a content-based approach to the development of an intellectual property in all its appropriate media forms throughout the life of the property. The firm's development and/or licensing capabilities in multiple media and markets will influence the types of properties sought and acquired. Faster product life cycles will make it increasingly difficult to publish new evergreen properties. They will also require firms to establish efficient procedures and technology and information infrastructures for effective and profitable sustained property management.

NOTES

1. Mark Manson, analyst at Donaldson, Lufkin, & Jenrette, as quoted by Richard W. Stevenson in "Paramount Pictures' Success Key to Revamping at G&W," *The New York Times,* 11 April, 1989.

2. As quoted in Glenn Rifkin, "Futuristic Lessons from a Public Television Station," *The New York Times,* 20 January, 1993, D2.

3. *See* Jay E. Rosen, "Turner Mines the Licensing Treasure of Its Cartoon Cache," *The New York Times,* 4 January, 1993.

4. Other tools introduced in this study that are appropriate for use in concept analysis and development include the Five Value-Added M's Matrix (Table 3-1) and the Content-Based Publishing wheel (Figure 4-1), cited above, as well as the Media Matrix (Figure 6-1), the Life Cycle of Media Technologies (Table 8-1), and the media matrices for the respective markets (Figures 10-2, 10-3, and 10-4).

5. *See also* Yoram Wind, *Product Policy: Concepts, Methods, and Strategy* (Reading, Mass.: Addison-Wesley, 1982), especially Chapter 8, "New Product Development Systems," and subsequent chapters in Part II, *New Product Development,* as well as the other sources cited earlier regarding product life cycles.

6. *See also* "The Ideas Business—Economy of the Mind," *The Economist,* 23 December, 1989, which refers to intellectual properties as "unreal estate."

PART VI

Conclusion

In the first five parts of this study we have seen how the publishing paradigm has shifted. We disaggregated the major elements of the publishing construct and enterprise for purposes of analysis and understanding. In this final part, consisting of a single chapter, we will reconsider four major themes for publishing in the Information Age: technology, strategy, management, and meaning.

CHAPTER 15

The Digital Enterprise and the Paradigm of Promise

THE MAN-MACHINE WORLD AND THE DIGITAL ENTERPRISE

The changes taking place in information technology are central to a broad technological sweep that continues to roll up its force as we stand at the brink of the 21st century. On a 1991 *New York Times* list of ten critical technologies, based on expert opinions, as "transforming the decade," six were information technologies: parallel computing, superconductors, digitized television-computing, microchips, fiber optic networks, and software programming.[1] Changes in biotechnology and medical technology, energy and materials technology, agriculture, manufacturing, weaponry, transportation and space travel, and others are also part of an inexorable trend toward a more highly technologized world, a world in which the fates of men and machines will intertwine more intimately than at any time in human history. Our individual and collective survival is already owed to a range of life-altering medical technologies. It is hardly a new observation that we have also created the technological means to annihilate our species.

Technology is arguably the primary lever of change throughout society and industry, fueling social upheaval and causing geopolitical realignment. Such change is often fomented by the invasiveness of both mass and personal communications media. Many observers feel the crumbling of the rigid eastern bloc was directly attributable to the invasiveness of information and communications technologies, including computers, copiers, fax machines, telephones, television, and radio.

In the long view of communications history, electronic multimodal publishing is something that has been waiting to happen all along, and we now stand at that cusp in the development of the media where previously separate technologies—video, audio, computers, printing, satellite, telecommunications, and the others discussed throughout this study—are converging to bring about major changes in our information universe. Many say there is a manifest destiny moving us toward a fully electronic information environment. In Gene Roddenberry's depiction of the 24th century on *Star Trek—The Next Generation,* nearly all information is digital and screen-delivered. (An exception to screen delivery is the Holodeck, which creates 3-dimensional walk-in computer-generated environments of the user's choice, the extension of today's virtual reality.) In 1928, a futurist from another generation, Aldous Huxley, said, when speaking of advances in print technology: "It has become obvious that the machine is here to stay. . . . Machines exist: let us then exploit them to create beauty—a modern beauty, while we are about it. It is only from the man with the machine that I can hope for any amelioration of my lot as a reader."[2]

The vector of change in publishing also points away from product and toward process. As Christopher Burns has stated:

New information uses are being transformed from consumption to communication. It is less a product and more often a process. . . . The idea of an information "package" which solved so many of our problems several centuries ago may not be the best intellectual model for the newest and fastest growing aspect of information. In business, science, health care and government—and prospectively in future home information systems—the role of the author and the publisher, even the role of the printer, is being disintermediated by technology, and the package has become increasingly a "connection."[3]

The publisher of the Information Age, in Koji Kobayashi's terms, is an information service center, a packager and provider of information to physical and electronic delivery systems, which allow for two-way feedback, selection, on-demand publishing, and other technology and market-driven information forms. The information service center, like the full-service publisher, is managed computerized data that feeds physical and electronic distribution networks—VAN, fiber optic, satellite, and physical packages—for end-users in home, business, and education markets. It is akin to cyberpunk author William Gibson's depiction of a jointly created virtual reality, "mankind's unthinkably complex consensual hallucination, the matrix, cyberspace, where the great corporate hotcores burned like neon novas, data so dense you suffered sensory overload if you tried to apprehend more than the merest outline."[4]

Even in Frederick Lancaster's vision of an all-electronic, paperless environment, some organizations, whether today's publishers and diversified media firms or others, will be the chief producers and purveyors of information and entertainment in its myriad forms. Were an all-electronic world to materialize, or even if digitally-based computers were to be replaced by biochemically-based information processors or some wholly new medium, media formats and attributes would not disappear. Nor would the other four M's, Material, Mode, Means, and Market, the basic components of the communications construct. The various media formats will continue to be part of an evolving equilibrium, with formats jockeying for position, forced to accept new positions and undergo re-evaluation as new formats are introduced. We can already see new electronic media being affected by even newer electronic media. Magnetic disk storage technologies are threatened by read-write optical discs, and optical discs by superconductors. We can be certain that there are other new technologies just around the corner, waiting to challenge these.

Now, in the final decade of the second millennium, all aspects of the publishing enterprise continue to be automated. While newspaper and magazine publishers automated production in the 1970s and 1980s, book publishers are confronting the same challenges in the 1990s. Moreover the evolution of information technology for enterprise management from mainframes to PC's to client-server networked computing has brought the need for infrastructure automation to the forefront, a necessary element for survival in a cost-conscious and competitive industry environment. The appropriate use of information technology not only leads to organizational efficiencies and cost savings by improving processes, information access, and knitting the organization together. It also provides a strategic advantage over competitors by enabling access to critical operating data more quickly, more accurately, more thoroughly, and for a variety of planning and operational purposes.

Successful publishing firms of the 1990s, then, by automating process, product, and support technologies, will emerge as nothing short of the digital enterprise. As banks and airlines automated their operations in the 1970s and 1980s not just to keep pace but to survive, so publishing firms will automate in the 1990s to survive. The vision is of a lean, highly automated, networked organization developing digital properties that it feeds into print and electronic formats and distribution systems. The organization supports product development with low-cost, high-powered workstations and interactive multimedia authoring tools, and it supports marketing strategists with an array of print and electronic communications vehicles. The entire organization is supported throughout by an infrastructural information system that provides interpersonal and intragroup communications and yields key operating and strategic information to users in any requested form on demand.

THE PARADIGM OF PROMISE

It is technology, then, which drives changes in markets and products and thus has a profound impact on corporate strategy. Publishers today are faced with a choice, not unlike previous communities of practitioners faced with major decisions about the direction and philosophical foundation of their futures. In the common understanding, and in the minds of many in the publishing profession, publishing is still synonymous with print products, ink on paper. This paradigm resists the invasion of electronics, excludes non-print forms, and sees television and computer screens as the enemy. Like astronomers in the time of Copernicus, biologists in the time of Darwin, physicists in the time of Einstein, publishers can opt for a relatively new and untested paradigm that offers a broader promise of growth and opportunity, or they can continue to adhere to the known and proven paradigm and pursue its limits. Many will remain undecided for some time.

But once the perceptual shift has been made and the world is viewed through new eyes, opportunities rather than threats unfold. Information Age publishers will come to predominate regardless of the attitudes of the unconvinced (after all, the Flat Earth Society still attracts adherents, albeit in limited numbers). Those publishers seeking to fulfill their mission to inform, educate, inspire, or enlighten, will see and seize the opportunities afforded by the new technologies, thereby participating in the mainstream tradition of publishing which has historically sought growth through opportunities presented by new formats and processes.

The new paradigm decouples publishing from its adherence to exclusively print formats and embraces the selection, packaging, and delivery of information in all media forms. In the new paradigm, decisions regarding electronic processes and formats are seen as everyday business concerns, not as foreign threats. In the new paradigm, the symbolic embodiment of material is emphasized equally with its physical embodiment. In the new paradigm, there is a coexisting plurality of traditional and new media forms, an evolving equilibrium as information and media technologies continue to change. In the new paradigm, complementarity and synergy are sought rather than displacement and competition. In the new paradigm, the past is both incorporated and built upon, for the new paradigm lays the groundwork for the new way of working, new areas of experimentation and exploration. It defines the scope of the new work and defines what the central problems are to be addressed. For those publishers not making the perceptual shift, the competitive environment will eventually force them to change or lose out. Authors, artists, designers, producers, and other content providers will go elsewhere, as will employees, investors, and customers.

The Information Age publisher sees this challenge, for his mission is to communicate and enable and his objective is to profit in so doing. The increased technological complexity of his industry and the plurality of content, medium, and market choices now presented to him make fulfillment of his mission and achievement of his objectives all the more challenging. He can choose to ignore this complexity, or he can choose to embrace it as the inevitable challenge of his times. A sort of professional Darwinism begins to take effect which mandates that not just survival but growth and prosperity will come to those that adapt to the demands of the changing environment.

The pragmatic attitude toward this change is to be found in communications professor Frederick Williams' assessment: "Our society is based upon change, and particularly technological change. That the communications revolution will have an effect upon us is not the critical issue. The challenge will be to manage the quality of this change."[5]

Urgency, reinvention, renewal, questioning oneself, looking forward, not back—these are the hallmarks of the Information Age publisher. Which firms will be around tomorrow? Which will thrive in the new environment, and which will die? As Paramount Publishing CEO Richard Snyder has stated: "The future belongs to the companies that do the best job of managing change. My job is to be sure that we're one of them."[6] Communications researcher and analyst Efrem Sigel has stated it thus: "Publishers will respond to public demands for information in whatever form the public wants it . . . [which] foreshadows . . . the inevitable diversification of publishers into new electronic media. The fruits of this diversification are either to fall to existing companies or, if they refuse to act to satisfy customer wants, to newer companies that grow up around newer media."[7]

Indeed, as noted earlier in the study, we are now at that stage in the industry's evolution where parties are seeking to align themselves with others to pursue emerging opportunities. The historically separate segments of the information industry are now colliding, symptomatic of the early phase of the paradigm shift, struggling to understand each other's perspectives, priorities, and working habits. The formation of strategic alliances signifies the movement to the second phase of the shift, wherein representatives from the different communities, while recognizing their differences, also recognize the benefits of cooperation, and therefore choose to work together for mutual benefit toward a common goal. As the shape of the new industry emerges, new organizations will also emerge, either from the transformation of existing firms, from combinations of existing firms, or as new-to-the-world entities. These new and transformed organizations will represent true new paradigm firms, digital publishers, interactive television program and service providers, multimodal network operators, and others. For the new paradigm firms there will be no clash of perspectives, no struggle to fit disparate pieces together, no struggle to understand the core strategic issues. They will by definition embody the necessary worldviews, will think in the new paradigm, will be the producers and purveyors of new paradigm goods and services, will be the pioneers of the digital information era.

THE SCIENCE OF MANAGEMENT, THE ART OF LEADERSHIP

To wield technology in the service of corporate strategy, firms need management tools and techniques. The 7M's framework presented in this study is one such tool for analyzing business performance. Along with the core concepts, it can be used to evaluate a firm as well as the competition. A firm can then rate itself against the competition: is management weak? Is the firm using technology properly in the infrastructure, in product processing, in media formats? Where is the competition weak, and where is it strong?

Perhaps we can glimpse the future in such places as the Media Lab at MIT. But publishers and developers are not about to throw overboard everything they currently have for some shimmering vision of an electronic utopia. Media are tools, means to an end, and the tools may change. But the publisher's mission, his raison d'être, won't change: to inform, to enlighten, to entertain. His job is to protect the valuable assets he already has and step incrementally into the future, maintaining profitability while seeking expansion and participation in opportunities opened up by new media.

But the successful use of technology is only one of management's tasks. They must also manage the engine of the enterprise, its people. They must attract, retain, develop, train, and motivate top quality employees. They must compete with other firms for talent and must provide incentives and opportunities for advancement. The publisher's industry environment will continue to change with rapidity, presenting new challenges and whole new worlds to fathom, technological and otherwise. The successful organization will therefore be a learning organization. Continuing education and training, both outside and in-house, are critical. Larger, more complex multi-market, multi-media, global firms require skilled, trained, and re-trained managers to make them run successfully. New technology means not just more to learn but more cultures to cross for managers, and it will require new types of cross-market, cross-media managers, the integrative leadership of the future.

While firms can learn the science of management, they must also practice the art of leadership. Vision, dreams, expression, new ground, boldness, risks, failures, success, growth, rewards, new horizons—these are the stuff of business too, required of an organization's leadership. Publishing ultimately distills down to some intuitive mix of experience and insight that emerges in a decision to publish or not to publish a given product. All business is risk, as Drucker tells us, the commitment of present resources to future return. Too mechanistic a view never works. Successful publishers have an understanding of the issues, technologies, and markets, then manage their resources toward their considered objectives.

At the same time as we can talk of value chains and professional management techniques and approaches to diversification, it is equally creativity and craft which define the publishing profession. The organization must not squash it but must allow it to happen, outside the organization, if necessary, as is often the case. Creative excitement is the lifeblood of the enterprise. All analytical aspects of management must be made invisible in service of the creative act. Indeed, the entire publishing organization should be a transparent conduit between creator and customer. Publishers do their best work when empowering creators. For the essence of their task is the meaning, the message, the movement beyond the work itself which is the embodiment in coded messages of thought—Gardner's symbolic products—of meaning, of emotion.

Successful leadership allows creators to thrive by providing the proper conditions for their work. Almost by definition, everything in an organization mitigates against free-thinking, new ideas, and change. Yet these are the very essence of the publishing enterprise. Moreover truly successful firms seek creativity not just in their products and their marketing, but in all areas— contractual arrangements with outside parties, company organization and structure, financial management, strategy, production techniques. Successful firms protect and reward creative individuals, seeking means to motivate their performance, for they are the key to the company's future.

MEANING IN A MEDIATED WORLD

Technology, the strategy which harnesses it, and the people who put it into play are all in the service of the organization's purpose. While real estate developers define the landscape and cityscape, working with architects and builders to create physical properties and the built physical environment in which we live, publishers, as intellectual property developers, define the mind-scape, working with authors, content creators, knowledge experts and other information providers, designers, and producers to develop intellectual properties which define the psychological environment in which we live. Either is capable of sins or genius, pollution or purity.

The essential task of publishers in the Information Age does not change. They are suppliers of information, of knowledge, of art, of tools, of entertainment. They are purveyors of meaning, in words, images, and sounds. For despite the progress of technology—and partly because of it—we still search for meaning in a mediated world.

The publishing function synthesizes, amasses, collects, and interprets the human enterprise in its myriad facets and forms. It is an essential social activity, a high calling. We will always continue to communicate, both among each other and across the generations. The knowledge pool now grows at such an exponential rate that we must keep educating ourselves throughout our lives. It is no longer enough to go to school once at the beginning of our lives and think we know what we need to get on in the world. The world now changes too quickly, moves on, learns new things, acts in different ways. And so we must relearn the world as it reinvents itself. This can cause anxiety. Information overload, dysfunctionality, and a retreat to the known are commonplace reactions in the mediated world. So is information impotence: we know everything but affect nothing. But as the world continues to change, more quickly and more drastically than ever before, we will continue to need instrumental knowledge. For knowledge precedes purposeful action, provides an understanding of the world and its ways, and allows us to move with confidence and correctness through our affairs.

While we need the purposiveness of information and the empowering force of knowledge, we also need tools to aid us in our work, entertainment to divert and amuse us, and art to ennoble, challenge, and comfort us, to illuminate our condition. Such is the breadth and depth of the publishing enterprise that it encompasses all of these.

Meaning, then, as embodied in the myriad symbolic forms of word, image, and sound, fragmentary and cohesive, ephemeral and enduring, is the publisher's trust. Thus, while market orientation serves the businessman in the publisher, content orientation serves the educator in him. For publishers have a social role as well as an economic role, a commitment to lead, not just follow, an obligation to make known the new, not just provide the expected or wanted. Publishers play an active role, are an outlet, a mouthpiece for the new and the novel and the important, and are not just passive purveyors of goods to an all-determining market. New and powerful ideas upset established orders, are not easily assimilated, nor expected. But they are necessary if we are to continue to grow and thrive as a society and as a civilization, and they are necessary if we are to surmount the difficulties that beset us. So leadership publishers serve a critical function by seeking out the new and the necessary. For many engaged in such an enterprise, it exerts a powerful force, like teaching or the ministry. For many, publishing is a vocation.

The publishing story is still being told. It is a dynamic industry that will continue to change, bridging the gap between technology and marketplace, between content and customer. In whatever segment of publishing he or she is engaged, a publisher can be infused with enthusiasm and vitality of purpose. For communication is essential to life, at once a basic function of biological existence and an essential function in a complex, interdependent society. A publisher is a connector, an enlightener, a facilitator of pleasure and knowledge and efficiency and purpose. He plays an essential role in maintaining an informed and effective citizenry, and the pursuit of this enterprise and ensuring that it is properly fulfilled in a changing world is no small challenge, and no mean responsibility.

The Orwellian vision in *1984* depicts a severe concentration of media power. We know that it can come true, that such concentration can lead to enslavement and repression. Thus it is vital that we maintain a multiplicity of channels, allowing many voices to flourish. Oldrich Standera has said: "Publishing has been traditionally the guardian of our cultural treasures and an effective instrument in recording, evaluating, editing, disseminating, preserving, and archiving the continuing progress of our civilization as we know it, and we all have too much at stake not to keep this mechanism alive and well. No matter what technology, this vital role of publishers must continue to function if our cultural heritage is to be preserved."[8] And, we should add, our freedom.

Information Age publishers will forge ahead into the new digital era, embracing the paradigm of promise. While this time of transition can be difficult, it is also a time of positive change, an opening up. There are many issues left to be resolved, as there always will be. More than ever there will be a challenge to the substance of publishers' products and services, a challenge to seek out, create, and deliver meaningful products and services, to provide information, knowledge, art, tools, and entertainment of true value in a mediated world. To sustain their role in a connected world, publishers must continue to wield the resources of their organizations to organize and present texts, images, and sounds in a meaningful fashion, and to reach customers with products and services of value. Those publishers who meet this challenge will also meet with success in the Information Age.

NOTES

1. *See* Andrew Pollack, "Transforming the Decade: 10 Critical Technologies," *The New York Times,* 1 January, 1991, 35ff. The other four technologies cited were micro motors, biotechnology-genetic engineering, renewable energy, and new materials. One could argue that each of these, in turn, has heavy information technology components.

2. As quoted in Alice D. Schreyer, "Books and Other Machines," The Center for the Book, Library of Congress, 1985, 79. Referring to the confluence of computers and communications, Stewart Brand has stated: "The world Machine is coming anyway . . . Earth is already wholly integrated. . . . All that will advance now is the rate of knowing, the structure of new immediacies."

3. Burns and Martin, "The Economics of Information" (Washington, D.C.: Office of Technology Assessment, 1985), VI-8.

4. As quoted in Stewart Brand, *The Media Lab: Inventing the Future at MIT* (New York: Viking Penguin, 1987), 245.

5. Frederick Williams, *The Communications Revolution* (New York: New American Library, 1983), 234.

6. As quoted by Edwin McDowell in "Is Simon & Schuster Mellowing?," *The New York Times,* 28 October, 1990.

7. Efrem Sigel, "The Future of the Book," in *Books, Libraries, and Electronics* (White Plains, N.Y.: Knowledge Industry Publications, 1982), 22.

8. Oldrich Standera, *The Electronic Era of Publishing* (New York: Elsevier Science Publishing Inc., 1987), 275.

AFTERWORD

Toward *Homo Digitas*

When *Publishing in the Information Age* was originally published in May 1994, I was aware that a good portion of the material contained in it was vulnerable to dating very quickly. While my major effort was to probe below the surface events of the information industries and construct a more solid foundation for my analysis, my arguments were supported by numerous examples drawn from the industry environment at the time. Moreover, a good deal of the less topical research was drawn from the period prior to publication going back to 1987, which meant that some of the material stretched even farther back. In a field moving as rapidly as this one, where every day there are striking reports of advances in technology, corporate maneuvers, personnel transitions, new government regulation (or deregulation), not to mention the unceasing flood of new products and services, the landscape changes too quickly for one snapshot to portray a wholly accurate picture.

I am therefore pleased to have the opportunity, on the publication of this edition of the book, to add a few words about the major events and trends in the industry in the two-year period since the book's original publication. While the 7M's infrastructure has held up well in its initial test, within those 7M's there has been incessant activity. The culture's tools for conversation continue to change, and with them the ways in which messages are created, processed, and delivered, as well as which types of messages hold sway in this increasingly mediated environment, such as the now-proven power of the sound bite and photo op of today's political campaigns (to which we are particularly attuned in this presidential election year).

Now, in addition to these familiar elements of the culture's mediascape, we are witnessing the emergence of new forms and habits, new types of messages, new bottles in which they are sent, and new ways in which those bottles are retrieved and the messages read. One example: numerous advertisements on television and in newspapers now carry a jumble of letters in small print at the bottom of the screen or page—"http://www.somethingsomething.com"— the organization's URL ("Universal Resource Locator") or address on the World Wide Web. This is new to the world in the last 12-18 months. This is but one change, but in their totality, the myriad instances of these penetrations of digital technologies into and throughout our daily lives are changing the way we live, and thereby changing who we are.

MATERIAL

Content-based publishing (Core Concept # 4) is still key: owning content or rights and reformatting and adding value in appropriate media for delivery in different forms to different markets. Curious George has now stepped out of books, where he started over 50 years ago, and onto the silver platter. Content franchises such as these, long successful and lucrative to their owners, will often determine the direction of the asset-rich firm entering the arena. Conversely, technology-based firms will continue to seek to license or partner with such content franchises—witness Living Books, a Random House-Broderbund joint venture to create multimedia Dr. Seuss and other titles, or Microsoft teaming up with Scholastic for *Magic School Bus*.

But all firms in the game, whether content or technology-based, must also seek to create new brand franchises. Old wine poured into new bottles will eventually run dry. Microsoft publishes an enormously successful new-to-the-world CD-ROM encyclopedia, *Encarta*, as well as a successful series of flight simulators, neither of which have brand precedents in other media. On the World Wide Web on the Internet, hundreds of examples exist of successful new brands and franchises: Yahoo, Netscape, GORP, InfoSeek, and others. This is new, wide open, unclaimed territory, and the traditional publishing mechanism—the organizations required to financially back, design and edit, manufacture, inventory, and distribute printed works for authors—is simply bypassed. The Web is already proving to be a significant revenue generator for some entrants, and it is these innovative young entrepreneurial firms that are in a position to cash in first through preemptive strikes. While it remains to be seen what the real value proposition is for content rights holders on the Web, there are many eager players who are not waiting to find out.

Author teams (Core Concept #9, the New Creative Powers) are emerging as the new norm. The complexities and constant evolution of digital authoring tools, as well as the magnitude of many projects, require collaborative teams that include a blend of skills and expertises in content, design, and engineering. Web site creators and digital development shops are springing up to meet the demand for the business. Significantly, the distributed nature of the work

—anyone anywhere can be empowered to publish with desktop equipment and a link to the grid—creates totally new-to-the-world outfits that are ushering in a new era of garage or even bedroom publishing that just two years ago was largely unforeseen. A Benedictine monastery in the Sangre de Christo mountains of New Mexico has gone online and is using their Web work as a source of revenue. They are attracting skilled programmers and designers away from secular paying jobs and offering the same work, plus the spiritual and physical rewards of monastic life in the 21st century scriptorium!

While the desktop publishing revolution of the 1980's still meant paper output and physical distribution, the desktop publishing revolution of the 1990's means Web sites and no physical distribution at all. With the Web, everybody's a publisher. Anybody can do it out of a back room, mount data on a server and let users pull off what they want when they want it. It is the new publishing paradigm: server-based, customer-driven, on-demand publishing. It disintermediates the elaborate and costly physical distribution chain of traditional publishing and replaces it with direct publisher-to-customer contact.

Text and still images are the norm on the net—today. With such tools as Java and Shockwave, moving images and sound will be the norm tomorrow, and these tools will be replaced by yet another generation of more robust multimedia authoring tools. Whether we believe Bill Gates' best-selling *The Road Ahead* that the true broadband information highway is 10–20 years away, or George Gilder and the upstart Silicon Valley alliance seeking to unseat Gates and company in the next wave of computing, the uber-communications environment of the future is now clear: ubiquitous multipoint access to and transmission of all modes of information at any time from any one point to any other point or points.

Proprietary content (Core Concept #5) is currently being challenged by an Internet netiquette that offers information on almost any topic free of charge. Most observers feel this will change. Proprietary content rights and remuneration for such are what fuel intellectual property development through the prospect of return. Even if coding tools cannot currently deliver one product capable of operating across all digital environments and platforms (e.g., CD-ROM and the Web), digital archives (Core Concept #6) of content assets are being assembled for repurposing in print, online, CD-ROM, and other delivery forms. The pendulum has swung in the last two years. Publishers of many kinds of material—professional, technical, and reference (more electronic encyclopedias are now sold than print), and increasingly educational and children's—are deriving multiple revenue streams from repurposed content. Even as distribution conduits continue to sort themselves out and user habits evolve in response to the new media available to them, traditional print-based publishers are realizing cost savings and revenue gains by digitizing assets once and re-formatting and updating as required for different uses. However it is quite clear that the infrastructure technologies for storing and redeploying these assets, including such critical elements as rights databases to track the material in its multiple forms and deliveries, is still lagging far behind product development mechanisms, despite initiatives by the AAP and other central industry bodies.   .

MODE

We are still in the early days of interactive media, still building the digital equivalent of Model T's until broadcast, broadband, and digital processing and the tools used to create content within them are fully integrated. We are still learning the best ways to use and combine the various modes in the new optical and online media, and there are few true examples of efforts that define the new grammar of interactive image, text, and sound. Farther out— even ten years into the next millennium—the interactive grammar of the mediascape will be so commonplace as to be unnoticeable to the average user, just as watching TV advertising or reading a book or making a phone call or formatting a spreadsheet are to us now. Some examples, such as *Myst*, which caught the popular imagination, or Pixar's *Toy Story*, the first fully computer-generated animated feature film, demonstrate the promise and help point the way. Games seem to be a clear area of success (nearly 50% of the CD-ROM market), as are simulations as learning tools. But these are all precursors, test rabbits of the future applications that we will incorporate in our personal, professional, and learning lives.

At this writing interactivity, as a screen-delivered experience, favors sound and image (still and moving) over text, a paradigm that originated with film and broadcasting. Sound and images move, while text is static and requires greater effort by the human eye and brain for consumption. Screen display also favors smaller chunks and evanescence to hold users' attention. Now, with the advent of truly large screen computers, such as Gateway's recently introduced 31" screen family console computer, things may change somewhat, though there will always be a sublimated role for text in the group viewing context as individual users read at different paces.

MEDIA AND MEANS

It is now abundantly clear that the publishing enterprise spans all three distribution cycles—list, periodical, and open channel (Core Concept #13). List and periodical publishing have been well established for centuries and will continue to thrive in the foreseeable future. But in the last two years we have seen a predominant trend toward open channel publishing, the electronic highways of Core Concept #16. Significantly, whether viewed as a marketing medium or as a revenue-generating information service, operating an open channel service means a sustained commitment, dedicated resources, editorial updating, responding to customers' queries and comments, and other tasks.

At the moment we are in a time of turbulence: will the menu fixe commercial online services continue to thrive and grow, or will the à la carte World Wide Web prevail? The signals are mixed. Some feel the big online commercial services are threatened, while others feel that these services will eventually migrate their delivery entirely out of closed proprietary systems to ensure their continued success. Nobody is sitting still: America Online bought GNN and started a separate Web service (1995); the Lexis/Nexis professional information service was sold by Mead Data Systems (1995); Delphi was dumped by Murdoch's News Corp. (late 1995); ATT revamped its Interchange Online Network into an Internet service, pre-launch; Sears sold its stake in Prodigy (2/96); CompuServe was put up for sale but announced it was starting a new family-oriented service, Wow, almost at the same time (2/96); Microsoft refocused the Microsoft Network—and indeed the entire company—around the Web and the promise of broadband delivery systems (2/96).

The emergent force has been the global meta-network, the Internet, and more specifically the World Wide Web, the Internet equivalent of the GUI (graphic user interface) that stimulated such tremendous growth in the personal computer industry with the introduction of the Macintosh computer in 1984. Like flying to San Diego, Lisbon, or Tokyo and getting in a rental car and driving away, the Web and the browsers that enable its navigation are part of the necessary infrastructure that paves the information highway. The infinite-node Web is the clearest pre-cursor of the broadband information highway. Some feel the Web is the highway itself.

After a twenty-plus year career as a government initiated, funded, and maintained effort for the exchange of academic and scientific information, the Internet emerged as a mass phenomenon in 1995, the year of the World Wide Web. Its reported tens of millions of users and untold thousands of home pages, coupled with the installed base of both office and home computers, made it the new media star, demonstrating the importance of standards (see Concept #22, Media Life Cycle)—in this case, international—for true growth. To anybody who had any contact with the Web, it was quite obviously something new and different from other mass media. Just like radio and television before it, the Web is a new environment, a new cultural tool for conversation. And like most new media, it incorporates parts of other media but is also unique, a thing unto itself because it merges all these things plus adds new attributes. It merges the telephone (point-to-point, connected, global, real-time), television (sound, moving images), books (text, still images, information), magazines and newspapers (updated, periodical, advertising), and software (interactive, navigable). It is the most stunning demonstration of Core Concept #27, Globalization and Segmentation, for by its definition the Web is both global, thereby mass, and niche, thereby segmented, at the same time.

Of existing media, only the well-established voice-to-voice telephone service comes close to the Internet's anywhere, anytime contact. But the Internet provides more. It can provide the Louvre on Thursday night in Des Moines and Indiana basketball (via Internet radio) in Johannesburg in March. It fits our publishing model (see Figure 2-1), transcending time and space. It is both international and point-to-point, and as such can knit together cultures, languages, and almost any type of community with any other. The Web is the first glimmer of the reality fulfillment of the visions of several data dreamers, such as Ted Nelson and Vannevar Bush. Its most critical new attribute is connectivity—to information sources, to other individuals, from one to many, from many to one. Connectivity is local as well as global: we can scan the menu and order a pizza from the local pizza parlor; find out the schedule of sports events, ticket availability, seat location, and order tickets to a local sports event. More remotely, we can download a song sample from the latest hot album on the charts, leave a message with a son or daughter at college about plans for the upcoming big weekend, or check out snow and weather conditions at the local ski areas.

A variety of players are jockeying for position on the information highway, whether it is today's Internet or some future meta-network. Cable television companies, for instance have recognized that the broader bandwidth of their coaxial cable provides a competitive advantage over telephone's twisted pair in delivery of so-called high speed data services, i.e., digital Internet transmissions versus video television broadcasts. U.S. West and Continental Cablevision combined forces in early 1996 to broaden their respective networks and subscriber bases, as well as to teach each other about delivering networked voice and video services. But even while they do so and invest significant dollars to realize their vision, no clear revenue model has yet emerged for these services. It is both the hope and the concern of all commercial purveyors. The Internet legacy noted above, as a government and academic information-sharing medium, sees the free and fair exchange of information as the right of all on the net and until very recently has been hostile toward commercial enterprises. But the rewritten communications act and the copyright laws currently undergoing revision, both with the support of the Clinton administration, will eventually ensure that the profit-motivated laws of intellectual property will prevail, the gates will drop, and the ticket takers will emerge. A handful of Web sites already have paid or subscriber tiers, and a few even generate six or even seven figure advertising revenue: 1996 may well be the first year of significant commerce on the net.

Like other organizations, publishers must learn how to take advantage of this new opportunity. But unlike most other organizations, publishers' wares—information and entertainment in the form of bits and bytes—are suited for delivery over the new medium. Revenue streams from electronic commerce will involve some combination of sale of hard goods for physical delivery (transactions), soft goods (software), advertiser and subscription revenue, pay-per-view, and others yet unexplored. Links to other, related sites for the right to post a billboard and draw traffic are now happening.

New media also provide enormous and undreamt of opportunities for suppliers of related goods and services. The automobile spawned tremendous growth in glass, steel, concrete, oil, rubber, and numerous other industries to feed its needs. The information highway has already spawned such early successes as Netscape, the current browser king, as well as so-called middleware suppliers such as InfoSeek, Yahoo, and Alta Vista, intelligent agents that search net sites and find information that meets individual needs. Other such opportunities will abound.

Publishers are also aware of the tilting mix of revenues in electronic versus paper formats (Core Concept #23, the Dynamic Equilibrium). Managing an evolving portfolio of media formats is critical to the success of formerly print-based firms that can no longer rely on business as usual. Encyclopedia Britannica found out the hard way that nothing is sacred, that customers can change their information usage habits and their buying habits. It is not just how to take advantage of the new media, but how existing media fit into the changing mediascape, and how they will be kept strong and remunerative. What is the proper role of books, for instance, in a connected, downloadable, multimodal, multiple format world? In new media, packaged electronic media, such as CD-ROMs, are clearly different from transmitted media, wired or wireless. Many see optical disc formats, no matter how high-volume their storage, as interim to the broadband highway. How can information providers gauge customer preferences for local data storage and ownership versus online connectivity and charges? Networked information delivery is a threat to publishers who are used to selling the whole printed package, only portions of which may ever be used, particularly in non-linear works such as encyclopedias. Network-proficient users may increasingly opt for downloading and printing (or not) only those portions they want, severely impacting sales of costly bound volumes that deliver an enormous amount of material that may never be used.

The dynamic equilibrium also tells us that the media formats affect each other. The aesthetic of interactive computer screen design is gradually infecting other media. With the rise of interactive media as the hottest and latest thing, broadcast and print designers are increasingly incorporating computer look and feel into their layouts and graphics, sometimes mimicking entire computer screens to great effect.

Increasingly, interactivity will come to be an expected attribute in nearly all media, a given behavior, not peculiar to certain formats. It is learned behavior by the older generation—starting in the workplace and coming home—and an accepted part of the mediascape by the next generation—starting in the home, taken to school, and then (when they are older) into the workplace. Once the world is seen through interactive eyes, the attribute is not only wanted but demanded: "Why is this *not* interactive?" Interactive media bend around you and your schedule and are customized to your information, entertainment, and communication needs. And interactive users have the power to control this because of devices at their command: distributed processing power.

In digital media, the passage of years means more machines that are both smaller and larger but that are always more powerful (Moore's Law). Prices for computing power also continue to drop. The marketing of the new release of a computer operating system, Windows 95, was arguably the biggest mass marketing event for any media product last year. Talk of the $500 communication device some call a teleputer is routinely dismissed by the PC makers. But viewed through the lenses of the network operators such as the phone and cable companies, it is a logical extension of the current voice-only device to a more powerful device that enables point-to-point data as well as voice communications. Meanwhile numerous hand-held and portable digital and cellular devices will only get smaller, more ubiquitous, more powerful, have better displays, be more portable, be more communicative, have more access to everything anytime anywhere, be cheaper, and be easier to use.

Content providers can choose to remain agnostic to the delivery conduit wars. The ticket takers will emerge, but the content can still travel via whatever conduits are present. Koji Kobiyashi's information service centers are emerging, digital cores of information linked to various distribution systems, available to users on-demand.

Meanwhile, and to some paradoxically, the consumption of printed matter continues to rise. Books and magazines are still vastly popular, their positive attributes reinforced in a screened environment. But over time such paper objects will come to be seen as a display alternative, a choice made between screen or paper, a chance for hard copy conveniently bound and formatted and portable, but lacking connectivity and responsiveness. They will be a costly and sometimes luxurious alternative to on-demand, screen-delivered information.

MARKET

The infusion of digital devices and services—voice-mail, e-mail, beepers, the Internet, cellular phones, digital satellite transmission, GPS devices, personal organizers, PDA's, and many others still in the lab—defines the new interactive environment. As they become part of our daily lives, just as television and radio or any other of our culture's major technologies did before, they are changing the way we live. They are becoming central and necessary components of our lives, depended-on technologies, expected and assumed, appliances. Moreover, this is increasingly true in all three major spheres of human activity—at home, at work, and at school.

The paradigm shift is to see the world through the customer's new eyes, through interactive eyes, through digital eyes, where all material is resident in servers and available upon command, for screen display, digital capture, paper output, combination with other material, re-formatting, or re-sending. *All* content becomes an interactive possibility, though at different levels: selection and play (performance) or selection and interaction (participation). The conversion experience for providers of information is to see the interactive screen, the user-controlled display, as the front-end that defines their information reality. Print is but one derivative output from the electronic whole, a customer format choice from the supplier's electronic inventory, available as an option when desired but also free to be ignored by the customer, as well, who has access to the underlying files in electronic form.

Increasing user power (Core Concept #26) is the force behind many of the changes now taking place. The new machines are always exponentially more powerful than the preceding generation. Users can now dip their hands into the publisher's cookie jar, the electronic inventory. As Jerome Rubin, founder of LEXIS and NEXIS observed (see page 164), putting *process* in the hands of the user allows them to control *format* and *substance* as well. The digital era of servers and networks allows multiple users infinite variations of the material to suit their needs, versus the monolithic, centrist print technology model which only allows multiple copies of the identical text to be created for all users. As Stewart Brand said, publishers must now "shift [their] perspective from how information is sent to how it is sought."

We are indeed now all RVLUs—readers, viewers, listeners, and users (Core Concept #25), and all media users will continue to be. The challenge for publishers, then, is to meet customers' information needs in all appropriate forms. Customer habits are indeed changing to include new formats. Interactivity is a growing norm. Connectedness is a growing norm. When use of one device displaces another, such as when users make a conscious choice to eschew prime time television in favor of the computer, information habits are indeed changing.

The job of building and extending brands and imprints (Core Concept #32) still remains one of traditional publishers' biggest leverage points. However it will never take them far enough. New brands will always be born: *Encarta*, Yahoo, *Myst*, Netscape. In an environment marked by constant change, where turbulence is the rule and attribute evolution a given, new brands must emerge. But the mediascape is also a tough and uncaring environment, littered with early successes now passed by, such as VisiCalc, as well as countless others that never rose to our consciousness.

MANAGEMENT

In a bold demonstration of the need for strategic vision (Core Concept #35), earlier this year Bill Gates once again shook up and re-invented the world's largest computer software maker, Microsoft. In fact Gates was more afraid *not* to change for fear that he would be left behind in a new era based on the networked information highway, not the desktop PC. He knows the hard-earned lessons of IBM and other big iron firms that were left behind in the move from mainframes to PCs. But taking such steps means constant awareness of markets and technology and competitors and trends, balancing these factors, and making decisions to keep the enterprise moving forward. This means integrative management.

No traditional print publisher is not in the electronic game in some way or other now. Most are finding that matching their resources (Core Concept #39) with others is the best way to learn to walk before they run. In a turbulent environment with uncertain outcomes, alliances can provide access to knowledge and skills and reduce risk. But it is clear that those who do not practice some entrepreneurship (Core Concept #42) will fall behind. If they are not entrepreneurial, they risk losing franchises, customers, and market value, and will decline as nimbler, faster-moving companies pass them by.

If the tilt is toward online information delivery, then, as Christopher Burns observed, publishing becomes a service business as much as a product business, responding to customers' needs for information on-demand, data which they access from servers and recombine as they choose: what they want when they want it. The commercial information services such as America Online prefigure this model, but most publishers will mount their own information services on the Web.

Digital is a young game. Where will the best and brightest be attracted? Usually where the growth and opportunity is, where the excitement is. The new publishing paradigm offers all kinds of jobs—editorial, design, engineering, product development, technical support, quality assurance. All is bent toward the design and presentation of the interactive experience. Whether it is narrowband and CD-ROM now or broadband later, it is essentially the same skill set. Personnel from existing industry paradigms and cultures often clash, for example software channel marketers versus book editors, but those who start their careers in the new media will not be similarly burdened with existing industry worldviews.

Constant industry and technology change also means constant organizational dislocations. Re-engineering around the 7M's in order to create, format, distribute, and maintain the content enterprise is by definition disruptive. But the value gained always outweighs the short-term losses. The reinvented company is infused with new spirit, a new perspective, new urgency, and a new sense of purpose.

MONEY

Harvey Poppel called it the trillion-dollar opportunity. The success of such companies as Intel and Microsoft in the microcomputer era, while definitely part of this opportunity, is only part of the news. New wealth is being created through mergers, acquisitions, initial public offerings, and other financial vehicles. Many new personal and corporate fortunes will be made in the digital arena in the years ahead. For some the fortunes have already been made: Steve Jobs and Pixar's *Toy Story*, Marc Andreesen and Jim Clark of Netscape, and a number of others who will never make the headlines. They are the new robber barons, what Time magazine calls "instantaires" or nerd-entrepreneurs. Many feel the market is crazy, too insanely hot. But there always seem to be enough investors ready to come to the table for the next digital offering.

HOMO DIGITAS

What does all this add up to? Two years ago I placed these words at the beginning of this book: "At our present juncture something indeed appears to be happening on the grander scale . . . a general reconstitution of the information procedures of the world." Today, in 1996, Erik Barnouw's words ring more true than ever, and they are a testimony to ENIAC's 50-year legacy as the first electronic digital computer, the machine that launched a thousand more machines. With each passing year the picture defines itself a bit more clearly. And now, even in the midst of this "reconstitution," it is becoming apparent that we are undergoing a change so fundamental that it is defining a new type of person, a person whose life is different because the way he approaches his daily activities is different, and the way he relates and communicates to other people is different, a person called *Homo Digitas*.

Despite 50 years of exponential technological growth, we are still in the early days of the digital era. There is much more change to come. For the optimistic and the strong of heart, change always equals opportunity and the possibilities that implies. Underneath the change, the fundamentals remain: the need to connect with one another, the need to trust and work with one another, the need to be informed to carry on our lives, the need to be entertained and enlightened and inspired and uplifted. Above all, and perhaps more than ever as the world's familiar touch-points also seem vulnerable to change, we need meaning in our lives—when we work, when we learn, and when we are at play. Though we are defining a new person, our technologies must continue to be in the service of human needs, the overriding objective. How we shape the new technologies toward these human ends is the continuing challenge of our time.

APPENDIX

List of Core Concepts

Core Concept #1—The 7M's of Publishing

Core Concept #2—Information Technology and the 7M's

MATERIAL

Core Concept #3—Information, Knowledge, Entertainment, Art, and Tools

Core Concept #4—Content-Based Publishing

Core Concept #5—Proprietary Content

Core Concept #6—The Digital Library

Core Concept #7—The Content Franchise

Core Concept #8—Recombinant Publishing

Core Concept #9—The New Creative Powers

MODE

Core Concept #10—The Three Major Modes: Textual, Visual, and Aural

Core Concept #11—Cross-Modal Conversion

Core Concept #12—Multimodal Publishing

MEDIUM AND MEANS

Core Concept #13—The Three Distribution Cycles: List, Periodical, and Open Channel

Core Concept #14—The Media Matrix: Modes and Means

Core Concept #15—Convergence: Publishing, Broadcasting, and Telecommunications

MARKET

MANAGEMENT AND MONEY

Selected Bibliography

Adler, Richard. "Technologies for Electronic Publishing and Computer Software: An Essay on Technical Invention and Social Innovation." Unpublished paper presented at Aspen Institute Conference on the Future of Electronic Publishing and Computer Software for Personal Use, January, 1988.

Ambron, SueAnn, and Kristina Hooper, eds. *Interactive Multimedia.* Redmond, Wash.: Microsoft Press, 1988.

Asheim, Lester. "The Reader-Viewer-Listener: An Essay in Communication." Washington, D.C.: Library of Congress/Center for the Book, 1987.

Association of American Publishers. "The Accidental Profession: Education, Training, and the People of Publishing." New York: Association of American Publishers, 1977.

Bailey, Janet, and the editors at Knowledge Industry Publications. *The El-Hi Market, 1986–91.* White Plains, N.Y.: Knowledge Industry Publications, 1986.

Bell, Daniel. *The Coming of Post-Industrial Society.* New York: Basic Books, 1973.

Beniger, James. *The Control Revolution.* Cambridge, Mass.: Harvard University Press, 1986.

Berg, A. Scott. *Maxwell Perkins: Editor of Genius.* New York: E.P. Dutton, 1978.

Bloom, Benjamin S., ed. *Taxonomy of Educational Objectives, Handbook I: Cognitive Domain.* New York: David McKay Company, Inc., 1956.

Bloom, Benjamin S., David R. Krathuol, and Bertram B. Masia. *Taxonomy of Educational Objectives, Handbook II: Affective Domain.* New York: David McKay Company, Inc., 1964.

Boorstin, Daniel J. "A Nation of Readers." Washington, D.C.: Library of Congress/Center for the Book, 1982.

———. *Books in Our Future.* Washington, D.C.: Joint Committee on the Library, Congress of the United States, 1984.

————. "Gresham's Law: Knowledge or Information?" Washington, D.C.: Library of Congress/Center for the Book, 1980.

————. *The Image.* New York: Atheneum, 1962.

————. *The Republic of Technology.* Colophon reprint edition. New York: Harper and Row, 1978.

Brand, Stewart. *The Media Lab: Inventing the Future at MIT.* New York: Viking Penguin, 1987.

Brownstone, David M. "Publishing Industry's Armageddon Postponed." *Publishers Weekly,* November 21, 1980.

Burns, Christopher, and Patricia A. Martin. "The Economics of Information." Washington, D.C.: Office of Technology Assessment, U.S. Congress, 1985.

Center for the Book. *The State of the Book World, 1980.* Washington, D.C.: Library of Congress, 1981.

Cohen, Stephen S. and John Zysman. "The Myth of a Post-Industrial Economy." *The New York Times,* May 17, 1987.

Cole, John Y., ed. *Books in Our Future: Perspectives and Proposals.* Washington, D.C.: Library of Congress, 1987.

————. *Television, the Book, and the Classroom.* Washington, D.C.: Library of Congress, 1978.

————, and The Center for the Book. *Responsibilities of the American Book Community.* Washington, D.C.: Library of Congress, 1981.

Compaine, Benjamin. "Information Technology and Cultural Change: Toward a New Literacy?" Cambridge, Mass.: Harvard University Program on Information Resources Policy, 1984.

————, ed. *Understanding New Media: Trends and Issues in Electronic Distribution of Information.* Cambridge, Mass.: Balinger Publishing Company, 1984.

Compaine, Benjamin, Thomas Guback, J. Kendrick Noble, Jr., and Christopher H. Sterling. *Who Owns the Media?* White Plains, N.Y.: Knowledge Industry Publications, 1975.

Coser, Lewis A., Charles Kadushin, and Walter W. Powell. *Books: The Culture and Commerce of Publishing.* New York: Basic Books, 1982.

Dahlin, Robert. "Electronics and Publishing, 1: Watch That Book!" *Publishers Weekly,* March 20, 1981, 24–30.

————. "Electronics and Publishing, 2: Consumer as Creator." *Publishers Weekly,* March 27, 1981, 21–27.

————. "Electronic Publishing: Steps Forward—and Back." *Publishers Weekly,* June 4, 1982, 26–31.

Darnton, Robert. "Toward a History of Reading." *Princeton Alumni Weekly,* April 8, 1987, 19–32.

Davis, Robert T., and F. Gordon Smith. *Marketing in Emerging Companies.* Reading, Mass.: Addison-Wesley, 1984.

Day, George S., Allan D. Shocker, and Rajendra K. Srivastava. "Customer-Oriented Approaches to Identifying Product-Markets." *Journal of Marketing* (Fall 1979): 8–19.

Deal, Terrence, and Alan Kennedy. *Corporate Cultures.* Reading, Mass.: Addison-Wesley, 1982.

Dertouzos, Michael L., and Joel Moses, eds. *The Computer Age: A Twenty-Year View.* Cambridge, Mass.: MIT Press, 1979.

Doebler, Paul A. "The Book Industry 1981: From 'Business as Usual' to ???." New York: Book Industry Study Group, 1981.

Drucker, Peter F. *Innovation and Entrepreneurship.* New York: Harper and Row, 1985.

———. *Technology, Management, and Society.* Colophon reprint edition. New York: Harper and Row, 1977.

Duke, Judith S. *The Technical, Scientific and Medical Publishing Market.* White Plains, N.Y.: Knowledge Industry Publications, 1985.

Eames, The Office of Charles and Ray. *A Computer Perspective: Background to the Computer Age, New Edition.* Cambridge, Mass.: Harvard University Press, 1990.

Ehrenhalt, Samuel M. "Work-Force Shifts in 80s." *The New York Times,* August 15, 1986, D2.

Eisenhart, Douglas. "The Best NeXT Seat at Symphony Hall." *BCS Update,* 12 (February, 1989): 14–17.

———. "1-2-3 Goes TV: Interactive Multimedia at Lotus." *BCS Update,* 12 (September, 1989): 14–17.

———. "The Future of Publishing." Unpublished lecture presented at 40th session of the Harvard/Radcliffe Publishing Course, Cambridge, Mass., July 15, 1987.

Fairfield Group, Inc. *Home Video/Disc Publishing: The Dynamics of Distribution, 1984 and Beyond.* White Plains, N.Y.: Knowledge Industry Publications, 1984.

Fedler, Fred. *An Introduction to the Mass Media.* New York: Harcourt Brace Jovanovich, 1978.

Fiske, Edward B. "Combining TV, Books, and Computers." *The New York Times,* August 7, 1984.

Foster, Richard N. *Innovation—The Attacker's Advantage.* New York: Summit Books, 1986.

Freiberger, Paul. "The Dream Machine: A Quest for the Ultimate Computer." *Popular Computing,* April 1985, 56–65.

Gano, Steve. "A Draft of a Request for Proposals Covering the Adoption of Computer Technology in the Home." Unpublished paper presented at Aspen Institute Conference on the Future of Electronic Publishing and Computer Software for Personal Use, January 1988.

Gardner, Howard. *Frames of Mind: The Theory of Multiple Intelligences.* New York: Basic Books, 1983.

Grannis, Chandler B., ed. *What Happens in Book Publishing.* 2d ed. New York: Columbia University Press, 1967.

Greenberger, Martin, ed. *Electronic Publishing Plus—Media for a Technological Future.* White Plains, N.Y.: Knowledge Industry Publications, 1985.

Hackett, Alice Payne, and James Henry Burke. *80 Years of Best Sellers: 1895–1975.* New York: R.R. Bowker Company, 1977.

Hamilton, John Maxwell. "Awash in the Age of Information." *The Boston Globe Magazine,* August 18, 1991, 20ff.

Harrigan, Kathryn Rudie. *Strategies for Joint Ventures.* Lexington, Mass.: Lexington Books/D.C. Heath and Company, 1985.

Hillis, W. Daniel. *The Connection Machine.* Cambridge, Mass.: MIT Press, 1985.

Horowitz, Irving Louis. *Communicating Ideas: The Crisis of Publishing in a Post-Industrial Society.* New York: Oxford University Press, 1986.

Kahn, Paul. "CD-ROM in the Scholar's Environment." *Optical Insights*, 1 (Fall, 1987): 8–11.

Kay, Peg, and Patricia Powell, eds. *Future Information Technology—1984: Telecommunications* (NBS Special Publication 500-119). Gaithersburg, Md.: Institute for Computer Sciences and Technology, National Bureau of Standards, U.S. Department of Commerce, 1984.

Kelly, Kevin, ed. *Signals: Communications Tools for the Information Age.* New York: Harmony Books, 1988.

Kiplinger Washington Letter. *The New American Boom.* Washington, D.C.: Kiplinger Washington Letter, 1986.

Klopfenstein, Bruce C. "Forecasting Consumer Adoption of Information Technology and Services—Lessons from Home Video Forecasting." *Journal of the American Society for Information Science,* 40(1) (1989): 17–26.

Knowledge Industry Publications. *Consumer Media Expenditures, 1982–7.* White Plains, N.Y.: Knowledge Industry Publications, 1983.

Kobayashi, Koji. *Computers and Communications: A Vision of C&C.* Cambridge, Mass.: MIT Press, 1986.

Kotler, Philip. *Marketing Management: Analysis, Planning, and Control.* 4th Ed. Englewood Cliffs, N.J.: Prentice-Hall, 1980.

Kuhn, Thomas. *The Structure of Scientific Revolutions.* 2d ed. Chicago, Ill.: University of Chicago Press, 1970.

Lambert, Steve, and Suzanne Ropiequet, eds. *CD ROM: The New Papyrus.* Redmond, Wash.: Microsoft Press, 1986.

Lapham, Lewis, ed. "Will Books Survive?" *Harper's,* August 1985.

Lazer, Ellen A., ed. *Guide to Videotape Publishing.* White Plains, N.Y.: Knowledge Industry Publications, 1986.

Levitt, Theodore. *The Marketing Imagination.* New Ed. New York: The Free Press, 1986.

Lippman, Andrew. "Computing with Television: Paperback Movies." Unpublished paper, MIT Media Laboratory, revised version, January 1987.

———. "Electronic Publishing." Unpublished paper, MIT Media Laboratory. January 1986.

McGraw-Hill, Inc. *Annual Reports, 1983–1991.*

McKenna, Regis. *The Regis Touch.* Reading, Mass.: Addison-Wesley, 1985.

McLuhan, Marshall. *Understanding Media: The Extensions of Man.* Signet reprint edition. New York: New American Library, 1964.

Mageau, Therese. "Redefining the Textbook." *Electronic Learning* (February 1991) 14–18.

Mahony, Sheila, with Nick DeMartino, and Robert Stengel. *Keeping PACE with the New Television: Public Television and Changing Technology.* New York: Carnegie Corporation of New York/VNU Books International, 1980.

Mander, Jerry. *Four Arguments for the Elimination of Television.* Quill reprint edition. New York: William Morrow, 1978.

Miles, Raymond E., and Charles C. Snow. *Organizational Strategy, Structure, and Process.* New York: McGraw-Hill, 1978.

Molotsky, Irvin. "Smithsonian Flight Archives to Be Sold on 10 Videodisks." *The New York Times,* November 21, 1983.

National Science Board Commission on Pre-college Education in Mathematics, Science, and Technology. *Educating Americans in the 21st Century.* Washington, D.C.: National Science Board/National Science Foundation, 1983.

Neustadt, Richard M. *The Birth of Electronic Publishing.* White Plains, N.Y.: Knowledge Industry Publications, 1982.

Noble, J. Kendrick, Jr. "The Media Megamerger Wave of the 1980's: What Happened?" *Publishing Research Quarterly,* 7 (Summer, 1991): 3–9.

Norman, Donald A. *Things That Make Us Smart: Defending Human Attributes in the Age of the Machine.* Reading, Mass.: Addison-Wesley, 1993.

Paisley, William, and Matilda Butler. "The First Wave: CD-ROM Adoption in Offices and Libraries." *Microcomputers for Information Management,* 4(2) (June 1987): 109–27.

Paramount Communications. *Annual Reports,* 1984–1992.

Patten, David A. *Newspapers and New Media.* White Plains, N.Y.: Knowledge Industry Publications, 1986.

Pinchot III, Gifford. *Intrapreneuring.* New York: Harper and Row, 1985.

Pollock, Roy V.H. "Computer-based Knowledge Nets to Store, Index, and Retrieve Medical Information." *Proceedings of Symposium on Computer Application in Health Sciences,* Tuskegee University, Tuskegee, Alabama, September 1985.

———. "PROVIDES: A Complete Veterinary Medical Information System." *Proceedings of the Second Symposium on Computer Applications in Veterinary Medicine,* Mississippi State University, May 1984.

Pool, Ithiel de Sola. *Technologies of Freedom.* Cambridge, Mass.: Harvard University Press, 1983.

Poppel, Harvey L., and Bernard Goldstein. *Information Technology: The Trillion-Dollar Opportunity.* New York: McGraw-Hill, 1987.

Porter, Michael. *Competitive Strategy.* New York: The Free Press, 1980.

———. *Competitive Advantage.* New York: The Free Press, 1985.

———. "The Harvard View of Hanson." *The Economist: The World in 1987* (London), 120–23.

Postman, Neil. *Amusing Ourselves to Death: Public Discourse in the Age of Show Business.* New York: Viking Penguin, reprint edition, 1986.

Powell, Walter W. "The Good Books Business." *The New Republic,* September 15 and 22, 1986, 32–38.

Prichard, Peter. *The Making of McPaper: The Inside Story of* USA Today. Kansas City, Mo.: Andrews, McMeel, and Parker, 1987.

Raman, V.V. "Communication and Civilization: 1985–86 Kern Lectures." Rochester, N.Y.: Rochester Institute of Technology, 1986.

Reich, Robert. *The Work of Nations.* New York: Alfred Knopf, 1991.

Rice, Ronald E., ed. *The New Media: Communications, Research, and Technology.* Beverly Hills, Cal.: Sage Publications, 1984.

———. "Toward Enhancing the Social Benefits of Electronic Publishing." New York: Aspen Institute for Humanistic Studies, 1987.

———. "Toward Improved Computer Software for Education and Entertainment in the Home." New York: Aspen Institute for Humanistic Studies, 1987.

Rogers, Everett M. *Communications Technology: The New Media in Society.* New York: The Free Press, 1986.

Ropiequet, Suzanne, ed., with John Einberger, and Bill Zoellick. *CD-ROM: Optical Publishing.* Redmond, Wash.: Microsoft Press, 1987.

Roszak, Theodore. *The Cult of Information: The Folklore of Computers and the True Art of Thinking.* New York: Pantheon Books, 1986.

Rubin, Jerome. "Life After Print." *The Bookseller,* August 17, 1990, 395–98.

Schreyer, Alice D. "Books and Other Machines." Washington, D.C.: Library of Congress/Center for the Book, 1985.

Sculley, John, with John Byrne. *Odyssey.* New York: Harper and Row, 1987.

Seybold, Patricia B., and David S. Marshak. "Optical Technology in the Office." *Optical Insights,* Boston Computer Society, 1 (Fall, 1987): 1–5.

Sigel, Efrem. *The Future of Videotext.* White Plains, N.Y.: Knowledge Industry Publications, 1983.

Sigel, Efrem, Erik Barnouw, Lewis Branscomb, Dan Lacy, Anthony Smith, and Robert D. Stueart. *Books, Libraries, and Electronics.* White Plains, N.Y.: Knowledge Industry Publications, 1982.

Snyder, Tom, and Jane Palmer. *In Search of the Most Amazing Thing: Children, Education, and Computers.* Reading, Mass.: Addison-Wesley, 1986.

Sobel, Robert. *IBM: Colossus in Transition.* New York: Times Books, 1981.

Standera, Oldrich. *The Electronic Era of Publishing.* New York: Elsevier Science Publishing, 1987.

Tarter, Jeffrey. "Groupware: Charting the Flow." *Soft Letter,* 5, December 1, 1987.

———. "Pro Forma." *Soft Letter,* 5, November 15, 1987.

Tenner, Edward. "The Paradoxical Proliferation of Paper." *Princeton Alumni Weekly,* March 9, 1988, 17–21.

Time Inc. and Time Warner. *Annual Reports,* 1983–1991.

Toffler, Alvin. *Future Shock.* Reprint edition. New York: Bantam Books, 1971.

———. *The Third Wave.* New York: William Morrow, 1980.

Trelease, James. *The Read-Aloud Handbook.* Revised edition. New York: Penguin Books, 1985.

U.S. Office of Technology Assessment. *Intellectual Property Rights in an Age of Electronics and Information.* Washington, D.C.: U.S. Department of Commerce, National Technical Information Service, #PB87-10031, 1986.

Weber, Robert. "Copyright in the Electronic Age." *Publishers Weekly,* March 22, 1991, 52–53.

Wendroff, Michael. "Should We Do the Book? A Study of How Publishers Handle Acquisition Decisions." *Publishers Weekly,* August 15, 1980.

Wiese, Michael. *Home Video: Producing for the Home Market.* Westport, Conn.: Michael Wiese Film/Video, 1986.

Williams, Frederick. *The Communications Revolution.* Mentor reprint edition. New York: New American Library, 1983.

Wincor, Richard. *Literary Rights Contracts.* New York: Law & Business, Inc., Harcourt Brace Jovanovich, 1979.

Wind, Yoram. *Product Policy.* Reading, Mass.: Addison-Wesley, 1982.

Index

About the Author

DOUGLAS M. EISENHART is Director of Electronic Development and Licensing at Houghton Mifflin Interactive, where he is a producer of CD-ROM and online interactive products and services. He formerly held management positions with Houghton Mifflin Company's Software and Trade Divisions, Westinghouse Group W Cable Television, and Harcourt Brace Jovanovich.